ALSO BY THE AUTHOR

*The Accidental Housewife™: How to Overcome
Housekeeping Hysteria One Task at a Time*

The Ultimate Accidental Housewife™

Your Guide to a CLEAN-ENOUGH House

Julie Edelman

HYPERION
New York

ISBN : 978-1-4013-2226-7

Hyperion books are available for special promotions and premiums. For details contact Michael Rentas, Proprietary Markets, Hyperion, 77 West 66th Street, 12th floor, New York, New York 10023, or call 212-456-0133.

Design by Renato Stanisic

First Edition

10 9 8 7 6 5 4 3 2 1

In Loving Memory

This guide is dedicated to my loving father, who passed away while I was in the throes of writing it. It is his sense of humor and love for living life that daily gives me the strength and optimism to embrace and never give up on my pre-accidental housewifely dreams. I miss you, Daddy, but I'm sure you're up there making everyone smile and enjoying a Dewars and soda or two, knowing your little girl loves you and will never give up, thanks to you.

Ac-ci-den-tal House-wife (noun): *An individual of no particular gender or race; married, single, or divorced; working or home-based; with or without kids who, due to circumstance, intent, or nuptial bliss finds him- or herself tasked with taking care of everyday household chores and activities regardless of interest, skill, or time.*

Contents

Never Enough Thanks

In the beginning there was the word and the word was housewife. And that is where my first words of thanks begin. Without you there would be no book called *The Ultimate Accidental Housewife: Your Guide to a Clean-Enough House* because it is our shared angst that propelled me to find simple solutions to our everyday household tasks.

The second and third word of thanks goes to the indefatigable Kevin Miller of ABC Radio Networks or *oh capitán* as I like to call him, who as I played food hockey with my salad called up the wonderful Ellen Archer at Hyperion and told her she must meet me. The rest, as they say, is history: We met with the fashionable and fab Ms. Archer and my stellar and incredibly brilliant and witty editor Brenda Copeland and the next accidental housewifely bestseller was born. Then there's Kathleen Carr, Brenda's amazing assistant, who was always perky when I called and insured my edits were clear and readable. Next up: my two terrific agents at William Morris, Andy McNicol and Jason Fox, who kept me from losing it along the way; and Andy's assistant, Ken Graham, who insured that this queen of technological darkness got her manuscript through cyberspace intact and on time. And, thanks to Kate "PMS" Sweeney (my nickname for her, which stands for "Pretty Manageable Stains" that you'll read about in Chapter 10) for her *stately* research.

Then kudos are in order to my dear friend and advisor, Harvey Stein, who introduced me to my incredibly talented and kind chief designer, John-Michael Eckeblad and the legendary creative branding guru Alan Seigel and his très artistic mates Seth Sever and Lloyd Blaner. Thanks guys for bringing Julie Edelman and *The Accidental Housewife* together as one entity! Next up: Peter Cohl and his wife, Zoe, for the amazing photograph of me that you see in the back of the book—good lighting and makeup are beautiful things!

On the personal side: never-ending hugs and all my love go to the most important person in my life: my extraordinarily warm and gifted son and the future number-one ranked player in the PGA, Luke, who once again was unselfish enough to play golf during every minute of sunlight when not in school so that I could write, and resourceful enough to keep us fed when this guide's deadline loomed. And, *salut* to my dear friend Vinnie for always welcoming me with open arms and a glass of Santa Margarita—see, I told you I'd thank you!

Lastly, thanks again to my mother, who was born ahead of her time. As a result she didn't have the choice nor chance to pursue her hopes and dreams nor be an accidental housewife, but encouraged me to pursue mine so long as I didn't walk on her beige carpeting.

I think that covers it. But, if I've forgotten you, please don't be upset—you are in my heart if not in my current overloaded memory, so the oversight is truly accidental.

Preface

TIME TO SPREAD THE GLOVE

Hello, my fellow accidental housewives! I'm back to spread the glove—so to speak. Yes, I've returned after months of touring for my first book, *The Accidental Housewife: How to Overcome Housekeeping Hysteria One Task at a Time*—which thanks to you made the *New York Times Bestseller List*. And, forgive me while I digress for a moment, but when it made the list I went into shock for a couple of reasons: One, it happened only a few weeks after the book came out. Two, my family and friends didn't buy every copy available. But most importantly it shocked me since I had connected with you in a very real way that validated my belief that there are millions of you out there like me yearning to come out of your broom closets and embrace your housewifely imperfections. Misery needs company and you shared how you would love some fresh, fun, and simple ways to deal with your daily tasks on what I lovingly refer to as Hysteria Lane.

That doesn't mean you and I don't enjoy watching Martha and envy her ease and skill at faux-painting or making hand-dipped candles, particularly since she makes it look like an activity a child could do. No, we too would love to have that kind of time and talent. But the truth is these hopes and dreams pass quickly when confronted with the day-to-day realities of being a housewife: endless laundry, stuffed toilets, soccer practice, misplaced bills, and all else in between. No, for us homekeeping perfection is not a viable option.

Speaking of hopes and dreams, back in college it was my hope and dream to become a household name—which leads me to a fun story from my first book tour. I had just appeared on the *Today* show sharing some of my manicure-friendly bathroom-cleaning tips. As you might imagine, I was riding high on having finally made it to the big time, when my college roommate called to tell me she'd seen the segment. Well, after she'd told me how wonderful I'd looked, she asked a question that quickly brought me down to earth: *"Did you ever expect when you graduated magna cum laude from Duke that you'd be cleaning toilets on national TV someday?"* Her question stirred up a wide range of conflicting emotions that I had thought I'd come to terms with once I'd embraced my accidental ways. But I guess that wasn't so. Fact is, during my Duke days I had envisioned being on *Today* but as an anchor like Meredith Vieira. And, though I had included marriage and children as part of my vision, I never imagined that I'd be the anchor for a story about cleaning poop and whiz. But there I was . . . millions of you watching me with my toilet scepter instead of a microphone in hand, having fulfilled my pre–accidental housewifely hopes and dreams in a truly accidental way—funny how life works.

The other thing I learned during these past months is that while you want simple solutions to your everyday household problems, you enjoy being able to have a sense of humor about it all. After all, and to put it bluntly, housework sucks. But it's just housework and we're not being asked to go to war or find a cure for the big C. So we need to have both a healthy perspective and a lighter attitude. Simply put, we need to smile and keep our wits about us. It's an approach to our housewifely lives that I've come to refer to as real life, resimplified. Resimplified as in putting a new spin on the ways we do our chores that bore that blends them into our real-life, everyday routines and uses items that are not always the tried and true but accessible and convenient to keep our homes clean enough. And, perhaps more importantly, resimplified as it refers to giving you, today's housewife, a new face: one with a smile, some fashion, flair, and frivolity.

Which leads to what's inside this ultimate guide to accidental housewifely homekeeping nirvana (that's a mouthful!). Inside you'll find just enough cleaning basics to keep your home acceptable to your mother, mother-in-law, and the health inspectors; your living spaces organized; your laundry relatively clean and stain-free; and manicure-friendly ways to prevent your home from falling apart. I'll also help you save our planet. That doesn't mean you'll need to become the Queen of Green, but like everything else in our accidental housewifely life there are simple ways to blend protecting our planet into our everyday routines and lives. And you may even save some money by doing so, which should put a smile on your face. There are also ideas to help you deal with things that bug us like mold, mildew, bacteria, dust mites, mice, moths, ants, and roaches.

Oh yes, and let us not forget a very handy-dandy homekeeping tool that many of you have—your kiddies (if you don't have any, you may want to consider having or borrowing one)! Yes, they are a wonderfully cheap homekeeping resource and there are many ways to put them to work, which I've labeled "Child's Play."

So there you have it. Take a breath, grab that libation, and let's recapture some of our pre-accidental hopes and dreams as we spread the glove together. Imperfection is our new perfection. *Vive today's housewife! Vive la Accidental Housewife!*

Just Enough Accidental Housewifely Disclaimers

Putting together a guide like this takes lots of trial and error and coffee and libations. It also made me realize that not everything in here may work exactly the same for each of you, nor provide you with all the homekeeping solutions you may face in your housewifely life. That said, please read and heed the disclaimers that follow so my publisher doesn't lose sleep in the months and years ahead:

- The overriding goal of each and every tip or word of wisdom in this guide is to help you achieve a clean-enough home (as the title says) and not homekeeping perfection.
- I am an accidental housewife, not a professional cleaning expert nor Ty Pennington, so my tips and solutions are based on my finding the easiest and most manicure-friendly ways to conquer chores that bore in a manner that is good enough for most overworked, overscheduled, and underpaid housewives like ourselves.
- This guide has been tested and retested by myself and others whom I trust and whose homes are still standing and clean enough that the board of health has not visited them nor have they fallen or floated away. That said, this does not mean that you will enjoy the same results, since your individual tolerance, diligence, and time will determine when something is clean enough or the repair is good enough. As I've often said, it's like using a recipe—you may follow all or most of it, but it

may not come out exactly the same as expected due to your own personal deviations, distractions, or the way your oven may cook.

- All products, experts, Web sites, companies, retailers, agencies, organizations, family, friends, and fellow accidental housewives who are mentioned in this book are in here solely because I have either used and liked their products; shopped and found what I was looking for easily; provided valuable information that applied to our real homekeeping lives; and, perhaps most importantly, wouldn't cause you any more stress or ruin your manicures. This is not to say that I haven't worked with some of the companies or spoken about some of their products in a professional capacity. But as it relates to their being in this guide, not a penny did they give *moi*. My only two sources of financial generousity came from my publisher and my mother.

- Cleaning products often contain toxic ingredients, so please use with care. For best results make sure to read all labels and follow manufacturers' instructions. And remember, always exercise caution. (It's far easier than going to the gym!)

- When enlisting children to help with chores, please keep their safety in mind at all times. That means keeping them away from all electrical appliances and any product or activity that may cause harm or injury. And remember: *Children (as well as some adults) should always be supervised.* SAFETY FIRST!

- The information in this book is not intended to be a substitute for professional advice. Although every effort has been made to ensure that information is presented accurately in this book, and every care has been taken to ensure that the home repairs listed in this book are simple, safe, and manicure-friendly, neither the publisher nor the author assumes any responsibility for errors or for any possible consequences arising from the use of information contained herein.

Introduction

CONQUERING CHORES THAT BORE

My theory on housework is, if the item doesn't multiply, smell, catch on fire or block the refrigerator door, let it be. No one cares. Why should you? —Erma Bombeck

Let it be . . . no one cares . . . why should you? Truly words of wisdom and a very good question. I mean, why should you care so long as you and your loved ones are safe and you can breathe the air without gasping or calling 911 as you open the fridge? Well, try as you may, the truth is that you need to care since clutter mounts, microscopic life forms multiply, dirty laundry smells, and stuff breaks down. So how do you balance not caring with your need to keep the house intact? Face two simple facts:

1. Like it or not there are certain chores you need to do to keep your family healthy and your home in good working order. These include cleaning, organizing, laundry, and home repairs.
2. Unless you're Heloise, homekeeping chores are generally boring, which is why I lovingly call them "chores that bore."

I mean really, do you get excited when you have to vacuum those pesky dust bunnies? Does walking into your bathroom only to discover that your toilet bowl looks like a paintball target jazz you? Or does organizing your closet make you feel revitalized for more than twenty minutes? I suspect not.

Thus, the main goal of this book is to make homekeeping a breeze, not a burden.

Your interest, time available, or state of disrepair will be your true guide to do what follows and to know when to call in the professionals. And, though I won't promise you that these tasks will become chores you adore, you will find simple, time-saving ways to get them done so you can balance your need to care with not wanting to. In short, this is your one-stop guide to a clean-enough house.

We begin:

Make a Judgment—Do It or Leave It!

I often find that once I decide it's time to do any of the chores that bore I get bogged down trying to figure out where to start, since everywhere I look needs some TLC. So to help make this decision easier ask yourself the following:

1. Which room of your house has the greatest chance of housing living organisms that multiply or smell?
   - bathroom
   - kitchen
   - bedroom (master or other)
   - family room
   - all of the above
   - other

2. Which rooms can you shut the doors to without fear of men in white suits, firefighting garb, or Ty Pennington making an unexpected visit?
   - bathroom
   - kitchen
   - bedroom (master or other)
   - family room
   - all of the above
   - other

If neither of these questions helps you decide where to begin, then this may indicate that your home is in an emergency state, so my advice is to call in the experts immediately, sell it as soon as possible, or level it.

Judgment delivered! Now, on your mark, get set, divide and conquer!

Divide and Conquer

You've made your judgment and unless you wound up calling in the real estate agents, demolition squad, or Ty, it's time to get cracking. Start by dividing your accidental housewifely home into the following two zones. By doing so you'll be able to judge whether you clean it pronto, organize it, or can leave it for another day.

1. TOXIC ZONES: These are the bathroom and kitchen, since they have the greatest chance of housing living organisms that multiply, smell, or attract the most clutter, resulting in blocked passageways and potential harm. Recommended choring frequency:
- CLEANING: Weekly
- ORGANIZING: Monthly
- REPAIRS: Immediately

2. NOT-SO-TOXIC ZONES: These are central living spaces such as the living room, bedrooms, and family room, which may house and attract things that multiply but don't generally smell unless your child has left a half-eaten sandwich under his bed for days or perhaps for weeks on end. That's the good news; the not-so-good news is that even though you need to focus on these rooms less often, you need to be aware of dust mites, which take up residence in your bedroom, multiply ad nauseam, and can cause physical discomfort. You'll need to deal with them on a regular basis. More on this in Chapter Seven. But as a rule, here's the recommended choring frequency:
- CLEANING: Every one to two weeks
- ORGANIZING: Monthly
- REPAIRS: Case by case; manicure by manicure

Practice Offensive and Defensive Choring

As you go through each zone you'll find room-specific tips and tricks on offensive cleaning, organizing, and home repair to help you put off till tomorrow (or the next day and the next) what your mother would have done today. Now, this may sound like you're engaging in an extra step, but trust me when I tell you that you're not. Offensive choring is actually comprised of those little tasks that can help keep those big tasks at bay. As the saying goes, "An ounce of prevention is worth a pound of cure." That's a weight-loss goal we can all achieve.

On the flip side, you'll also learn enough defensive tips and tricks to help when accidents and everyday realities of housekeeping rear their ugly heads.

Do Just Enough

From cleaning well enough to keep health inspectors away, to organizing well enough to keep passageways clear, to repairing something just enough to prevent disasters, this is the nuts and bolts of how you're going to achieve your goal of living in a clean-enough home. And in the process you will engage one of the accidental housewife's least expensive and most accessible taskers—your children. Throughout this guide I've indicated those activities that are so simple a child can do them. Just look for the heading "CHILD'S PLAY." If you don't have any children, perhaps you can borrow or rent one, two, or several from a family member, friend, or neighbor who will probably be delighted to share them.

Time to spread the glove and maintain your home, sanity, and manicure.

PART **1**

THE TOXIC ZONES

Chapter 1

The Bathroom

There is only one immutable law in life—in a gentleman's toilet, incoming traffic has the right of way. –Hugh Leonard

We'll begin with the most toxic zone in the house: the bathroom. The bathroom is a breeding ground for so many different types of germs and bacteria that it might as well be someone's science project. Try as you might, you can't ignore it. As if that weren't bad enough, the bathroom also seems to be a clutter magnet. Towers of magazines line the floor; makeup, brushes, and shaving stuff clog the drawers; and curling irons, hair dryers, toothbrushes, and toothpaste carpet the vanity. And let's not forget how this room can live up to its truly "toxic" classification from the numerous times the toilet can overflow thanks to loved ones' "doo" diligence when it comes to wiping. All of which should lead and inspire you to learn just enough cleaning, organizing, and home repair know-how to deal with this yuckiest of home zones without losing your mind or ruining your manicure.

Cleaning

Okay, now it's time to spread the glove; that is, put on those rubber gloves and start dealing with that yucky stuff—mold, mildew, and soap scum—that just loves taking up residence in your bathroom with a smile and some pizzazz. We'll start with just enough defensive and offensive cleaning tips.

SPREAD THE GLOVE FASHIONABLY

In the preface I shared how you and I have begun to "spread the glove" by coming out of our broom closets and embracing our housewifely imperfections regardless of their origins. Well, another way you and I can spread the glove and make these chores that bore more fashionable and functional is to put on a pair of rubber gloves. Not just because your hands will be going in places and coming in contact with things that excite only your plumber and perhaps your internist, but to protect your manicure and elevate these tasks to ones that may cause us to smile! So "spread the glove" and treat yourself to a pair with flair versus those oh-so-yesterday yellow ones found in the cleaning aisle. You can find some oh-so-current ones at Target, Bed Bath & Beyond, Linens 'n Things, or online.

Defensive Cleaning—Toxic Targets

MOLD AND MILDEW: WHAT IT IS AND WHAT YOU CAN DO ABOUT IT

Mold and mildew (M & M) have become inseparably linked as buddies and buzz words in the news, particularly as they relate to our health and homes. Not like the good ol' days when I associated the word *mold* with tasty cheeses and *mildew* with a spring scent. No, today's M & M have reached "celebrity" status as new and sometimes toxic enemies that come in a variety of colors and forms that unfortunately don't melt in your mouth or your hands.

So what exactly are M & M? Mold and mildew are fungi, which I've learned means they're microscopic plant life without chlorophyll. Since they like warmth and humidity, and a steady supply of them, they usually take up residence in places like our bathrooms and basements. It is there that they come home to roost or, as the experts say, "form colonies"—reproducing (they form spores) on anything and everything that remains wet for more then twenty-four to forty-eight hours*: showers, tubs, toilets, floors, and even junior's tub toys. And that's what we see—their colonies, which are actually spores preparing to reproduce and grow. Are you thoroughly grossed out yet? If not, read on.

Lots of allergies and allergy symptoms (sneezing, runny or clogged noses, coughing, itchy eyes, and so on) are attributed to the common types of mold and mildew that in-

---

* Depending upon the research you read or the mold masters you talk with, mold can form (i.e., begin to reproduce) within twelve to forty-eight hours if the conditions are right. The key is to keep in mind that they are very quick to call your bathroom home, but if you read what follows you'll be safe enough in fending them off.

habit our homes. That means it's a good idea to stop them as best you can before they take up permanent residence.

DEALING WITH THE FUNGUS AMONG US

As far back as the Old Testament, folks have been living with the fungus among us, which I guess means it's not going to cause the end of civilization as some news reports might suggest. But it's good to know what's sharing your living space and what you can do to help make it go away. First, I'll share what the wise men of yesteryear suggested:

From Leviticus, chapter 14, verses 33–57

- On the seventh day the priest shall return to inspect the house. If the mildew has spread on the walls, he is to order that the contaminated stones be torn out and thrown into an unclean place outside the town. He must have all the inside walls of the house scraped and the material that is scraped off dumped into an unclean place outside the town. Then they are to take other stones to replace these and take new clay and plaster the house.
- If the mildew reappears in the house after the stones have been torn out and the house is scraped and plastered, then the priest is to go and examine it, and if the mildew has spread in the house, it is a destructive mildew: the house is unclean. It must be torn down—its stones, timbers, and all the plaster—and taken out of the town to an unclean place.

Nowadays, in the event that your priest or priestess is doing lunch or on sabbatical, here are a few things you can do to defend against and defeat the fungus among us:

- *LET THE SUN SHINE IN!* Keep windows open to let steam escape. Less humidity will mean less mold growth since M & M flourish in humid conditions.
- *KEEP FANS RUNNING:* Leave bathroom fans on during and after your shower or bath.
- *TOSS IN SOME VINEGAR:* Studies show that white vinegar can kill 90 percent of the bacteria in our homes and more than 80 percent of mold and germs. So put some in a spray bottle, squirt it on a paper towel or microfiber cloth, and wipe. If the smell grosses you out, finish off with a bit of disinfecting air freshener spray either shot onto a paper towel or directly into the air. Wiping areas with a fabric dryer sheet will also help take the V-scent away.

- *ADD SOME OIL:* Mix a few drops of lavender oil and a cup of water and put it in a spray bottle to evict germs.
- *DRY 'EM OUT:* Since mold, mildew, and bacteria love damp, moist places be sure to let items like sponges, toothbrushes, and washcloths dry out. Toss moist sponges in the microwave and damp clothes and towels in the dryer, or let them hang out to dry in the good ol' sunshine.
- *USE DEHUMIDIFIERS:* Dehumidifiers suck the moisture out of the air, which is exactly what you want to do to cut off M & M's lifeline. The moisture is collected in a tank, which needs to be emptied regularly. That said, when looking for a dehumidifier consider those with a larger tank so you don't have to empty it so often. And, like all good eco-friendly appliances, be sure to buy an Energy Star model. Keep in mind that you may want to use your dehumidifier in other rooms, so look for a portable one. If so, and if you'll forgive the pun, "weigh" in on whether one with a smaller tank may make more sense than a larger one in regards to having to empty the water, unless you have Arnold Schwarzenegger residing with you.
- *SPRAY 'N' RUB THEM OUT WITH STORE-BOUGHT STUFF:* From bleach to ready-mades, here are a few to consider. Be sure to read the instructions before using any of these and wear your gloves when using!
  - Tilex Mold & Mildew Remover
  - Clorox Clean-Up Cleaner with Bleach
  - Moldzyme—an eco-friendly one you can find at www.ecodiscoveries.com
  - Lysol Mildew Remover with Bleach

HOLD THE MOLD

Though you may be doing everything to prevent and defend you and yours from those toxic little critters, sometimes you just can't stop them from moving in. After all, mold and mildew takes only twenty-four hours to start forming colonies. So if you see white patches on your wall or smell something with a musty, almost urinelike scent and no one has tinkled, you've probably got mold, which means start cleaning pronto.

Please note: According to the Centers for Disease Control and Prevention (CDC), if the mold covers more than ten feet of any room you should consult an Environmental Protection Agency (EPA) expert. My suggestion: If that's the case, immediately put on your Hazmat suits and have everyone in your household evacuate with gusto.

What you'll need:

You can use a store-bought mold and mildew product (such as Tilex Mold & Mildew Remover, Clorox Clean-Up Cleaner with Bleach, Moldzyme, or Lysol Mildew Remover with Bleach) or try the following simple cleaner-upper:

- 1 cup bleach
- 1 gallon water
- Measuring cup
- Spray bottle or bucket
- Sponge
- Rubber gloves
- Mask

What you'll do:

Mix the bleach and water in a spray bottle. Please remember to ventilate the room and wear gloves and a mask. Then:

- Spray ceiling and walls or wipe them with mixture
- Leave it on for ten to fifteen minutes
- Wipe with warm water and a sponge
- Let dry thoroughly
- Throw away the sponge so you don't spread the love!
- Repeat if necessary

If after several tries the mold holds, call in the pros pronto!

- ***REPAIR LEAKY PIPES OR TOILETS* TOUT DE SUITE** (that's French for right away!): You don't want moisture accumulating unless you want M & M as houseguests. You can find easy home repairs for your leaky sink or toilet beginning on page 224.
- *PAINT!* As Oscar Wilde implied when he said, "Either the wallpaper goes or I do" you should forget the wallpaper and paint your bathroom so you don't have to worry about our M & M buds growing betwixt the paper and the wall. For more helpful hints on this see "Giving M & M the Brush Off" on page 12.
- *USE MOLD-and-MILDEW RESISTANT STUFF:*

- Products like DampRid are terrific since they absorb, dissolve, and last up to forty-five days (www.damprid.com).
- Hang mold-and-mildew-resistant shower curtains. Be sure that they're also machine washable
- *GO BARE:* Forget carpeting and replace with flooring. For more on this go to "Homeschooling: The Bare Facts on Bathroom Flooring" on page 16.

GIVING M & M THE BRUSH OFF

Painting your bathroom walls is a terrific way to limit mold and mildew buildup and you don't have to be Michelangelo to do it with ease if you follow these two simple steps. If minimal sanding is required you can use one of your jumbo, heavy-duty emery boards. If this isn't enough or your walls require you to also scrape and spackle, please seek guidance from your local paint or home improvement store experts.

1. *CLEAN THE SCENE:* Before you paint, remove any mold and mildew that may be hanging out on your walls and ceilings. There are lots of store-bought mold and mildew products to choose from, such as Tilex Mold & Mildew Remover, Clorox Clean-Up Cleaner with Bleach, Moldzyme (an eco-friendly product you can find online at www.ecodiscoveries.com), and Lysol Mildew Remover with Bleach. However, according to Denise, my local bathroom paint guru at Wyckoff Paint and Wallpaper, the best way to get rid of it is to do the following:
   - Open all your windows so the area is well ventilated.
   - Put on gloves and a mask (not Spider-Man or SpongeBob).
   - Fill an empty spray bottle with a 1:3 ratio of bleach and water (that's one part bleach and three parts water).
   - Spray walls and ceiling and leave it on for five minutes.
   - Wipe with warm water and sponge.
   - Let dry thoroughly before going to step 2.*

FYI: If the area with mold is larger than ten square feet, call in the pros.

---

*If you have water and smoke stains:
PRIME TIME: After you finish step one and you're sure the walls and ceilings are dry it's time to prime with a "stain kill" or "stain blocker" to get rid of any water and smoke stains. Ask your neighborhood Denise which product will be best for your bathroom.

2. *PAINT:* Now the fun begins! It's time to paint. The best type of paint to help protect against mold and mildew redotting your newly painted bathroom are those that specifically say "bathroom paint" (some may include the words *and kitchen)* since they are formulated specifically for those rooms. Benjamin Moore and Perma-White are good choices for M & M–prone areas, plus they include a self-priming product, which means one less step for you to do. FYI: these paints are acrylic compositions, which means they dry harder and prevent moisture from seeping through, unlike oil-based, enamel paints, which tend to never dry thoroughly. Latex paints are not toxic either so you'll be able to paint without wearing a gas mask or smudging your lipstick! Lastly, latex paints specifically formulated for the bathroom or kitchen generally come in a satin finish, which is easier to clean and won't show fingerprints. Love that!

Please note that you can find most of the products referred to in this section at your local supermarket, paint or hardware store, and/or home improvement retailers such as Lowe's, Ace Hardware, and Home Depot.

Offensive Cleaning—Not-So-Toxic Targets

Less is more when doing housework, particularly in the bathroom, which has the dubious honor of being both the grossest and most used room in your home. As such it ranks as the number-one chore that bores on the "I hate but have to clean" scale. That's why knowing how to prevent things like mold and mildew from multiplying are key, as are knowing simple, manicure-friendly ways to maintain the image of a clean-enough sink, tub, shower, floor, and toilet. Here's how to do just that:

- *KEEP DISINIFECTING WIPES EVERYWHERE AND USE THEM LIKE TISSUES:* Wipe faucets, sinks, tubs, toilet seats, blow dryers, and anything in your "swiping" range whenever the mood hits you.
- *REPLACE BAR SOAP WITH LIQUID BATH SOAP:* This will limit the amount of soap scum that can form.
- *USE LEMON OIL OR BABY OIL:* At least once a month (twice will be better if you can remember!) put some lemon oil or baby oil on a paper towel and wipe key "scum zones" (sinks, tubs, and showers). The oil will cause the dirty water to bead and roll down into the drain.
- *DROP A TAB OR TWO INTO YOUR TANK:* In between cleanings, put

The Fine Print on Toilet-Cleaning Tabs

Toilet tabs, though a very effective, easy, and manicure-friendly way to keep our toilets clean, are poisonous. So if you have a doggie, cat, or toddler who enjoys drinking from your toilet bowl, then toilet tabs are not a good option. Of course if you have those who are older than tots, walk on two feet instead of four, and can remember to keep the lid down, then drop in those babies. But who are we kidding: If you have males in your home, their affinity for leaving the seat up or lack of memory for putting it down after they tinkle is an accident waiting to happen, so my advice is to nix using the tabs.

toilet-cleaning tabs in your tank to reduce residual poop, whiz, and rust from sticking.

- *SHAVE YOUR MIRRORS:* Next time you're shaving your legs or face spread a thin layer of foam (nongel) shaving cream all over your mirror and let it sit until you're finished shaving or showering. Wipe it off with paper towels. This will result in a clean mirror and one that will stay defogged after hot, steamy showers for up to three weeks!
- *LIMIT THRONE ACCESS!* There's no reason household members have to use every bathroom in the house. So if you have more than two, pretend that this is all you have and limit access to those that are near highly trafficked areas, even if that means locking doors or putting DO NOT CROSS tape on them. Key areas include:
  1. Bedrooms
  2. Kitchen
  3. Family Room
  4. Basement

Defensive Cleaning—Not-So-Toxic Targets

Okay, you've got your offensive moves, and though the best offense may be a good defense, accidents happen. The following are ways to mount a good enough defensive when they do. In each case please remember to spread on your rubber gloves:

BOWL RUNNETH OVER

Clearly it isn't a pretty sight when your toilet bowl overflows and you're faced with a cleanup that is off the charts on the grossness scale. Once you get past your disgust and dismay, the key is to act quickly and efficiently while keeping a realistic barrier between you and that which overfloweth.

Note: If you need a small dinghy, wet suit, snorkel, and goggles to deal with this problem do not attempt to do so. Instead, call your plumber and leave the premises *tout de suite.* If the situation is manageable, albeit gross, proceed as follows:

What you'll need:
- Gallon-size Ziploc bag(s)
- Old rags, towels, or microfiber mop
- Bleach-based disinfecting or sanitizing product

What you'll do:
- Turn a Ziploc bag inside out and use it to pick up any poop or large alien objects. Seal and toss the bag out—preferably not in your kitchen garbage can but in one that resides outside your home or apartment.
- Sop up any liquid with old rags, towels, or a microfiber mop. Please note: If you decide to keep these cloths rather than throw them out, launder them immediately with bleach, an enzyme laundry product, and hot water—other than the mop, give them a "special storage spot" and use them only for future emergencies that are equally gross and disgusting.
- Wash bowl and floors with bleach-based, disinfecting, and sanitizing products to rid the area of germs and odors.
- Machine wash mats. If you have carpeting, you might want to consider pulling it up and replacing it with flooring that doesn't retain moisture, is easy to clean, and won't cause you and your loved ones to slip.

CLOSE SHAVE
New blades or disposable shavers may give you baby-smooth skin but they also often give you a nick that just won't quit! So, unless you're hemorrhaging, place a damp piece of tissue or bandage on your cut and start cleaning your bathroom mat, nightie, or T-shirt as follows:

If it's your mat:
Run cold water through it until most of the blood washes out. Like most stains, the faster you deal with them the more likely they'll come out. Then launder per instructions.

Homeschooling: The Bare Facts on Bathroom Flooring

You step out of the shower and your bare, wet footsies are looking for comfort, warmth, and a nonslip surface so you and yours don't wind up on your rears. Though carpeting and mats may seem like a good way to go, they retain moisture, which is a no-no in our battle against mold and mildew. Here are flooring options to help prevent against mold and mildew, and a few to help you from going bottoms up:

1. VINYL TILE: If you're a Do-It-Yourself-er, this flooring's for you, and it could make a fun family project. Vinyl tile is easy to put down and comes in tons of different designs. It's also cheap and simple to clean. The downside is that after a while the tiles may start lifting up since moisture can seep between the cracks, which is why they make sheet vinyl. Laying sheet vinyl, however, is not an accidental housewifely DIY-er unless you're handy since it comes in rolls and you have to cut it to size.

2. STONE: You've probably heard the expression "stone cold"—well, that's the downside of using stones such as marble, limestone, and granite. They're cold on your footsies and they're a lot more expensive than vinyl. They can also be slippery unless you buy a textured variety. But there are upsides: They're easy to clean and moisture isn't a problem.

3. CERAMIC TILE: It's waterproof, easy to clean, inexpensive—relatively speaking—and there are lots of shapes and types to choose from. It is cold on the feet and can be slippery, but if you decide on smaller mosaic tiles there is more grout betwixt them, which will reduce slippage. Same holds true for ceramic tiles that have more texture.

4. LAMINATED: This option is last on my list since it's got the greatest chance of all these options for moisture to seep through and ruin it. But if you're dying for a "wood-like" look this is the best way to go versus solid hardwood, which is mold and mildew's favorite flooring.

If it's your nightie or T-shirt try one of the following:

1. Spit on it! That's correcto, put some of your own saliva on the bloody spot and then flush it with cold water until most of it is gone. It's a medical mystery to me but it must be your saliva and not someone else's to work!

2. If the nightie or T-shirt is white and your care instructions say it's okay to use bleach, try a spot cleaner first like the Clorox Bleach Pen or do the following:

- Flush immediately with cold water
- If the stain remains use color-appropriate bleach applied with an eye-dropper or sponge, unless care instructions note otherwise.
  - For whites only:
    - Use chlorine bleach diluted with equal parts water
  - For whites and colors, use one of the following:
    - Oxygen bleach
    - White vinegar
    - 3 percent hydrogen peroxide—1:3 ratio peroxide to water
    - Isopropyl alcohol (rubbing alcohol is not as strong but you can use it if that's what you have handy)

Launder per garment instructions with an enzyme laundry product.

For more tips on removing blood and other protein stains flip to "United Stains of America," which begins on page 144.

LOST YOUR COOKIES

Like it or not, someone in your household is going to chuck up one of your epicurean delights or come down with a stomach bug. Hopefully, adults who do will be kind enough to clean up after themselves. That, of course, is far too optimistic, and besides, even if they do remnants may remain in nooks and crannies and the stench can linger. That means it will be time to grab that gas mask and start cleaning.

By the way, vomit, like blood, is a protein stain and you can learn more about how to deal with more of their kind later in "United Stains of America," which begins on page 144.

What you'll need for hard surfaces such as toilets and floors:
- Super-absorbent paper towels, old rags, microfiber cloth or mop
- Garbage bag
- Disinfecting cleaner, bleach, or ammonia and water

How you'll clean up your cookies:
- Sop up the "cookies" with paper towels and chuck (not in the same way as they originated).
- Use a disinfecting cleaner per product instructions on a disposable or microfiber mop or cloth and wipe floors or any objects that were within range thoroughly (toilet, walls, tubs, and so on). Though a bit more toxic, I like to use a 1:3 ratio bleach or ammonia

and water mixture to clean up, since it eliminates the smell pronto, but that's your call. If you do decide to go this route, please remember to keep the room well ventilated. And don't forget your rubber gloves.

What you'll need for bath mats:
- Plastic spoon
- Garbage bag

How you'll clean your "cookies" off the bath mat:
- Remove as much as you can with the plastic spoon and either deposit the yuk into the toilet or a garbage bag. Throw both the spoon and bag away.
- Toss the mat in the washing machine. Launder according to its instructions.

What you'll need to get rid of the stench:
- White vinegar
- Microfiber mop
- Disinfecting spray

How you'll get rid of it:
- Unless it's sub-below and you're at risk for developing pneumonia, keep any and all bathroom windows open for as long as possible.
- Mop floors and wipe the toilet with white vinegar. You may want to leave a bowl filled with vinegar behind the toilet for a few days since vinegar is a great odor absorber.
- Spray liberally and often with an aromatic disinfecting spray.

How you'll clean the cookies off your nightie or T-shirt:
Never use hot water to flush or to soak out a protein-based stain, since hot water will set the majority of them. Instead:

- Scrape off remnants with a plastic spoon (no dishwashing this way!) or knife and blot up excess with white paper towels or a cloth.
- Flush immediately with cold water.
- If stain remains, use color-appropriate bleach applied with an eye-dropper or a sponge unless care instructions note otherwise.
  - For whites only:
    - Use chlorine bleach diluted with equal parts water

- For whites and colors, use one of the following:
  - Oxygen bleach
  - White vinegar
  - 3 percent hydrogen peroxide—1:3 ratio peroxide to water
  - Isopropyl alcohol (rubbing alcohol is not as strong but you can use it if that's what you have handy)

Launder per garment instructions with an enzyme laundry product.

COLOR FAUX PAS

You haven't had a chance to go to the colorist and so you took it upon yourself to say nay to gray. Great in concept but if you're like me, you tend to splatter color onto whatever surface you're working on or near. So, girlfriends and gents, here's how you can have your color and clean it up too:

- *DIP A TIP:* Put some nail polish remover on a Q-tip and dab away—for larger splats use a cotton ball or rag.
- *GET PROFESSIONAL HELP:* Visit your local salon and promise them you'll never try this at home again if they let you buy or give you their hair color–removal products.
- *BE ABRASIVE:* Good ol' Ajax, Comet, or a store-bought generic abrasive will do the trick if you use a little elbow grease.
- *KNOW WHEN TO LINE 'EM:* Avoid any cleanup next time beauty calls by coloring your do in the sink, not the shower or tub, and lining it with a garbage bag. Adhere with either duct tape or bandages.

SPLAT GOES THE MIRROR

Should you be feeling a bit klutzy and drop your hand mirror or bathroom cup, don't try to pick up the pieces by hand unless you wish to cut yourself and do a double cleanup. If you choose that route and bleeding ensues, refer to the "Close Shave" cleanup tips on page 15. If not, wise decision and try one of the following:

- Use a dust pan to brush up the larger pieces.
- Dampen an old rag to pick up remnants.
- Take a slice of fresh bread and press it on the area where the mirror fell to pick up the remaining slivers.
- Hand vac is optional.

How to Clean the Rest Just Enough

You'll need to decide which cleaning tasks blend into your everyday routines and the order in which you should do them. But to get you started, we'll begin with a list of what you'll need and move right into the least offensive chore—cleaning your bathroom mirror. Please note: Many of the cleaning tasks have more than one simple cleaning solution. This is intentional and meant to provide you with alternatives that fit your routines and preferences. Now roll up your sleeves and let's get to it. A cup of coffee in hand is optional.

YOUR MULTITASKING, MANICURE-FRIENDLY SHOPPING LIST

My rule of thumb when cleaning any area of my home is to try to *blend it into my everyday routines* so that it's less of a chore, requires less thought, and I get it done on my terms. It's my way of multitasking and it enables me to use items that are handy, which is a great time-saver too. So what follows is a manicure-friendly shopping list that combines traditional cleaning items with those that may cause your mother or mother-in-law to look at you aghast and wonder if indeed you've lost your mind. A downloadable list is available on my site at www.theaccidentalhousewife.com.

CLEANING PRODUCTS AND TOOLS
Here are the basics you'll need to clean this toxic zone just enough:

- **DISPOSABLES:** I love these since you use them and lose them. This may not be the most eco-friendly way to clean but the reality is that you and I are not going to turn into the Queens of Green overnight but over time, and we're about saving our sanity and our planet. Enviro-friendly taskers follow on page 21.
  - Disinfecting multipurpose, multisurface antibacterial wipes (such as Windex Clean & Shine Microfiber Cloths, Lysol Sanitizing Wipes, Clorox Disinfecting Wipes)
  - Mr. Clean Magic Eraser—great for removing soap scum
  - Toilet cleaning tools (Scrubbing Bubbles, Clorox ToiletWand, Scotch-Brite Toilet Scrubber, and so on)
- **MOLD AND MILDEW CLEANERS:** These are must-haves in this toxic zone. Here are a few that are easy to use and to find:
  - Tilex Mold & Mildew Remover
  - Clorox Clean-Up Cleaner with Bleach

- Moldzyme
- Lysol Mildew Remover with Bleach
- ***MULTIPURPOSE, MULTISURFACE CLEANERS:*** A multipurpose cleaner is another accidental housewifely must-have since it'll mean you can clean almost any surface (or at least those you're most likely to care about) without thinking about what to use for which surface. Here are some of my picks:
  - Fantastik Orange Action All Purpose Cleaner
  - Formula 409 All Purpose Cleaner
  - Lysol All Purpose Cleaners
  - Mr. Clean Antibacterial MultiPurpose Spray
  - Clorox Disinfecting Floor and Surface Cleaner
  - OxiClean Miracle Foam
  - Windex Multi Surface Cleaner with Vinegar

TOOLS

- *Microfiber cloths, mops, or any other form in which microfiber is available.* I love microfiber since it cleans every surface, is machine washable, and is safe for the environment. For cobwebs and other hard-to-reach areas look for the ones with the rotating heads and extendable handles so you don't have to strain yourself!
- *Portable/battery-operated hand vac:* My fave is Dirt Devil's KONE—even if you don't use it, it looks good since it has a sleek design and it comes in lots of colors. Check it out at www.dirtdevil.com.
- *Paper towels*—Go the recycled route if you can deal with the fact that they're generally not pretty but on the flip side they'll keep our forests looking lush and lovely since trees will be left to do what they do best!

THE ACCIDENTAL ENVIRO-KEEPER'S CLEANERS

In the pages that follow you'll see exactly how you can use these manicure-friendly cleaners, but meanwhile here's a quick heads-up (pardon the pun for what immediately follows):

- *Effervescent denture or antacid tablets, Kool-Aid, or Tang:* for toilet bowls.
- *White vinegar or vodka (your fave or a cheap kind is fine!):* for toilet bowl exteriors, shower doors and walls.
- *Biodegradable baby wipes (Avalon—see the "Resource Guide"):* for toilet bowl exterior, counters, and tub rims.

- *Foam shaving cream:* to defog mirrors.
- *Newspaper:* for lint-free wiping on mirrors and chrome; odor absorption.
- *Toothpaste (nongel) and toothbrush (dedicated to cleaning nonteeth items only); a battery-operated toothbrush is good too:* for faucets and chrome fixtures.
- *Leftover white wine:* for shower doors.
- *White vinegar:* for shower heads.
- *Handheld spinning brush massage or electric toothbrush:* for tubs, tile, and grout.

Here are some enviro-friendly manufacturers and products I've tried and liked, to help make it easy being clean and green!

- Mrs. Meyer's (www.mrsmeyers.com)
- Greening the Cleaning (www.imusranchfoods.com)
- Method (www.method.com)
- Seventh Generation (www.seventhgeneration.com)
- LifeTree (www.lifetreeproducts.com)

MANICURE-FRIENDLY, MULTITASKING CLEANING TIPS
There are three things to keep in mind as you gather and store these items:

1. *PORTABILITY:* Put them all in a lightweight, easy-to-carry caddie or basket that comes with a comfy handle and/or wheels.
2. *ACCESSABILITY:* Keep them in a storage space near your target area so that when the need or mood hits you aren't searching all over the house.
3. *VERSATILITY:* There are lots of ways to skin a cat (have you ever wondered what that means—sorry, I digress!); same thing when cleaning. That's why the products on your manicure-friendly shopping list can be used to do a multitude of tasks.

Warning!

Never mix any ammonia-based products (such as Windex) with a bleach-based product (such as Ajax, Comet, or bleach) or you will truly have toxic consequences, since together they produce toxic fumes.

Homeschooling: Microfiber

As the name sort of implies, microfiber is a man-made material made up of thousands of tiny (micro) fibers that act like a magnet, collecting dirt, dust, lint, hair, and a bunch of other stuff. In fact, it's one hundred times thinner than a strand of human hair. I know, fascinating—but the big news for us is that because of its makeup it holds and absorbs more dirt, grime, and water and won't smear or smudge your mirrors—plus, it's superabsorbent, which makes it great for cleaning up spills. It's also environmentally friendly, since it's chemical-free and hypoallergenic. And, as if that isn't enough, it can be used over and over again before you give it a spin in the washing machine. This is truly the definition of a perfect multipurpose, multitaskin' accidental housewifely must-have tool.

MIRRORS

Mirror, mirror on the wall, don't tell me who's the fairest one of all at six a.m.! Ah yes, the mirror, the bane of our existence and vanity, which gets covered with spit, toothpaste, finger marks, and fog—not always a bad thing after a sleepless night! Here's a simple way to defend against dirt.

What you'll need:
- Microfiber cloth or paper towel
- Multisurface spray, streak-free wipe, water, or white vinegar

What you'll do:
- Wipe the mirror with a microfiber cloth or paper towel, since it leaves no lint and does not smear or smudge.
- No liquid is necessary, but feel free to put some water, store-bought spray, or vinegar on if it makes you feel better!

FAUCETS, SINKS, AND COUNTERS

SHINE YOUR PEARLY WHITES

What you'll need for the faucets:
- Toothpaste (nongel, nonwhitening)
- Toothbrush (not the one you use to brush)
- Paper towels or a microfiber cloth

What you'll do:
- As you're brushing your pearly whites, put a dab of toothpaste on the faucet and use an old toothbrush to clean. (C'mon—you've got two hands!)
- Wipe with a paper towel or dry microfiber cloth.

READ ALL ABOUT IT!

What you'll need for the faucets:
- Newspaper

What you'll do:
- Crumple a piece of newspaper and wipe the faucet. Newspaper ink is a terrific polishing agent.

WIPE AND SWIPE

What you'll need for your faucet, sink, and counters:
- Disinfecting wipes or baby wipes
  or
- White vinegar, vodka, or multipurpose disinfecting spray
- Rag
- Paper towel or microfiber cloth

What you'll do:
- Swipe with wipe of choice.
  or
- Douse an old rag with vinegar or vodka.
- Rinse with water and dry with paper towels or a microfiber cloth (alternatively, you can also use a multipurpose disinfecting spray and wipe with a microfiber cloth or paper towel).

SHOWERS

Soap scum, mold, and mildew tend to congregate in our stalls, so while you're singing in the shower here are some easy, "blended," spur-of-the-moment ways to scrub as you rub both you and your shower.

Vinegar Splash

What you'll need to remove soap scum, mold, and mildew:
- White vinegar or leftover white wine
- Spray bottle
- Disinfecting spray
- Paper towels, microfiber cloth, or newspaper

What you'll do:
- Fill a spray bottle with white vinegar or use that leftover white wine you have from two days ago. Leave it in your shower between cleanings and washes.
- While showering, use spray and then rinse shower walls and door with water.
- If the vinegar or wine stench doesn't please your nozzle, spray a bit of scented disinfecting spray on a paper towel or microfiber cloth, and wipe.

If you have some nooks and crannies on your tile that need a bit more elbow grease, to remove soap scum use a toothbrush and some dishwashing liquid.

For those less adventurous or if you've been banned from the shower due to your horrible voice, feel free to use a traditional alternative such as Scrubbing Bubbles Automatic Shower Cleaner or Shower Shine, Clorox BathWand System, Tilex Fresh Shower Daily Shower Cleaner, or an eco-friendly one such as Method's Daily Shower Spray Cleaner, which can be found at Target and online.

Baby Your Tub and Shower

If you apply baby oil or lemon oil to the sides with a dry microfiber cloth, clean rag, or paper towel it will help keep scum to a minimum since it'll cause the dirty water to bead up and drip down the drain. Be sure to remove any excess oil that may trickle down by sprinkling some baby or talcum powder on the bottom of your tub and removing it with a damp paper towel or cloth—you don't want to accidentally slip after finally indulging in your long overdue soak!

If you have shower curtains:
- They should be machine washable and mold resistant. If not, chuck them and buy new ones.
- If they are machine washable and mold resistant, wash them separately from your other laundry but throw in a few bath towels to help "scrub" off any yuk.

TUBS

My tub stays fairly clean since I never have time to take a bath and my son has outgrown both its size and its playtime appeal. But, for those of you who still use the tub as your child's indoor swimming pool, have bathing-age tots, or are lucky enough to have the time to take baths, here are three simple ways to keep rings and rot to a minimum:

1. What you'll need:
- Nonoily bubble bath or baby shampoo

What you'll do:
- Wash the kiddies and the tub simultaneously with nonoily bubble bath or baby shampoo.
- Rinse the tub with clean water when through.

2. What you'll need:
- Leftover white wine, white vinegar, or vodka (the cheap variety!)
- Spray bottle
- A dry microfiber cloth, paper towel, or newspaper

What you'll do:
- Pour the leftover wine, vinegar, or vodka into a spray bottle and squirt it on the tub.
- Wipe it dry with the microfiber cloth, paper towel, or newspaper.

3. What you'll need:
- Antibacterial multipurpose/multisurface product
- A microfiber cloth
- Newspaper (optional)

What you'll do:
- After bathing: Spray the tub and let the product sit per instructions as you dry off your little ones or yourself.

- Dry it with the microfiber cloth.
- Optional: Shine the faucet and chrome with newspaper.

DECALS

Decals often become permanent works of art in our tubs, staying there long after our kiddies have said bye-bye to their favorite mermaid, duck, or fishie. They can also get gross-looking and harbor mold and mildew under them so you should remove them.

Please note: If the decals have been there for a long time you may need to repeat the following once, twice, or thrice. After that give up and cover with a Brad Pitt decal!

What you'll need:
- Vinegar, mineral oil, or nail polish remover
- Credit card of choice*
- Vinegar, liquid soap, or hand sanitizer

What you'll do:
- Drench a dry rag with vinegar, mineral oil, or nail polish remover and put it over the decals.
- Let sit for five to ten minutes.
- Lift the rag and remove the decals with the credit card.
- Remove any leftover yuk by rubbing it with vinegar, liquid soap, or hand sanitizer.

Another option:
- WD-40 is terrific for removing both floor and wall decals. Apply directly to the decal and let it sit for fifteen to twenty minutes.
- Remove any residue by scrubbing it with liquid soap.

TUB TOYS

If you're noticing that rubber ducky's looking yucky it's probably not just from your little one chewing on it—tub toys are another "hot spot" for the fungus among us to set up shop, so every now and then do one of the following three things:

---

*It is suggested that you use one that has either expired or needs a rest since you may bend the edges in the desticking process.

1. Give them a vinegar bath in your sink, letting them soak for ten to fifteen minutes. (I know I've often suggested using vodka for this, but unless your toys are for adults, forgo that technique here. We don't want little Sammy or Samantha sucking on any residual drippings!)
2. Wipe them with disinfecting wipes. Be sure they're nontoxic.
3. Wash them on the top shelf of your dishwasher—just check if there are any warnings on the toys to ensure you don't cook ducky or melt any of his other pals!

TOILETS

There are many words that I'd like to use to describe my absolute hatred of cleaning toilets, but my editor has told me that this book is rated G. I mean, come on, other than dogs who love to drink from toilets and plumbers who make their living from fixing them, who the hey wants to put their hands anywhere near that yuk? But, if you'll pardon the pun, a housewife's got to doo what a housewife's got to doo and cleaning poop and whiz is unfortunately what we got to doo! I promise, though, that my simple tips for this god-awful chore that bores and abhors will help us maintain our distance, our manicures, and, most important, our dignity!

ADD SOME FIZZAZZ

What you'll need for the bowl:
*   Effervescent tablets (denture or antacid)
*   Toilet brush with disposable head

What you'll do:
*   Plop two effervescent tablets in the bowl. Let them fizz and work their magic for at least twenty minutes. FYI: *You can also use these tablets to clean your diamonds. Just plop one in a glass of water and let the fizz bring some sparkle back to that carat!*
*   Flush and brush with a disposable toilet brush.

WHATCHA DRINKIN'?

What you'll need for the bowl:
*   Tang, cola, Kool-Aid (unsweetened lemonade), or Crystal Light
*   Toilet brush with disposable head

What you'll do, depending on your drink of choice:
- Tang: Hey, if it was good enough for the astronauts to take to the moon—why not your toilet!
  - Sprinkle a tablespoon or two of Tang on the inside walls of your t-bowl.
  - Let the Tang sit for about an hour, brush, and flush.
- Cola:
  - Pour a can of cola into the toilet.
  - Let it sit for an hour, then brush and flush. It'll also remove any rust rings or other mineral deposits, thanks to the phosphoric acid in it—which once again gives me pause as to what it's doing to our insides when we drink it.
- Kool-Aid or Crystal Light:
  - Put a few tablespoons in the bowl.
  - Let it sit for an hour, then brush and flush. In case you're wondering, it's the citric acid that does the trick!

What you'll need to clean your throne's exterior:
1. Disinfecting wipes or baby wipes
   or
2. White vinegar or cheap vodka and a paper towel or microfiber cloth

What you'll do:
1. Clean with disinfecting wipes or baby wipes.
   or
2. Dampen a paper towel or microfiber cloth with white vinegar or vodka and cleanse.

FLOORS

This is probably the one part of the bathroom that I clean the least since I have several bath mats scattered about and every few weeks (actually more like once a month) I throw them in the wash. But for those of you who are losing your hair faster than expected, creating a natural floor covering, here are three simple ways to clean up on a more regular basis:

1. *VAC:* Use your hand vac to pick up hair, nail clippings, and dust.
2. *DANCE:* Put on a pair of slippers or socks.

Who'd Have Thunk! The Bottom Line

As I researched this guide I found a lot of myths and facts on the varying levels of grossness we tend to assume are associated with the bathroom and our family throne in particular. One person, Charles Gerba, a professor of microbiology at the University of Arizona, seems to have taken these myths on a crusade of sorts. Everyone has their talents! At any rate, I was both amazed and grossed out by what he found and suspect you may be as well!

Public Bathrooms Are Less Germy Than Those in Our Homes
It may be hard to believe, but public restrooms seem to have cleaner door handles than those in our own homes. Gerber conducted a study that showed that 68 percent of folks who go on the run wash their hands before leaving public loos. And, since these usually disgusting places are cool and not humid, they aren't prime breeding grounds for our bacteria buds who hit the dust (not literally) after two hours in dry conditions! Hmmm, seems like a good reason to travel and eat out more often!

Microbes in Your Mist
Here's another gross factoid from our buddy Chuck. Every time you flush your toilet it gives off a microscopic mist, so if your toothbrush is within misting range it gets sprayed with bacteria—*yuk!* Some good news though—since bacteria aren't superhuman broad jumpers, you just need to keep your toothbrushes far away. If you live in a New York City apartment this may not be possible; therefore, close the lid before you flush and consider keeping your toothbrush near your kitchen sink.

- Attach a disinfecting wipe to the bottom of the slippers or socks with a rubber band or scrunchie.
- Turn on your iPod and dance away the debris.

3. *SWIRL:* Dampen a microfiber mop and put half a capful of mouthwash on it, then sweep. Mouthwash will give your bathroom a fresh, minty smell—feel free to take a swig for yourself. Use the time you're swirling it around in your mouth as a timer so you don't spend more time doing this task than you have to!

Chapter 2

The Bathroom

JUST ENOUGH ORGANIZING

Although you'll find our house a mess, come in, sit down, converse. It doesn't always look like this—some days it's even worse. —Anonymous

I've discovered that an easy way to maintain the image of a clean-enough bathroom (and most rooms, for that matter) is by doing some simple things to keep it organized. I also realize that the bathroom is generally the first and last stop of our day, which means we greet it weary and perhaps blurry-eyed, the result of our overscheduled days or sleep-deprived nights. That said, it's important to have all the things you need visible, within easy reach, and not blocking any critical passageways. Additionally, many of you have bathrooms that are no bigger than a broom closet, so the more you can keep off vanities and floors the better. Thus, we begin this chore by asking ourselves the following questions to ensure you do just enough organizing:

- Are any key bathroom stops such as the sink, tub, shower, or toilet blocked, thereby preventing easy access, which could result in physical harm of or "accidents" by loved ones or guests?
- Have your possessions surpassed the height and space available?
- What things do you use regularly and need to have handy?

This question in particular will help you figure out where to start. Things to consider include:

- toilet paper
- towels
- shampoo and conditioner
- styling aids (brushes, blow dryers, curlers, sprays, hair clips, scrunchies, etc.)
- makeup
- skin creams
- shaving stuff
- contacts and solutions for them
- medicines
- bath toys
- throne-side reading material
- air freshener
- coffeemaker—I realize many of you might wonder why this is on the list. Well, many of you have shared with me that you have or like the idea of having a single-pod brewsky in your bathroom to help start the day. So this brew's for you!

Living an Organized-Enough Life

Try as you might to keep clutter in check, your toxic zones are the accidental housewife's primary cause of disorganization. The good news is that over- and under-the-counter help is available to enable you to live an organized-enough life.

HOW TO KEEP CLUTTER IN CHECK

Please remember that as with all chores that bore, you should embark on the following preventive measures when you're in the mood, and not all at once, unless you've drunk too much caffeine and have energy to burn. For the rest of you, what follows is a simple three-step process to help keep things in check:

LEARN TO LET GO:
- Throw out things that you haven't used in the last month unless they are backups for things that you may use (for example, creams, contact lens cleaner, shampoos) or items that you use occasionally (razor refills, pedicure tools, scissors, teeth-whitening treatments, hair-coloring aids, and so on). The items that you may want to toss include:
  - multiple sample packets of makeup, lotion, or perfume from your fave department store;

- styling tools and aids that were must-haves from your last haircut or color treatment; and
- anything else that has dust rapidly collecting on it or leaves its imprint on your vanity when you lift it up.

Special-occasion makeup or that bought on a whim can be stored in Ziploc bags and kept under your sink or in a drawer. Put a date on the outside so you know how long it's been there and when to chuck it.

- Check expiration dates on medicines, condoms, and anything else that has a shelf life, including makeup, creams, and cleansers (see "You're Expired" on page 41).
- Recycle magazines that have a pub date older than three months ago and newspapers after a week. Not only will this keep your reading material fresh, it will also help minimize potential mold buildup. Remember mold loves dark, humid places, and the pages in your old magazines and newspaper are perfect hangouts for them.
- Toss any tub toys that have holes, tears, or are coated in anything foreign looking.

TRY GROUP THERAPY
- Keep items that relate to the same activity together. This means keep all your styling tools and aids such as gels, mousse, brushes, and sprays near your curling

The Fine Print on Newspapers

Before recycling old newspapers keep in mind that you can use them to:

- shine faucets and other chrome fixtures,

- clean windows—they don't leave lint;

- absorb odors both in your garbage and in the bathroom.

This last fact has always made me wonder if that's why so many of us choose to read the morning newspaper in the bathroom!

iron and blow dryer. Same therapy applies to your shaving items—keep your razor, cream, and lotions all in a drawer near your tub, sink, or shower side and not scattered about. This will limit your searching through drawers and under your vanity for things and then leaving them in disarray.

Control Urges
- Finish what you start before opening another bottle of lotion or shampoo.
- Don't buy another bottle of the latest youth-enhancing skin cream or this season's must-have eye shadow, lipstick, and pencil until your last season's is done—unless the next time you see your friend she looks ten years younger after having used them.

Simple Enough Solutions

Organizing is about finding easy-to-see, easy-to-reach places for the items you need. Need, of course, is personal and why I suggested you think about the things you use regularly. As a result, what follows are some tried, some true, and some things new to help you organize enough, regardless of your personal needs and habits.

- *STURDY NOT PURDY:* Something may look pretty but if it can't hold your new 5,000-watt blow dryer, pass on it. If you're not sure about its sturdiness, ask a sales rep or test it out while you're in the store.
- *NEED TO BREATHE:* The last thing you need are organizers that maintain moisture, so look for products that are well ventilated and/or are nonporous. Materials to consider: plastic, mesh, and wire. Stay away from wood or fabric organizers as well as anything that can rust.
- *GET A HANDLE:* Since you may keep your items in a handy organizer under your sink or vanity, buy one that you can easily lift. Look for one with a handle that preferably folds down so that it fits in tight spaces.
- *CLEAR THINKING:* The more you can see at a glance the better—particularly first thing in the morning or late at night—so buy organizers that are clear, or see-through. You'll thank me when you reach for the toothpaste instead of the hemorrhoid cream the next time you brush.
- *STACK 'N' SLIDE:* Look for organizers that easily stack and slide. These will save space, and you won't need to lift and replace them every time you need an item. Check the "Under- and Over-the-Counter Faves" on page 41.
- *MBA NOT REQUIRED:* If something comes with lots of directions, leave it on the shelf. Remember who you are and that your goal is to make life easy, so buy

only organizing solutions that don't require you to have an MBA from MIT or the latest laser drill to install. Best bets are to buy organizers that:

- come with over-the-door hooks or can be hung with double-backed tape,
- include instructions that require fewer than three steps to assemble completely,
- don't ask you to put holes in your wall (which may risk your breaking a nail),
- a seven-year-old child can assemble for you.

Resimplifying

What follows are some organizing ideas, tips, and items that give real meaning to the word *resimplified*. Resimplifying is about giving a fresh approach and look to things that may already provide simple solutions to all aspects of your everyday homekeeping in a manner relevant to *your* individual life, needs, time, and skills. That means I may repurpose, redirect, recycle, and get you to rethink how you look at everything, including things you have hanging around the house, find in stores, see on TV, read about in magazines, and yes, even when you look in the mirror and see your weary mug.

Another part of resimplifying means that I've given you a variety of solutions that you can use to solve a multitude of your organizing problems all at once. I like these multipurpose ideas, since they require little thought or effort, and they're terrific space-savers. They're followed by what I call "Baby Step" solutions that provide tips and tools on an item-by-item basis (i.e., tips for individually organizing makeup, shaving items, styling aids, etc.). Regardless of which idea you choose these simple solutions will organize your bathroom just enough.

MULTIPURPOSE SOLUTIONS

Pocket Pals Rock

Anything that has a multitude of pockets and can be hung is your organizing pal, since they can hold most of the items that cause bathroom clutter, save space, and don't cost a lot. Plus, they come in a variety of colors and fabrics to suit your decorative palette. You can also buy ones with clear pockets. That's my choice, since I'm usually reaching for my bathroom musts before I've put in my contacts.

To find the one that's right for you, visit a store like Target, Wal-Mart, Linens 'n Things, Bed Bath & Beyond, a local dollar store, or a thrift shop. Look at shoe bags, multipocket closet organizers, and, for smaller spaces, travel toiletry roll-ups. By the way, most of these pocket pals come with their own hanging attachments (over the door or pole hooks) or they can be easily attached using double-stick tape. If neither of these easy "hookups" applies to the one you find, fawgetaboutit and ask a salesperson for one that does.

Here are a few suggestions on how to organize your pocket pals row by row. The key is to start with the items you use frequently and put them in according to the order of your daily grooming and beauty routines:

- Row One: toothbrush, toothpaste, mouthwash, floss
- Row Two: shaving cream, razor, aftershave, and bandages!
- Row Three: skin cream, makeup, brushes, and makeup remover
- Row Five: styling aids—mousse, spray, gel, brushes, and combs

You get the idea . . . One more tip: Clip hairclips and barrettes to the sides of your pal.

Velcro Is Your Bathroom's New Black

In the world of fashion every season has its must-have colors and accessories. I look at homekeeping items in the same way, which helps me feel a bit better when I do these chores that bore. I've already shared one of my favorite, must-have fashionable and functional accessories for cleaning: rubber gloves, which you can flip back to and read more about on page 8. Another timeless accidental housewifely bathroom organizing must-have is Velcro. That's right—that oh-so-thin, versatile, sticky-backed, space-saving jewel that goes with and on almost anything. Just pull some out, snip, peel, and stick on items to turn your overstuffed bathroom drawer or vanity from bad to fab in minutes since this beauty works with so many of your bathroom's key clutterers, including:

- deodorant
- makeup and makeup brushes
- shavers and shaving cream
- tweezers
- hairspray
- hand mirrors (please note that most store-bought Velcro works only on items that are *no more than* three pounds, so please check the package for its exact limitations to avoid seven years of bad luck!)
- combs, brushes, and curling irons

And on and on . . .

Homeschooling: Velcro

Velcro is like bottled water—there's one for almost every need you have. For example, there's a heat-activated Velcro, which is a terrific and quick fix for when your child's pant or skirt hem has fallen—just cut, iron, and voilà! There's also a heavy-duty and waterproof variety, which would be a good choice in your moisture-rich bathroom to prevent an avalanche occurring after you Velcro all your items! Check out what's right for you either by visiting a home-crafting retailer like Michaels or Jo-Ann or go to their Web sites and enter the word *Velcro* in the search box.

CHIC AND SIMPLE TIPS

Of course, you'll need a chic and simple place to attach your bathroom bounty, so here are a few pocketbook-friendly ideas to keep it all together and make your bathroom look mahvelous:

- *STRIP STYLE:* Attach rows of Velcro strips, to any type of hanging board. Now, affix Velcro on the item you wish to display. Voilà—it's all together now. If you're feeling crafty, you can cover a plain board with a piece of coated fabric and place size-specific Velcro strips onto the fabric. Use heavy-duty double-stick tape or a hook to hang the board.
- *FRAMES ARE IN!* Buy or use an existing picture frame that fits the space you have available and hang it on your wall. Cut out and stick Velcro pieces to the space inside the frame so that you can attach items. Be sure that you don't care about what happens to the wall, since the strips will most likely cause damage if or when you remove them. An alternative idea is to put a picture or painting you don't care much about in the frame to preserve your wall and then attach the strips.
- *GLAM IT ON:* Take that dusty flower pot that's been sitting in the garage and fill it with an artificial plant (which is what I plant since I was not blessed with a green thumb!). Then stick a strip of Velcro around the perimeter and hang like items such as your makeup brushes, tweezers, razor, toothpaste, and toothbrush on it. Alternatively, you could glam on your items to that extra wine bucket or basket you've got lying around and fill the center with your brushes, curling or

flattening iron, and other related styling items. Stick straight items like makeup pencils, makeup brushes, combs, and so on around the outside.

Cosmetic Cover-Ups

As I mentioned in the introduction to this chapter, an accidental housewife's greatest homekeeping trick is to redirect the eye's focus in a room by doing simple things to make it look organized and therefore neat. So if you have styling tools and aids, makeup, and creams scattered all over your vanities but can't bring yourself to organize them you can still achieve some sense of order with "cover-ups." These results are similar to those achieved in what is often referred to as cosmetic cleaning—doing the minimum amount of surface cleaning to achieve the maximum effect in areas that are most visible. Cover-ups are particularly good for those of you who have trouble letting go or engaging in group therapy since it won't require you to move anything or make decisions about what to group with what or what to throw out. A few more baby steps toward your achieving an organized-enough bathroom.

Here are a few cover-ups that are listed in their order of ease:

- *SCREEN ZEST:* Floor-standing decorative screens are a perfect decoy that can hide a multitude of clutter and give your bathroom the appearance of being neat and tidy. There are some hang-up screens that have hooks and come with add-ons for magazines and shelves, as well. Check out a few at www.target.com. FYI: The models that have more accessories may also require installation, so ask or read the fine print before taking one home to ensure that an MBA (or a child) is not required.
- *MIRROR, MIRROR:* Self-standing mirrors come in a variety of sizes and they're great for hiding items. Just place them in front of the clutter you want to disguise. Place them: on vanities to hide blow dryers, curling or straightening irons, styling aids, lotions, shaving cream; on tubs to hide shampoos, bubble bath, and loofah sponges; and on floors to hide towels, laundry baskets, and so on. They're also a terrific way to give a small bathroom an illusion of being larger.
- *MADE IN THE SHADE:* Use S-hooks to hang lightweight shades or blinds made out of plastic, rattan, or waterproof fabric from your ceiling. Then roll them down to block out your chaos and up when you need to get to your blow dryer, styling aids, or shaving stuff.

Baby Steps

The ideas that follow allow you to ease your way into organizing on an item-by-item or category-by-category manner as you learn to deal with and overcome your bouts with chronic disorganization.

MAKEUP/COSMETICS

Everyday stuff (foundation, concealer, shadows, liners, mascara, blush, lipstick, and so on) should be kept in one place. Use a container that allows you to easily see its contents, such as:

- Small Ziploc bags
- Plastic utensil divider
- Tupperware
- Tiered cosmetic, art supply, or fishing tackle box

Two's Company's Home Chic Home designer Ziploc quart-sized storage bags are an attractive alternative to using your handy-dandy supermarket variety. They've got a purdy damask scroll pattern and come forty to a box. Check them out at www.vintageweave .com.

For straight items like eyeliners, lip pencils, and mascara use:

- Colored ponytail bands or scrunchies and group by item
- Multiple toothbrush holder
- Empty disposable tissue box cubes
- Small clay flower pot: Add a piece of Styrofoam and "plant" your brushes or other straight beauty pals in the foam

STYLING TOOLS AND AIDS

For blow dryers, curling irons, and flat irons:
- Use a bar towel rack to organize these tools.
- Hang S hooks, traditional or decorative door hooks on walls that are near outlets.
- Put up a decorative hand towel ring and place a towel under your blow dryer to hold and secure it when not in use.
- Put that extra wine bucket that's been sitting in your closet to use and throw these tools in it.

For styling aids:
- Gently toss them into a wine bucket, coated basket, or flower pot
- Place them in a hanging shoe bag.

CREAMS (SKIN, BODY, AND SHAVING)
- Display them on serving trays that have been collecting dust in the garage or attic.
- Use the four-cup cardboard drink or coffee cup holder you get from your local deli or bagel place. They're a great organizer for shaving cream cans and similarly shaped bottles of lotion or cream.

TWEEZERS AND RAZORS
- Use magnets with self-adhesive backs and attach them to tweezers and razors, then hang them on a magnetic board.
- Keep them in a multiple toothbrush holder.

MEDICATIONS AND CONDOMS
- Flush old medications down the toilet or ask your pharmacist if he or she can dispose of unwanted pills.
- Use different colored nail polish to color-code each household member's prescriptions.
- Condoms have expiration dates or manufacturing dates printed on their packaging, so check them. If the manufacturing date is listed here's how long they're worthy:
  - With spermicide—up to two years
  - Without spermicide—up to five years

TOILET PAPER
- Stack several rolls on a paper towel holder.
- Load them up on an old golf club and lean it in the corner near the toilet.
- Slide rolls onto a decorative broom.

TOWELS
- Hang a tiered pants organizer like those you would use in your closet on a wall or back of a bathroom door. This is a great way to let towels dry and keep them off the vanity or tub no matter how big a slob you and yours are.
- Use a towel rack that attaches to your door hinge.

- Install a swing-arm towel holder. Check out Rubbermaid's at http://www
.organize-everything.com/trswtobarch.html or Williams-Sonoma's at http://
www.williams-sonoma.com.
- Dust off those candlesticks that your grandma gave you and place them by your
sink to throw your hand towels and washcloths on.
- Roll hand towels up and place them in a wine rack.

NEWSPAPERS, MAGAZINES, AND CATALOGS
- Keep them on a free-standing laundry dryer rack.
- Roll them and store in wine racks.
- Use a towel rack.
- Hang a tiered pants organizer like those you would put in your closet on the wall
near the toilet.

You're Expired

I've learned from experience and several eye infections that bacteria love to grow in
makeup. But how are you to know when your favorite shade of blue mascara is living in a

---

Under- and Over-the-Counter Faves

Here are a few of my favorite store-bought organizers that are easy to install and are terrific space savers:

- Hook-on shelves by Grayline Housewares. These hook onto the edge of any
standard shelf or if you have space under your sink or vanity they're great there
too (http://www.organize-everything.com/17unshba.html).

- Slide and stack baskets—just pile these babies on to house a variety of items
(www.rubbermaid.com).

- Storage compartment boxes—these are great for makeup and brushes, hair
clips, coated rubber bands, scrunchies, and anything else that's currently in
disarray on your vanity top or in your drawers. They also have handles so you
can store things below them and easily lift them for access when you need it
(http:// www.organize-everything.com/lglimebox.html).

sea of it? It can be tricky, since manufacturers aren't required to provide expiration dates for makeup. Still, there are some things you should know to keep your eyes from flaunting a pinkish cast and bacteria from breeding in your makeup brushes. For more info on the good, bad, and ugly of kitchen-based bacteria go to page 47.

- Don't wet your eyeliner brush with saliva. Doing that will leave it damp and breed bacteria on both the product and the brush.
- Throw away anything that smells or is discolored, chunky, or hardened.
  - Water-based foundations last up to twelve months, so if they get chunky and start to dry out before that, add a few drops of alcohol-free toner and shake that baby.
- Lengthen the life of your lipstick and minimize bacteria from moving in by keeping it cool in your fridge.
- Limit pumping your mascara—the more you pump, the more you expose it to the air, which will dry it out faster.
- Use Q-tips or disposable applicators and sponges.
- Sharpen eyeliners and lip pencils regularly.
- Chuck the brush or product pronto if you get an infection.
- Toss stained or misshapen brushes.
- Never share your makeup or creams!

YOUR EXPIRATION GUIDE TO SAFE-ENOUGH BATHROOM TOILETRIES, MAKEUP, AND ALL ELSE IN BETWEEN

The expiration guidelines that follow are approximations gathered from makeup gurus. The reason: Manufacturers are not required to give dates, so even those in the know don't really know. The keys are to use good old common sense and let your god-given senses, such as your sense of smell and sight, guide you. Remember, if something looks chunky, lumpy, smells bad, or has changed color it's time for it to go—and if you've kept that must-have orange lipstick from three years ago, clearly it's not a must-use, so chuck it! Face it, girlfriends: The things we use generally don't last more than six months, so if they are still hanging around beyond that and you haven't gone into witness protection, here's your opportunity to *let go*. As you may recall, this is a critical step in helping to keep your clutter in check.

Makeup
- Face powder and powder blush: 2 years
- Foundation

- Water-based: 12 to 18 months
- Oil-based: 18 months
- Concealer: 12 months
- Lipstick: 1–2 years (remember, if it smells rancid, chuck it)
- Moisturizer: 12 to 18 months
- Lip and eye pencils: 2–3 years
- Eye shadow: 3 years, or until next season's hot color replaces it!
- Eye cream: 1 year
- Cream blush: 6 months to 1 year
- Mascara: 3–6 months
- Makeup brushes: 3–7 years, depending upon care and quality. If they become misshapen or stained, time to go.

Brushing Up on Makeup Brushes

I know you're probably thinking, *Oh great, another thing to clean.* Just keep in mind that your brushes are some of your best buds since they help make you look good every day! Keeping them clean will also help prevent bacteria from breeding and pimples from erupting. So take heed and read!

- **BABY THEM:** Most brushes are made of hair, so clean them as you would your own: use a little baby shampoo and warm water, reshape, then lay them on the edge of your sink to dry.

- **DIP IN VINEGAR:** Dip your brushes in a mixture of two parts water and one part white vinegar and rinse in warm water. Reshape and let them dry on the edge of the sink.

- **SIMPLIFY:** Ask your bud at the cosmetic counter what she likes, or you can check out two of my faves, which are quick and easy to use:
  - Trish McEvoy's Makeup Brush Cleaner is available at Nordstrom, Saks, and Neiman Marcus.
  - Japonesque Professional Brush Cleaner cleans and dries instantly, plus it has a terrific citrus scent to it. Visit their Web site (www.japonesque.com) for where to buy it.

Frequency of Cleaning:
- For brushes you use to apply liquid or cream-based products (foundation, concealer, creamy eye shadow, lipstick), shampoo or at least wipe them daily with a clean damp rag.

- All others can be cleaned every week or two—okay, every two weeks is fine—after all, we are accidental housewives!

Brush-Buying Basics
Buying makeup brushes can be confusing and expensive, since there seems to be a different kind for every step in our daily makeup ritual. Here are some guidelines to help you sort it out. The key is to go for quality, not quantity, when deciding what to buy:

- **Should-haves:** Unless you're a model, have unlimited time to apply your makeup, or can afford every brush available, select only those that you really need and will use regularly. The essentials include shadow (contour and lid), blush, and powder brushes.

- **Real vs. fake:** There are two main types of brushes: synthetic and animal-hair. Animal-hair brushes are generally considered best and they're usually made from sable, pony, or squirrel. If you're wondering how they get the hairs, fear not—PETA will not come knocking on your door. The animals are not scalped but brushed, and the hairs that fall out are gathered and grouped by color—I have to admit it's hard to imagine a squirrel sitting and having its fur stroked, but it's an entertaining visual.

You can find a wide range of brushes that are good enough at stores like Target, Nordstrom, Sephora, Rite Aid, CVS, or your local discount beauty supply shop.

Hair stuff
- Shampoo: 2–3 years
- Conditioner: 2–3 years
- Mousse and gel: 2–3 years
- Brushes—when bristles start to break or after a bout with lice

Creams
- Eye cream: 1 year
- Body: 3 years
- Shaving cream: 2 years

Dental hygiene (except for toothbrushes, these products usually have expiration dates printed or stamped directly on them or on the box)
- Toothpaste: 2 years, opened
- Toothbrush: 4–5 months, unless bristles start falling out or you've had a cold sore
- Mouthwash: 3 years from manufacturing date
- Tooth-whitening strips: 13 months

Miscellaneous
- Nail polish: 1 year
- Nail polish remover—indefinite
- Deodorant
  - Unopened: 2 years
  - Opened: 1 year
  - Antiperspirants follow FDA guidelines since they have active ingredients that prevent perspiration—check the bottom for an expiration date.
- Body bleach
  - Opened: 6 months
  - Unopened: 2 years
- Loofah: 3 months—be sure to squeeze out moisture after every use and hang dry. Discard if it starts deteriorating.
- Perfume: 1–2 years
- Rubber duckie: chuck when torn or holes appear.

Chapter 3

The Kitchen

The only thing that I have ever successfully made in the kitchen is a mess. —Carrie Bradshaw, *Sex and the City*

Ah, the kitchen. It's that wonderful room where everyone gathers at least once or twice a day to indulge in some food and frivolity and to navigate the day ahead or chat about the day behind. Those who like to cook see it as the center of the home, a place to prepare yummy meals. Those who don't like to cook see it as the room with too many appliances and a place to keep take-out menus. The thing is, no matter what you use your kitchen for, it's another high-traffic toxic zone like your bathroom with its own demands and its very own set of living organisms. That's why you're going to need a simple battle plan to keep it clean without losing your mind. And so we begin.

Cleaning

You learned in the first chapter that organizing is your first line of defense in maintaining the image of a clean-enough house. So with any luck (and a little manicure-friendly work) you'll get rid of many items that gather dust, dirt, and grime during your organizing soiree which follows. That's the good news. The bad news is that no matter how much organizing you'll do, the kitchen still requires more cleaning than any other room in your home. What's more, according to the *Journal of the American Dietetic Association*,

> ### Cell-O-Matic
>
> "One little, two little, three little bacteria, four little, five little, six little bacteria . . ." (sung to the tune of "Ten Little Indians").
>
> And then there were 8 million of these microscopic germs which can cover one of many surfaces in our kitchens. *YUK!* And that's just in twenty-four little hours since one little cell, if left to its own devices, may grow and divide into 8 million in one day! Amazing, isn't it? Disgusting too! As they say, what a difference a day makes!

"Food-borne diseases are estimated to cause approximately 76 million illnesses in the United States each year." Translation: The kitchen is the one place where you want to make sure that your clean-enough house really is clean. That means it's time to prepare for battle, mount that defense, and put on your fashionable and functional rubber gloves—the rolling pin is optional.

Defensive Cleaning: Toxic Targets

BACTERIA: WHAT IT IS AND WHAT YOU CAN DO ABOUT IT

There's the dirt you can see—the grime, the grunge, the grease—and the dirt you can't, those living organisms that set up house in your toxic zones, producing germs, smells, and even illnesses. I'm talking about bacteria. Bacteria, like its bathroom buddies mold and mildew (that's M & M to those in the know), multiplies with reckless abandon if not defended against. Unlike M & M, which are generally visible to the naked eye, you can't see bacteria, which makes it that much more dangerous (unless, of course, you have the resources of a CSI).

What exactly are bacteria? They're microscopic, single-celled life forms that are neither plants nor animals. They reproduce quickly and are always on the prowl for nutrients, which is why our kitchens are their number-one breeding ground though, as you've learned, they can also exist in your makeup. And, by the way, just as you and I have good and bad cholesterol there is good and bad bacteria. In fact, according to the experts, 99 percent of all bacteria you come in contact with are good guys, since they aid in activities like your digestive process and actually improve your immune system. But it's that other 1 percent—the bad bacteria—that can cause illness or infections.

In your kitchen that 1 percent of bad bacteria (commonly known as salmonella, E. coli, and staphylococcus—the long form of what is commonly referred to as "staph") can come from a variety of places. It is important to note the word *can*. *Can* means don't panic and throw on a biohazard suit and don't worry that you'll be running to the toilet, doctor, or therapist to ensure your family's health or sanity. On the other hand, perhaps knowing about bad bacteria is good news, since it provides us with an excellent reason to eat more chocolate, which studies have shown is good for you!

Where bacteria begins:
- Raw and undercooked meats, fish, eggs, and poultry
- Fruits and veggies that have not been properly processed, washed, and packaged—that is, produce that has been grown in cow manure or washed in contaminated water
- Unpastuerized juice—pasteurized products mean high heat was used to kill germs

So how do you conquer these microscopic critters before they mount their offensive? You do as any military strategist would:

1. Know thy enemy's whereabouts.
2. Cut them off at the pass.
3. Hit them where they live and grow.

Here's how:

- Avoid cross-contamination of raw meats, fish, eggs, poultry, fresh fruits, and veggies.
- Don't leave foods out too long—cook, refrigerate, or freeze meats, fish, and poultry within two hours.
  - Fridge temp should be 40° Fahrenheit or colder.
  - Freezer temp should be 0° Fahrenheit or colder.
- Don't overstuff your fridge or freezer, since that will prevent air from circulating and maintaining a cold enough environment. It'll also mean your fridge has to work harder to keep itself cold, which is not eco-friendly and will cost you more money on your energy bill. For more information on manicure-friendly ways to be eco-friendly go to page 245.
- Cook foods thoroughly. I'm a bit of a carnivore, particularly when I'm suffering from PMS, which my husband seems to think is 24/7/365 but that's fodder for

another book. At any rate, as such, I also enjoy my steak and burgers rare, which is a no-no unless you enjoy dining with bacteria and having them visit your digestive tract. For those who share my carnivorous craving or just would like to know when your fish, meat, or poultry is cooked enough, here are some simple tips:

- Fish
  - Use a fork to see if it starts to flake and check that the color is more opaque versus translucent.
  - Scallops and shrimp tend to get less flimsy and are firmer when they're good to go.
- Meats and poultry
  - Test their doneness by cutting into the center with a knife or stabbing it with a fork.
  - Make sure the juices run clear.
  - For meats: pink is the color
  - For poultry: white is the color
- Clean up pronto after prepping, cooking, and eating. Don't leave dirty dishes in the sink or in your dishwasher unwashed for too long. If you can't get to them right away at least rinse off the yuk in hot water, or start using more disposable paper and cooking products! Cleanup also includes washing your hands in hot, sudsy water and/or using a hand sanitizer, store-bought disinfecting product, or a natural disinfectant such as white vinegar.
- When in doubt throw it out! If it smells, looks funny, or is mooing, clucking, or growing, don't take a chance—chuck it!

Who'd Have Thunk! Toilets Are a Cut Above Cutting Boards in Cleanliness!

"If you have a choice between licking a cutting board or a toilet seat pick the toilet seat," advises Charles Gerba, Ph.D., University of Arizona. Professor Gerba did a study back in 1998 in which he swabbed different spots in the bathroom and kitchen to check for bacteria and E. coli. What he found was that our refrigerators' door handles are dirtier then our toilet seats. And—this is the one that really grossed me out—we'd be better off eating off our toilet seats than our cutting boards, since the cutting boards contained two hundred times more bacteria! Almost makes you want to serve dinner in the bathroom, doesn't it?

If you'd like to learn more about preventing bad bacteria from taking over your kitchen and tummies visit www.fightbac.gov. They've got lots of great info for your kids too and a food cooking safety chart that you can print out so you don't have to remember anything. *Bon Appétit!*

BACTERIA'S FAVORITE HOT SPOTS

CUTTING BOARDS
There are lots of conflicting theories on which board is better in your fight against bacteria: wood or plastic? The truth is, no one knows for sure. Studies have shown that bacteria die faster on wood surfaces since they're porous and the wood dries faster. Some in the know think that the nooks, crannies, and nicks from knife cuts on plastic boards provide a perfect place for them to hide. Plastic boards are also nonporous, so they stay wet longer, producing a perfect environment for bacteria to thrive. So as the debate continues, here are a few defensive tactics you can initiate regardless of which board you have. Have I bored you yet?

Buy a minimum of two boards. Use one for meats, poultry, and fish, and another for veggies and fruit.

After using, clean them immediately with one of the following:
- Soap and hot water
- A natural sanitizer like vinegar
- A combo of one teaspoon bleach with one quart of water

1. *If dishwasher-safe:* Wash in the dishwasher on full cycle to ensure that the temperature is hot enough to kill the bacteria. This is not the time to use your environmentally friendly dry cycles.
2. *If microwave-safe:* Zap it in the microwave for 30 seconds.

PLEASE NOTE: Once cleaned, *always store vertically* in a cool, dry place.

SPONGES
1. *WRING OUT DAILY.* After each use rinse thoroughly and squeeze out all the excess water. Leave in an open-air spot or buy a sponge dish so it can dry completely on all sides. If you don't have a specific dish, try one of the following:
   - Put it on top of a small juice glass.

Cutting-Edge Advice on Cutting Boards

Like everything else, there are different kinds of cutting boards available. Three simple guidelines to follow are:

1. Pick a board (or two or three) that's right for your food-prep needs to avoid cross-contamination.
2. When choosing boards, make sure you will be able to easily identify which board is to be used for what food.
3. Buy a board that's easy enough to clean (dishwasher and/or microwave-safe)

My advice is to go for boards that are either color-coded or have a picture that identifies what you should use it for (for example, a chicken, cow, carrot, or fish), which is why I like the idiot-proof color-coded flexible cutting boards from Sur La Table. Check these out online at www.surlatable.com. Target also has a bunch of multicolored coded boards (if you prefer color-coding to idiot-proof pictures), which you can view at www.target.com. And my bud Rachael Ray has a wood board combo called the Rachael Ray Gusto Grip 7-Piece Clean-Cut Cutting Board Set by Füri that'll cover all your needs. It's a hardwood board that comes with a medley of six dishwasher-safe polypropylene color-coded mats that offer you food safety across the board (forgive the pun!):

*   red for raw meat,
*   brown for cooked meat,
*   blue for seafood,
*   yellow for poultry,
*   green for vegetables, and
*   white for dairy.

It's available at www.amazon.com.

• Take a large black clip that you use to hold papers together, stand it upside down, and clip the sponge.
• Use a medium-size butterfly hairclip, turn it upside down, and put the sponge in between—the clip marks will go bye-bye once you wet it.

2. *DE-BAC-TIZE:* Try one of the following:
- *Microwave:* Squeeze out any excess water and then zap the sponge for three minutes. Let it sit before removing so you don't burn your hand (I add a spritz of lemon during or after as well to give my sponge a fresher scent).
- *Boil:* Float in boiling water for two to three minutes.
3. *ASSIGN:* Like bathroom plungers, which you should designate for specific jobs to avoid cross-contamination between the sink and toilet (more on this on page 224), you need to avoid cross-contamination with sponges. Have a few within reach and use one for cleaning counters and one for the sink. Better yet, switch to disinfecting wipes so you don't have to remember what assignment you gave the yellow, red, or patterned sponge.
4. *REPLACE:* Toss any that are falling apart and/or get smelly. Usually every month will do but for the fifty-nine cents it'll cost you to buy a new one and to be really safe, you should replace them every two weeks.
5. *ELIMINATE:* Junk them and use disposable, disinfecting wipes or microfiber cloths so you don't have to think about them at all! Particularly given the fact that a study published by the *Journal of Environmental Health* found that kitchen sponges were the number-one source of germs in our home sweet homes.

DISH TOWELS
1. *KEEP THEM DRY:* Wring them out when you're done and let them air dry or toss them into your dryer (clearly not as eco-friendly an option as air-drying, however!).
2. *CHANGE THEM DAILY LIKE UNDERWEAR:* Replace them immediately if they come into contact with raw meats, poultry, or fish.
3. *SWITCH TO PAPER!* It's an easy way to not have to worry about nuttin'! Consider buying the recycled kind and that way you'll be helping our environment as well as your well-being.

FAUCETS, FRIDGE HANDLES, AND COUNTERTOPS
Disinfect daily with one of the following:

1. *BLEACH:* Dampen a cloth with a teaspoon of bleach and water.
2. *DISINFECTING WIPES:* Every time you're chatting on the phone simply attack another one of bacteria's hot spots and swipe those critters away.

3. *STORE-BOUGHT, DISINFECTING KITCHEN CLEANERS OR ANTI-BACTERIAL OR SANITIZING SPRAY CLEANER:* Read the directions to see how long they need to sit to be effective and to confirm the surfaces you can use them on. Most of these products suggest leaving them on for at least thirty seconds to sanitize and four minutes to disinfect. Wipe with a paper towel when time's up.

4. *VINEGAR:* Pour some on a microfiber cloth and clean away!

5. *VODKA.* Put a shot on a cloth to rid you of those pesky critters. While you're at it, swirl some around in your mouth as a mouthwash to kill the bacteria lurking there—swallowing is optional! By the way, the higher the alcohol content the more effective so go for the absolute best!

GARBAGE DISPOSALS

Use one of the following biweekly:

1. *WHITE VINEGAR AND BAKING SODA:* Pour a bit of white vinegar and baking soda down the drain and watch it bubble. Follow with a dousing of very hot water.

2. *BLEACH AND WATER:* Give it a teaspoon of bleach followed by a very hot water rinse.

Finish with zest: Throw down a lemon, lime, or orange wedge and let it chop to give your disposal—and your kitchen—a fresh scent.

TRASH CANS

Daily:

1. Throw out food garbage

2. Clean handles or area you touch regularly with disinfecting wipes, sanitizing spray, or a cloth dampened with vinegar or vodka.

Weekly:

Spray your can with disinfecting or sanitizing spray or wash with a cloth dampened with vinegar or vodka.

Immediately:

• Buy a touchless electronic trash can. (I love these, and so does my son!) All you do is wave your hand over the top or put your foot near a sensor and—presto!—it automatically opens and closes, preventing you from spreading or touching any bacteria. I'm a big fan of products from a company called simplehuman, since they've got a bevy of sleek and simple (duh) solutions to your everyday household needs. Check out their touchless can at www.simplehuman.com or Google the words *touchless trash can.*

HANDS
Immediately:

- *WASH:* As the saying goes, the obvious is often overlooked, and the same holds true for your hands. Be sure to wash them with hot water and soap or wipe with a hand sanitizer or disinfecting wipe after you're done cleaning to avoid spreading those little tykes.

MOLD: WHAT IT IS AND WHAT YOU CAN DO ABOUT IT

Mold, whether it's in the kitchen or the bathroom, is a nuisance. And, though we usually think of kitchen mold as that green or bluish kind that carpets our old bread and cheese, it also rears its ugly head on nonfood items, just as it did in our bathrooms. For those who missed the scoop on what mold is in the bathroom cleaning section, here's a brief recap: Mold is a fungus that forms colonies on anything and everything that remains wet for more than twenty-four* hours, though some research says twelve hours and others forty-eight hours. These colonies are made up of spores, which are mold's darling offspring. Thus, you need an easy birth control plan to stop their taking over your kitchen counters, sinks, and anywhere else that's moist or dark.

Here's how you can hold the mold:

- *WIPE SPILLS PRONTO.* Mold thrives in moist, dark conditions, so don't let things like spills or drippings seep underneath appliances, remain on counters, or sit in the fridge for any extended period of time (i.e., more than twenty-four hours).
- *CLEAN THE DRIP PAN UNDER YOUR FRIDGE:* The moisture down yonder is a perfect breeding ground for our mold militia. Be sure to clean around your fridge's molding since moisture can get trapped in there as well—hmmm, do you think that's why it's called molding? Note for apartment dwellers: The drip pan is also a perfect drinking fountain for roaches, so clean and dry the pan often.

---

*Please note: I made an executive decision to settle on twenty-four hours vs. twelve or forty-eight. Why? you may ask. Well, though mold is an unpleasant toxic pal it is not so dangerous that it will cause fatal harm should it start to germinate and form colonies if left more than twelve hours. Read more about these toxic pals in "Dealing with the Fungus Among Us" on page 9.

- *CHALK IT UP IN THE BREADBOX!* As for the green mold forming on your bread, my aunt Annie told me that putting a box of chalk in my breadbox would stop mold from growing. It seems that chalk absorbs the moisture in the air. I'll chalk that one up to experience!

Offensive Cleaning: The Not-So-Toxic Targets

COUNTERS

Wipe Out

Keeping our counters clean can be one of the easiest and most mindless things to blend into our everyday routines such as yakking on the phone. Just keep the following close at hand and you'll be able to yak and attack the dirt, crumbs, grit, and grime:

What you'll need to do for:

- *DIRT AND BACTERIA:* Disinfecting wipes—keep them at arm's reach just as you would a box of tissues.
- *CRUMBS:* Lint roller—keep one in an easy-to-reach drawer or cabinet and let it roll!
- *SPILLS AND M & M (MOLD AND MILDEW):* Microfiber cloths—they're terrific for sucking up liquids (see "Homeschooling: Microfiber" on page 23). Keep one under your kitchen sink, faucet, or hanging on a cabinet handle. Paper towels are okay, but you'll have to use lots of them to absorb spills.

SINKS

Got Streaks? Baby Them!

What you'll need:
- Baby oil
- Paper towel or cloth

What you'll need to do:
- Put some baby oil on the paper towel or cloth and wipe the sink to help keep it from spotting and streaking. It will also help deter mold from colonizing.

Counterattack: How to Keep Kitty Off Your Kitchen Counter

I don't have a cat but my editor does, so these tips are for her and all the other cat lovers out there to help mount a purr-fect defense against your furry friends' affinity for jumping onto your kitchen counters. I also want to thank my friend Connie for letting me use her loving kitty Newport as a lab rat, or rather test cat!

STICK IT TO THEM: Seems our feline friends don't like having their paws get stuck, so put some double-sided tape, Velcro, or contact paper on the edges of your counter. If you're concerned about removing the tape, Velcro, or paper from your counter once he or she gets the message, fold in half one of the following and stick it to your counter's edge:

- Disposable lint roller sheets or

- Adhesive bandages

FOIL THEIR FOOTSTEPS: Cats are very sensitive to the feeling and the noise their little paws make when they come in contact with aluminum, so cover your counters with sheets to foil their footsteps. Use large pieces vs. strips, so they aren't tempted to munch on any.

SPICE UP THEIR ACT: Try sprinkling a little chili powder or any other hot spice on your counter. Then let it do its stuff as it clings to your kitty's paws—next time they lick them it'll be with a kick! It may take a couple of times and be a bit messy but it will work without hurting them.

ALARM THEM: There are several products out there to scare them off. One, called the ScatMat, gives little harmless zaps when your cat prances on your countertop. You can find it at www.safeproducts.com. Another is called Tattle Tale and it detects even the slightest motion, causing it to vibrate and sound a two-second alarm. Go to www.kiienterprises.com/tattletale.

GOT GUNK? TRY SOME MAGIC

What you'll need:
- Mr. Clean Magic Eraser

What you'll need to do:
- Dampen Mr. Clean Magic Eraser and wipe away any gunk or debris immediately after washing your dishes.

Got a minute?
- **Wipe:** Use those disinfecting wipes like tissues and give your sink a quick swipe.
- **Boil:** Next time you're making a cup of coffee or tea boil up some extra water in your kettle or microwave and pour some down your drain to prevent clogs.

FLOORS

Child's Play
A youngster and a stick vacuum—now that's my idea of offensive cleaning! Kids love to vacuum and it's a safe way to let them share in the joy of housekeeping and to keep debris at bay. If you don't have a stick vacuum, give them a Swiffer, along with their iPod, and then go take a break!

Mat Quest
Make your life easy and buy some decorative, machine-washable kitchen mats to catch the debris. Place them in front of your sink, oven, stove, key work area, and trash can.

FRIDGE AND FREEZER

Line Them Up
Invest in shelf liners for your fridge. That way when those veggies you've been hoping will cook themselves have turned limp and slimy or the milk or ice cream drips you can toss the liner out along with the rotten stuff. Paper towels work but they won't absorb as well and might leak through, making a bigger mess for Momma. Dishwasher-safe, plastic mats are another good alternative, as are rubberized liners which you can find at your local supermarket or retailer. Here are two of my accidental housewifely faves—the first is disposable and the second is machine-washable:

1. *FRIDGE FRESH LINER.* These are terrific since they have some kind of patented fiber that absorbs and locks in liquids, making them great for spills. Plus they've got baking soda so they're wonderful for absorbing odors. In fact, they claim to be seven times more absorbent than your handy-dandy paper towels so spills and drips won't be traveling. They come in packs of four and fit any space, so give these disposable wonders a try.
2. *SPILL-N-WASH LINERS.* These are your machine-washable option that look cute and you can can find at www.Mom4life.com. Besides, they were invented by a mom so we should show our thanks for her helpfulness!

3. *FOIL LINERS.* Line your freezer shelves with aluminum foil, which will make cleaning up easier when your hubs or kiddies finally remember to put back the tub of melted ice cream they left on the counter hours ago. Wax paper works too, but food can stick to it. I prefer foil because it also helps to maintain the cold.

Time to Toss

Every week or two check the expiration dates on foods in your fridge and toss any that are past due, particularly if they're lumpy, sporting a greenish cast when they should be white or yellow, or require you to wear a nose clip. There's a really cool disposable device called Timestrips that can help you keep track of stuff you open like pasta sauce or baby food by automatically counting down the days to their demise. Truly an accidental housewife's must have. Go to www.timestrip.com.

Shake It Up

- It's an oldie but goodie: Keep an opened box of baking soda in the fridge and freezer and replace it every three months. It's a good idea to shake up the box once a week and empty out a little bit every two weeks to ensure freshness. FYI: The actual life expectancy of baking soda is usually found on the bottom of the box. If you can't find it but want to check on its potency, put a teaspoon into a bowl and add some vinegar. If it starts to bubble with gusto, it's still good to go. If it makes a clump, it's time to dump!
- I've become a big fan of Arm & Hammer's Fridge Fresh Refrigerator Air Filter, which you just stick on a wall in your fridge or freezer and let it do its thing. It even lets you know when to replace it—simply idiot-proof and why I love it!
- Another cool inexpensive odor buster I like is Fridge It, which you can use and hang from a shelf in both your fridge and freezer. You can find these little wonders at Linens 'n Things or check them out online at www.innofresh.com.

Suck It Up

Dust and debris can accumulate in your fridge's coils and decrease the efficiency of the unit. So take your vacuum out every month and clean the coils, which are located above, below, or on the back of your fridge.

Seal the Deal

Every few months wipe the gasket on your refrigerator door (that's the rubbery looking rim) with a small amount of petroleum jelly to help limit sticking and tearing. It will also tighten the seal so your fridge will run more efficiently.

OVENS, RANGES, AND COOKTOPS (OH MY!)

GENERAL ADVICE: PRAY FOR OLD AGE
- Check how old your non-self-cleaning oven is and keep your fingers crossed that it's time to consider buying a new self- or continuous-cleaning model.
- Consider cooktops that have as few crevices as possible and sealed burners instead of open ones, since they are easier to clean of grease and burned-on spills (especially if you cook as sloppily as I do!).

FOR ALL OVENS, RANGES, AND COOKTOPS:

READ MANUAL:
If you haven't misplaced or thrown it out it's best to read your owner's manual, since each model varies. If you've misplaced it you can call the manufacturer for how-to info.

CLEAN PRONTO:
When a spill happens, wipe it up immediately before it has a chance to get baked on. Be careful not to burn yourself if the cooktop, range, or oven is still hot or warm.

MAKE IT A HABIT:
After every cooking soiree and once the appliance has cooled, get in the habit of wiping off your cooktop, the inside of the oven door, or any other area that you can easily reach or is easily seen by others.

What you'll need:
- Mild dishwashing detergent
- Clean cloth
- Dry microfiber cloth

What you'll do:
- Put some detergent on the cloth and wring out any excess water.
- Wipe thoroughly and buff with the microfiber cloth.

This will prevent grease spots and other food debris from building up, making less work for you in the future. If you have any grease remaining, use a little white vinegar on a cloth and buff with a dry microfiber cloth.

FOIL TO AVOID TOIL:

For those of you who don't have self-cleaning ovens, line your oven with foil to avoid having to clean the splatters from your reheated culinary delights.

FOR SELF-CLEANING OVENS

General rule of thumb is that you should never use store-bought oven cleaners to clean your self-cleaning or continuous-cleaning oven since it can affect the finish and ruin the walls. However, being an accidental housewife, I took a chance in the interest of simplifying our oven-cleaning lives and tried Easy-Off Fume Free Max Oven Cleaner, which purports to work on self-cleaning ovens. And good news, my friends! I didn't die from toxic fumes, which is what many spray-on products emit, *and* my self-cleaning oven was spick-and-span the next morning. I can't guarantee results will be as good with your oven, but it worked for me. Best advice: Read the directions and cautions on the Easy-Off package and ask your friendly salesperson where you bought your oven or contact the manufacturer to confirm it's okay to use it.

Self-cleaning ovens will do most of the work but for baked-on spots do the following:

- *BEFORE YOU TURN ON CYCLE:* Apply a 3:1 ratio mixture of baking soda and hot water, which will look like a paste. See "Homeschooling: Baking Soda—Nature's Miracle" on page 76.
- *AFTER CYCLE IS OVER:* Remove the paste and debris by wiping it away with a cloth dampened with white vinegar.

REMOVE RACKS:

When the self-cleaning function is in play it's best to take out the racks and let them sit overnight in your sink or bathtub in hot, sudsy detergent water. You want to remove them before cleaning since the heat created during the cleaning cycle can discolor the metal and make removing them tough.

However, if you're like me and forget to take them out, here's an easy way to keep them from sticking the next day—and yes, you will have to remove them to do this:

- Use a steel wool pad to scrape away any debris.
- Spray the edges with a little bit of cooking spray or wipe them with salad oil.

Homeschooling: The Wrap on Aluminum Foil

I always thought that aluminum foil and tin foil were the same but I've learned I was wrong, and perhaps that's why the Tin Man in *The Wizard of Oz* wasn't made of aluminum! It seems that tin foil is stiffer than aluminum foil and tends to give food a slight tin taste (duh!), which is probably why the folks at Reynolds Wrap replaced tin foil with aluminum foil. Another interesting misnomer is that it doesn't matter if you pack, cook, or reheat foods on the shiny or dull side since they're the same. The only reason one side is dull is due to manufacturing. If you have been using this as an excuse for why din-din didn't turn out quite as you had hoped, fear not, this will remain our accidental housewifely secret!

MICROWAVE

LAYER IT
Put ten to twenty sheets of paper towels on the bottom, so if anything leaks or spills all you'll have to do is remove a sheet or two—very manicure-friendly!

COVER IT
Unless otherwise directed, cover all foods with microwave-safe tops to prevent splatters when heating.

DISHWASHER

PICK THE RIGHT SOAP STUFF
Never use anything but automatic dishwashing products unless you want to give your floor a bubble bath. I know from experience, having used my dishwashing liquid in my dishwasher. What resulted was like a scene from an *I Love Lucy* episode—my kitchen was filled with soapsuds. The same holds true with laundry detergent or soap. So the moral of this tip is: Don't use anything but automatic unless you're auditioning for Nick at Nite.

GIVE IT FIRST AID
Rinse aids are invaluable for keeping comments about ugly water spots and dirty glasses to a minimum. Newer-model dishwashers generally have a designated area to pour in liquid

rinse aids. But, regardless of whether you have an old or new model, the best rinse aids are those that hang from a shelf or rack. Why, you ask? Solid rinse aids work throughout the wash *and* rinse cycle while liquids do their thing only at the end of the wash cycle. Jet-Dry is a good store-bought liquid or solid option and, in case you were wondering, its Web site shares that it's kosher! Finish and Glisten are also good rinse-aid choices but I was unable to find out if they're kosher. By the way, if you're lucky enough to have a water softener you don't need a rinse aid, so consider going soft to eliminate one more thing to think about during the high holy days or any day!

Toss in Some Vinegar

Every two months pour a thirty-two-ounce bottle of white vinegar into the dispenser and run it on a full cycle without any dishes to remove gunk, debris, and those fishy smells.

GARBAGE

Load Up on Layered Look

- Layer up to five plastic garbage bags in your trash can. As you do, be sure to let the air out between each one. Not only will this eliminate your having to put new bags in every other minute, but it's a great way to deal with leaks or tears, thus avoiding a bigger mess and the need to clean.
- If layering isn't your look, keep extra garbage bags folded on the bottom of your trash can so they are right there when you empty it.

Keep Yesterday's News

Put old newspapers on the bottom of your trash can to absorb leaks, not to mention odors!

Defensive Cleaning—the Not-So-Toxic Targets

Okay, you've got an array of ways to stave off some of the potential cleaning challenges the kitchen may pose, but what about those unforeseen spills, burns, and overflows that you can't predict? And they will occur unless you plan on eating out every meal, starving your family, or are fortunate enough to have a full-time chef along with domestic help. (If the latter is so, and you're a single male, please call me immediately!) The following are ways to help you win the battle if not the war when your pasta sauce boils over or the fat from your steak catches fire, accidentally of course!

STOVETOP SPLATTERS

What you'll need:
- Salt
- Spatula or overextended credit card
- Pastry brush or toothbrush
- Microfiber cloth
- Dishwashing liquid

What you'll do:
- As soon as it happens, without burning yourself wipe up as much of the spill as possible with a microfiber cloth or sponge.
- While it's still hot, carefully sprinkle on a thick layer of salt and leave it until the stovetop cools and the splatter has hardened—that is, baked to a crisp.
- Continue cooking—*sorry, this splatter is not a pass to order in!*
- When cooled, lift away the hardened mixture with a spatula or overextended credit card.
- Use a pastry brush or toothbrush to sweep away any remaining debris.
- Wipe with a damp microfiber cloth and a little dishwashing liquid.
- Resume eating.

BAKED-ON CRUNCH

What you'll need:
- Boiling water
- Spatula
- Paper towels or microfiber cloth
- White vinegar

What you'll do:
- Pour boiling water onto spills that have hardened.
- Let it sit before scraping it off with a spatula.

- Wipe dry with a paper towel or microfiber cloth.
- If you care about any water spots that may remain, use some white vinegar to erase them. Vinegar will also help cut the grease residue.

CHILD'S PLAY FOR BAKED-ON CRUNCH

What they'll need:
- Baking soda
- Water
- Measuring cup or measuring spoons
- Plastic bowl
- Spatula
- Timer
- Damp paper towels or microfiber cloth

What they'll do:
- Bring out your good ol' baking soda and have them mix it with water in a small bowl. It's three parts baking soda to one part water so, depending upon how big a mess it is, you may need to help them measure out the amount required. Use a measuring cup or measuring spoon. For an exact recipe and other uses for baking soda go to "Homeschooling: Baking Soda—Nature's Miracle" on page 76.
- Spread the mixture on with a spatula.
- Set the timer for ten minutes and when it ringy-dingys tell them to wipe it up with a damp microfiber cloth or paper towels.

BROKEN GLASS

Being the klutz I am, I have dropped more than my share of glasses. Same holds true for friends and family who've enjoyed one too many of my accidental housewifely dirty martinis—a cocktail that I am especially fond of since it reminds me of the 1950s housewife who paved the way for us to come out of our broom closets and embrace our imperfect homekeeping ways. As a result, dirty martinis have become my signature drink as well as a key element in my preentertaining cleaning strategy. You see, by serving a dirty martini to my guests upon their arrival it helps blur their focus of any dust and debris and thereby gives the illusion of a clean-enough house. Brilliant, yes? They taste really good too. The recipe for this perfect offensive cleaning tool is on page 66. Of course, an easy alternative to prevent glass breaking is to use single-serving disposable drinks or plastic glasses, which are available in a variety of decorative styles and sizes. Many are also dishwasher-safe should you prefer to wash and use them again rather than toss.

What you'll need:
- Duster and dust pan and/or hand or stick vacuum
- Lint roller paper
- Play-Doh (color optional)

What you'll do:
- **FOR LARGER PIECES:** Use the duster and dust pan followed by the hand or stick vacuum.
- **FOR SLIVERS:**
  - Roll the lint roller over the area.
  - Spread out Play-doh and press until all slivers are removed.
  - Go over the area one more time with the vacuum.

Here's the one you learned for picking up broken glass in the bathroom should you wish to go this route instead.

What you'll need:
- Duster and dust pan and/or hand or stick vacuum
- Loaf of fresh bread (sliced)

What you'll do:
- **FOR LARGER PIECES:** Sweep up with the duster and dust pan and then use the hand or stick vacuum.
- **FOR SLIVERS:** Gently press a piece of fresh bread firmly down on areas where glass slivers may be and lift. It may take several slices to get them all. Be sure to throw the slice out to avoid anyone in your household inadvertently using it to make a sandwich or your pooch from wolfing it down.

GREASE FIRE IS THE WORD!

I've had many incidences where I've gotten distracted by my son or have been yakking on the phone only to find those oh-so-fatty and tasty lamb chops have sparked a fire. Sound familiar? Well, before you burn dinner again or those hunky men in the red trucks arrive

Homeschooling: The Dirt on the Absolute Best Dirty Martini

Martinis have a long and varying history dating back to the mid to late 1800s. The history we'll go with is that it was originally called a Martinez since a version of it was first served to gold prospectors in Martinez, California. Its real popularity, though, seems to have skyrocketed during prohibition since whiskey required too much aging and distillers couldn't keep up with the demand at speakeasies. Thus, gin became a fave alternative.

It has received historic words of praise: The author E. B. White referred to it as "the elixir of quietude," H. L. Mencken called it "the only American invention as perfect as the sonnet," and James Bond put a new spin on it by switching its main ingredient from gin to vodka and asking for it "shaken not stirred."

As for me, I associate the martini with our 1950s pre–accidental housewifely heroines who dutifully went about their daily homekeeping chores with a smile and feather duster in tow and who, no matter how busy a day they had, would stir up a martini for their hardworking hubs. You see, the 1950s housewife's days were considered insignificant compared to her husband's day. As I've said many times before, that was then, this is now. Times and we housewives have changed and it is you and I who should enjoy an end-of-day elixir. And a dirty martini aptly reflects our homekeeping attitude: A little dirt never hurt anyone, which is why a clean-enough house is good enough. Bottoms up!

The Accidental Housewife's Dirty Martini

What you'll need (per cocktail):

- 2 ounces vodka or gin
- ½ ounce of dry vermouth
- Splash of dirt—olive juice from olive jar
- 3 queen-sized olives
- Shaker
- Chilled plastic martini glass (in case you are truly accidental!)

How you'll shake it up (stirring optional)

- Combine vodka or gin, vermouth, and olive juice in a shaker filled with ice and shake.
- Strain it into the chilled martini glass.
- Add olives and let them marinate for a bit as you sip!

If you like your dirty martini hot, use pepper-flavored vodka and olives stuffed with jalepeños!

to prevent your kitchen from going up in a blaze of glory, here are some easy ways to fend off the fire just enough. Please note: If the flames look like a scene from the classic movie *The Towering Inferno* do not attempt any of the following and immediately dial 911 *from outside* your home.

A NOTE OF CAUTION: Though most of us instinctively think water is the way to stop a fire, it isn't unless you have a fire engine handy with hoses specifically created to do just that. According to the U.S. Department of Energy using water to douse a grease fire can actually cause the grease to splatter and the fire to spread. Instead, you should try one of the easy fire putter-outers that follow. And at the very least be sure to have a fire extinguisher handy. There are several to choose from but I'm a fan of First Alert's Tundra Fire Extinguishing Spray, which you just point and spray. It's very manicure-friendly, since there is no pin to pull, and it's small space–friendly, since it's the size of a jumbo can of hairspray. Go to www.firstalert.com to check it out or Google *Tundra Fire Extinguishing* to learn more.

Simmering the Hot Stuff

What you'll need:
- Flame- and/or heat-resistant pot holders or oven mitts
- Lid from a pot or pan
- Baking soda, salt, or flour
- Fire extinguisher
- *Optional and highly recommended:* Hunky men in red trucks

What you'll need to do:
Fires need oxygen to spread, so your first defense is to smother the fire—deprive it of air as quickly as possible. Be sure to put on the mitts or holders before doing any of them:

- *PUT A LID ON IT!* Smother the fire with a lid from one of your pots or pans.
- *BAKE, SALT, OR FLOUR:* Pour as much baking soda, salt, or flour as needed on the fire until it goes out.
- *EXTINGUISH IT:* Ready, aim, and fire your extinguisher directly onto the flames.

POP GOES THE MICROWAVE

Popcorn explodes, reheated sauce bubbles over, and your paper coffee cup from the bagel shop cracks after reheating it five times. Here are two ways to clean the yuk away in your microwave:

What you'll need:
- White vinegar
- Microfiber cloth

What you'll do:
- Wipe the mess up immediately with a microfiber cloth dampened with vinegar.
- Don't forget to clean the seals. Built-up yuk may cause the door to not close tightly, which means your number-one mealtime pal may not work properly.

What you'll need:
- Lemon, cut in half
- Small microwaveable bowl filled with water
- Paper towels or a dampened cloth

What you'll do:
- Squeeze the lemon into the water, add the lemon halves, and put the bowl in the microwave.

Firefighting Ifs, And, and But

If a fire starts in your oven, don't panic or start toasting marshmallows. Stay calm and try one of the following:

- If your food is burning, douse it with baking soda, salt, or flour and then order in.

- If the gaskets or heating elements have caught fire, immediately turn the oven, range, or stovetop off.

- If it's an electric stove, unplug it pronto.

- AND, if it's smoldering . . . that is, the fire is not completely out, after you're attempted to put it out, be doubly safe and call your buds at Local Ladder 101 to check. Be sure to ask them to bring their most recent calendar!

- BUT to be really safe, avoid greasy foods and go on a fat-free diet!

- Zap for five minutes.
- Let the bowl cool before removing to avoid burning your hands, since it will be hot.
- Wipe the microwave with the dampened cloth to remove any remaining yuk.

DE-STUFFING—STUFFED DRAINS

It seems natural to scrape and push all the debris left on dishes, pots, and pans down ye old drain, but after a while it's going to stuff up and back up. The best way to avoid this is to let fats cool and harden enough to easily scrape the debris directly into the garbage. If you don't want to wait for that to happen, wash your dishes, pots, or pans pronto with hot, soapy water and then continue running hot water down the drain for two to three minutes. This will also help avoid buildup on your sink's garbage disposal. If you've already OD'd your drain, here's how to free it up and clean the yuk that may remain:

What you'll need:
- Baking soda
- White vinegar
- Measuring cup
- Boiling water
- Mr. Clean Magic Eraser
- Disinfecting wipes—low streak formula
- Microfiber cloth

What you'll do:
- Pour a half cup of baking soda down the drain followed by a half cup of vinegar and let sit. It should get bubbly and foamy.
- When the bubbling stops, immediately pour down a fresh kettle of boiling water—depending upon how clogged your sink is you may need to repeat.
- Clean any remaining debris on sink with dampened Mr. Clean Magic Eraser.
- Wipe with disinfecting wipes and dry with the microfiber cloth.

TOASTER TROUBLES

Here is an easy way to clean your toaster before you need to wear gloves to cover hand scars or your toaster's coils become inactive.

HARDENED STUFF ON COILS

What you'll need:
- Baking soda
- Toothbrush
- Dampened microfiber cloth
- Mild dishwashing liquid

What you'll do:
- FIRST: UNPLUG THE TOASTER!
- Sprinkle some baking soda on the coils and rub them with the toothbrush.
- Wipe with a cloth dampened with a bit of dishwashing liquid to remove any remaining residue.

How to Clean the Rest . . . Just Enough

Now it's time to learn how to maintain a clean-enough kitchen when it comes from everyday dirt, debris, gunk, and goo that mounts simply because it's your home's hub and because it has more appliances—both large and small—and more nooks and crannies than any other room in your home. You'll do so by dividing your kitchen's cleaning targets into three categories:

1. *SURFACE AREAS*—sinks, counters, backsplashes, cabinets, and floors
2. *LARGE APPLIANCES*—fridge, freezer, oven, stove, cooktop, range, and dishwasher
3. *SMALL TO MIDSIZE APPLIANCES AND GADGETS*—microwave, toaster oven, auto-drip coffeemaker, blender, electric can opener, coffee bean grinder, and cheese grater

YOUR MULTITASKING MANICURE-FRIENDLY SHOPPING LIST

In the kitchen, as in the bathroom and every other room in your home, there are a host of traditional and nontraditional multipurpose products that you can use to keep your kitchen clean enough. Many of them will also enable you to blend cleaning activities into your general routines, so these cleaning tasks will seem less like chores that bore. A downloadable list is available on my site at www.theaccidental housewife.com.

CLEANING PRODUCTS AND TOOLS

Here are just enough of the basics you'll need to clean this toxic zone:

- *DISPOSABLES:* I love these since you use them and lose them. This may not be the most eco-friendly way to clean, but the reality is that you and I are not going to turn into the Queens of Green overnight but over time, and we're about saving our planet and our sanity. Enviro-friendly taskers follow on page 72.
  1. Disinfecting multipurpose, multisurface antibacterial wipes (Windex Clean & Shine Microfiber Cloths, Lysol Sanitizing Wipes, Clorox Disinfecting Wipes, Mr. Clean Wipes, Method Cleaning Wipes)
  2. Mr. Clean Magic Eraser
  3. Specialty wipes such as Carbona's Clean It! for stainless steel, ceramic stovetops, and refrigerator and microwave
- *MULTIPURPOSE, MULTISURFACE SPRAY CLEANERS:* These are great for cleaning almost any surface—check labels just to be sure if any are a no-no for the surface you're attacking. Here are some to check out:
  1. Fantastik Orange Action All Purpose Cleaner
  2. Lysol All Purpose Cleaner
  3. Mr. Clean Antibacterial Multi-Surfaces Spray
  4. Clorox. Any disinfecting kitchen cleaner
  5. OxiClean Miracle Foam Spray
  6. Windex Multi-Surface Cleaner with Vinegar
- *BACTERIA BUSTERS:* Disinfecting antibacterial and/or sanitizing wipes or sprays made by the biggies like Clorox, Lysol, and Mr. Clean
- *MUST-HAVES:*
  1. All-purpose orange oil cleaner (degreaser)
  2. Mild dishwashing liquid (antibacterial)
  3. Aromatic disinfecting spray

TOOLS

- *MICROFIBER CLOTHS, MOPS, OR ANY OTHER FORM IN WHICH MICROFIBER IS AVAILABLE.* You'll read over and over again throughout this guide how I love microfiber, since it cleans every surface and is machine-washable and safe for the environment. They're a wonder tool, particularly when it comes to their ability to absorb spills!
- *DISPOSABLE MOPS AND BROOMS* (I like all the Swiffer floor cleaners and Clorox ReadyMop)

Warning

Never mix any ammonia-based products (for example, Windex) with a bleach-based product (for example, Ajax, Comet, bleach) or you will truly have toxic consequences, since together they produce toxic fumes.

- *PORTABLE/BATTERY-OPERATED HAND VACUUM*
- *PAPER TOWELS*—go the recycled route if you can deal with the fact that they're generally not pretty but on the flip side they'll keep our forests looking lush and lovely.
- *DISH BRUSH*
- *SPONGES* (optional—I prefer disinfecting wipes and microfiber, but you'll decide what you prefer after reading "Bacteria's Favorite Hot Spots" on page 50)
- *OPTIONAL:* iRobot Scooba Floor Washing Robots or a French Maid

THE ACCIDENTAL ENVIRO-KEEPER'S KITCHEN CLEANERS

Here are a few items you may have handy that will help you easily clean and be mindlessly green in your kitchen:

- White vinegar
- Baking soda
- Baby oil
- Vodka
- Toothpaste (nongel, nonbrightening)
- Toothbrush
- Lemon
- Salt
- Powdered lemonade drink (Tang, Kool-Aid, or Crystal Light)
- Disposable lint rollers
- Newspaper
- Eggshells

Here are some eco-friendly manufacturers and products I've tried and liked as well:

- Bio-Kleen (www.biokleen.com)
- Mrs. Meyer's (www.mrsmeyers.com)

Homeschooling: Antibacterial, Disinfecting, Sanitizing—*Oh My!*

If you're anything like me, you're confused by the information on the exterior of certain household cleaning products. So here's a little homeschooling to get us all in the know.

Disinfectants, antibacterials, and sanitizers do not clean unless their packaging specifically says so. Their purpose is to limit and kill bacteria and/or germs, so read the fine print to make sure they also clean.

Here are some attempts at clarifying what the heck you're buying and what they do:

- **ANTIBACTERIAL:** Anything that has the power to destroy or stop the growth and reproduction of bacteria—that is, kills it—is called antibacterial. However, just because a product is antibacterial does not mean that it kills viruses. Confused yet? Antibacterial products are regulated by the FDA and have an ingredient in them that kills bacteria on the skin, but they do not kill germs that cause colds and flu. You often see these words on dishwashing liquids and hand soaps or liquids. Even white vinegar is considered an antibacterial product. So next time you toss that salad, toss some on your hands!

- **DISINFECTING:** This means that the EPA has established that these products have a higher level of germ killing than antibacterial products. (Not for use on or in the body.)

- **DISINFECTANTS:** These products must be registered with the EPA if they want to be referred to as disinfectants. They remove, kill, or immobilize bacteria before they cause infections like salmonella and staph. Disinfectants come in the form of bleach, spray, and my fave store-bought cleaning product, disposable disinfecting wipes.

- **SANITIZING:** This is a lower level of killing germs that is acceptable by regulators and pubic health codes.

- **SANITIZERS:** These reduce the bacteria, making it safe according to the "acceptable health codes," but unlike a disinfectant they don't completely kill or eliminate those suckers. Sanitizers come in the form of wipes, sprays, and in 5 percent distilled white vinegar—one of my natural faves! FYI: According to the folks at Good Housekeeping, a sanitizer needs to sit for at least ten minutes to be effective in killing bacteria. But here's where I begin to lose it again: In order to be registered as a sanitizer, the

> product has to show at least a 99.9 percent kill rate—which means it's off by a mere .01 percent, which would make it a disinfectant. . . . So I ask you, are we splitting hairs here or germs? I'd say with 100 percent certainty that we are!

- Greening the Cleaning (www.imusranchfoods.com)
- Method (www.method.com)
- Seventh Generation (www.seventhgeneration.com)

You now have enough of the stuff needed to clean this toxic zone, so it's time to begin.

MANICURE-FRIENDLY, MULTITASKING CLEANING TIPS

There are a few things to try to keep in mind as you gather, store, and get ready to clean:

- *CONSOLIDATE:* Put all cleaning items in a lightweight, comfy carry-all.
- *KEEP HANDY:* Store items in a convenient spot, such as under your sink.
- *DRESS FOR SUCCESS:* Wear fashionable and functional rubber gloves, a pair of comfy shoes (preferably liquid resistant), and perhaps an old T-shirt and sweats or jeans. (This is definitely not the time for a little black dress.)
- *BE MOODY:* Clean only when you're in the mood, unless you're dealing with a mess that requires immediate attention.
- *TUNE IN AND OUT:* If you don't like to whistle while you work, make sure to put on your favorite tunes to help pass the time as you clean.

SURFACE AREAS

Sinks, counters, and floors are constantly being used and abused by you and yours, so they require more frequent cleaning to prevent crumbs, crud, and other food-related embellishments from taking up residence. They're also areas that you can clean while you do your everyday routines.

SINKS

You may think that sinks get cleaned as often as they get used with all the water and washing that you do, but that's not the case. Sinks are like magnets and no matter how many times you wipe them, soap gunk, food bits, coffee grounds, streaks, and a host of other junk coat their walls. Here are three simple ways to keep them clean enough.

Perfect Pastry Uses

CHILD'S PLAY: Paste Recipe

What they'll need:

- Three parts baking soda
- One part water
- Bowl
- Spoon (plastic so you can dispose pronto!)
- Spatula or hands

How they'll make it:
- Mix the baking soda and water together until it forms a pasty consistency. The exact amount will vary depending upon how big a mess you or your loved ones have made.

How to use it:
- Spread the paste on the dirty area, mess, or spill with a spatula.
- Let the mix sit for ten to fifteen minutes. If you let it sit too long it will harden and crumble, creating more of a mess for you to clean up.
- Wipe with a damp microfiber cloth or paper towel when the time's up. CAUTION: Though we may be accidental we do not want to put our children in harm's way so do not let them apply the paste to a hot surface. I don't want you to accidentally burn yourself either, so please be sure that you've let the appliance or surface cool "just enough" to avoid a burn yet warm enough to keep yuk from hardening. When the surface is just right, apply the paste with the spatula.

Where you can use the paste:
- Oven windows: Spread it on the inside of the window to clean off the brown junk.
- Oven floor: Coat it to remove yuk from leaks and spills—this may require a bit of elbow grease, too!
- Cooktops: Apply the paste to baked-on spills from sauces overflowing, splatterings, and so on.
- Drip pans on stovetop: Removes baked-on overflows.

Homeschooling: Baking Soda—Nature's Miracle

There are dozens and dozens of things you can use baking soda for throughout the house, which is terrific since not only is it inexpensive (okay, cheap), but it's also one of the best natural cleaners and deodorizers around. So what follows are ways to use this natural cleaning miracle worker in the raw (as is). It can also be used to create a perfect paste (see previous page), which also qualifies as a terrific "Child's Play" activity—love that!

In the Raw Uses

- **Refrigerator doors:** Sprinkle some on a damp microfiber cloth and wipe.

- **Faucet stains:** Try rubbing some on dry or sprinkle a bit on a sponge to remove water spots.

- **Stainless steel sinks:** Sprinkle and wipe with a damp sponge or microfiber cloth.

- **Dishwasher:** Load it up with baking soda—use the same amount as you would of dishwashing powder.

- **Clogged sinks:** Send down a cocktail of baking soda and vinegar. Use a half cup of each, let it foam and bubble, then pour down hot water.

- **Coffee or tea stains on mugs, pitchers, etc.:** Put in three tablespoons and mix with hot water. Let sit overnight.

- **Flatulence:** *I had to add this one!!!* I learned this tip courtesy of my aunt Dora: If you put a tablespoon of baking soda into a pot of beans while you're soaking them, you'll minimize farting—I did notice that the air was a bit "fresher" last time we dined on her franks and beans!

1. What you'll need:
- White vinegar or vodka
- Microfiber cloth
- Optional: Fabric dryer sheet

What you'll do:
- Seep microfiber cloth with vinegar or vodka and then wipe the sink. Put the liquid directly onto the cloth to reduce smudging and smearing.
- If it stinks since you used the vinegar, wipe the sink with a dryer sheet.

2. What you'll need:
- Baking soda
- Damp microfiber cloth
- White vinegar
- Dry microfiber cloth or paper towels
- Optional: Fabric dryer sheet

What you'll do:
- Sprinkle baking soda on the damp cloth and wipe the sink all over
- Buff sink to shine with white vinegar
- Optional: Wipe with fabric dryer sheet if vinegar stench bugs you

3. What you'll need to remove lingering crud: (by the way, crud is a professional term)
- Sponge with "rough" side, sink scrub brush, or Mr. Clean Magic Eraser
- Baking soda
- White vinegar
- Microfiber cloth
- Optional: Fabric dryer sheet

What you'll do:
- Use the rough side of the sponge, brush, or Eraser, dampen it and apply a bit of baking soda
- Use a cloth dampened with vinegar to buff
- Optional: Remove the vinegar stench if it bugs you by wiping with a fabric dryer sheet

CHILD'S PLAY

My son wears a retainer and getting him to remember to clean it is no easy task—on the other hand, he loves plopping denture tablets in water and watching them fizz, so with this simple solution, I accomplish two things: I don't have to clean my sink or his retainer!

What they'll need:
- Denture tablets

What they'll do:
- Fill your sink with warm water and drop in the retainer.
- Depending upon how large a sink you have, plop in four or five denture-cleaning tablets. Let them fizz and sit for a bit.
- Remove the retainer and rinse, then drain your sink. Both will be nice and clean!

FAUCETS

I look at faucets like I look at my nose—front and center and where the eye goes first. And if your nose has a zit, people notice it. Your faucet clearly doesn't have zits but it does get covered with more than its share of water marks, fingerprints, soap scum, bacteria, and debris from washing dirty dishes and hands (or at least my son's hands, since he uses our kitchen sink as his primary hand-washing spot simply because "it's right there"). Here is a simple way to keep your faucet zit-free.

What you'll need:
- Nonwhitening toothpaste
- Old toothbrush
- Newspaper, paper towel, or microfiber cloth

What you'll do:
- Put a dab of toothpaste on the faucet and brush gently with the old toothbrush.
- Dry with the newspaper, paper towels, or microfiber cloth (you can clean your stainless steel basin this way as well).

A Moldy Oldy Tip

As the old saying goes, oil and water don't mix—in fact they repel one another, so wiping your sink with oil will help deter mold from growing there since the water won't stick—and it also minimizes streaking!

THE TOUGH STUFF—LIME STAINS

Got whitish-greenish stuff covering your faucet's tap? Relax, it's not mold but most likely some kind of lime or mineral deposit.

What you'll need to remove lime stains:
- Vinegar
- Old cloth or paper towels
- Hair clip

What you'll do to remove them:
- Wrap a vinegar-saturated old rag or paper towel around your faucet. Clasp it with a hair clip.

Stuck on You

You'll find my picture in the dictionary next to both *accidental housewife* and *klutz.* I am notorious for dropping and knocking stuff over—accidentally, of course! At any rate, one of my most popular accidents is breaking wineglasses. It's not that I drink too much wine (hic!), it's that I have a nasty habit of leaving the glasses precariously close to the edge of the sink after I've hand-washed them, which is why I often find myself buying new glasses and chipping a nail when I remove the price tag or label on them. That was until I discovered this manicure-friendly removal tip that I now share with you.

What you'll need:
- White vinegar

What you'll do:
- Zap a small amount of white vinegar in the microwave for about twenty to thirty seconds.

- Pour the heated vinegar directly on the label and let sit for a few seconds.

- Lift off the label and start pouring your next glass of vino!

You may need to repeat this a few times, depending upon how cheap the glasses are since I've found the cheaper the glass, the more stubborn the sticker!

- Leave it on for about an hour.
- Remove the rag and wipe the faucet with a microfiber cloth or paper towels.

Alternate method: Make a baking soda paste (remember it's a 3:1 ratio of baking soda to water) and apply. Leave on for an hour and then wipe dry.

COUNTERS

They're the prime target for dirt, crumbs, and spills, but if you keep a few items within easy reach and in clear view they can be one of the easiest and most mindless things to clean on a whim or in an instant—like when you're chatting on the phone or yelling at your kids to do their homework for the fifth time!

What you'll need:
- Lemon juice or white vinegar
- Water
- Spray bottle
- Paper towels or microfiber cloth

What you'll do:
- Mix equal parts of lemon juice or vinegar with water in the spray bottle.
- Spray counters, wipe, and then dry with the microfiber cloth.

TLC—CLEANING MARBLE, GRANITE, AND CORIAN

Your beautiful stone counters require some special care due to their composition. The first and foremost thing to remember when cleaning them is to *never* use anything on them that you wouldn't use on your own hands. Here's the 411 on the TLC required:

Marble and Granite
- Since they are porous and stain easily, sop up stains pronto with a microfiber cloth. Try to avoid putting down items like wine, coffee, tomato sauce, vinegar, lemon, oil, and fruit juices on them, since their acidic makeup can stain, etch, or dull these surfaces.
- Don't clean with vinegar, lemon, or any products with ammonia, since they can damage the surface and dull the finish.
- Don't use anything or any product that's highly abrasive unless it says it's scratch free—bottom line, read the fine print.
- Clean them with a sponge or microfiber cloth dampened with warm water. If

something stronger is required, try a product specifically formulated for these stone wonders, such as Method's daily granite and marble cleaners. Check it out at www.methodhome.com.

Corian

- Use warm, soapy water or a store-bought mildly abrasive product like Soft Scrub or Scratch-Free Comet to clean Corian. Ammonia-based cleaners are also fine to use. If your counters are really disgusting and require a tougher cleaner, ask your local home improvement store guy or gal for a recommendation.

Here's a simple way to clean each of these surfaces.

What you'll need:

- Whitening toothpaste
- Microfiber cloth
- Damp cloth

How you'll clean them:

- Gently rub a little bit of toothpaste onto the surface with the microfiber cloth.
- Wipe off any residue with a damp cloth.

Backsplash

Splish splash, your backsplash takes a bath from everything you're slicing, dicing, or serving—grease being one of its favorite embellishments. So before the flying debris becomes permanent backsplash decor, try the following:

What you'll need:

- Vinegar or multisurface degreasing cleaner
- Baking soda
- Old toothbrush
- Microfiber cloth or paper towel

What you'll do:

- Spray vinegar or cleaner directly on grease spots.
- Wipe with dry microfiber cloth or paper towel.
- For debris that's become more permanent, apply some baking soda paste (3 parts baking soda, 1 part water) and work it in with the toothbrush.

Homeschooling: Rock On

For those of you who are armchair geologists, here's a quickie course on what marble, granite, and Corian counter slabs are made of and their maintenance issues or lack thereof.

- **Marble:** It's the softest and more porous of the stone surfaces available, so it's *très* susceptible to nicks, cuts, stains, and burn marks. It requires periodic maintenance to keep it from becoming dull and needs to be resealed to protect it from stains.

- **Granite:** Second to marble on our accidental housewifely care scale—it's more durable, since it's made from hard volcanic rock, but like marble, it needs to be resealed periodically to prevent stains and cracking.

- **Corian** (a solid surface product made up of materials from natural stones created by DuPont): The best and most mindless to care for of the three, since it's pretty much maintenance free. It's stain resistant, doesn't scratch as easily, and you can pick a finish that looks like marble or granite . . . clearly an accidental housewifely way to go!

- Let it sit for a bit (about fifteen minutes).
- Wipe with warm water.

CABINETS

Open, close, push, slam, and what's gracing your cabinet's outside doors can be a lovely recipe of cooking ingredients, leftovers from sticky fingers, or licks from Fido. Here are three ways to keep them clean enough.

1. *What you'll need:*
   - Baking soda
   - Damp microfiber cloth
   - Disinfecting wipe

What you'll do:
- Put some baking soda on a damp microfiber cloth or paper towel. Remove any soda-due with a damp cloth.
- Finish with a streak-free disinfecting wipe.

2. What you'll need:
- White vinegar or vodka
- Microfiber cloth or sponge

What you'll do:
- Dampen a microfiber cloth or paper towel with vinegar or vodka. Finish with a warm water wipe. If using vinegar and you can't stand the smell, spray some aromatic disinfecting spray onto a paper towel and wipe.

3. What you'll need:
- Multipurpose, multisurface spray, or orange oil cleaner
- Dampened microfiber cloth or sponge

What you'll do:
- Any store-bought multipurpose, multisurface spray will do. If they're really greasy, buy an orange oil cleaner or degreaser. Then wipe with a damp cloth.

FLOORS

They're the catchall for what lies above and finds a home below, be it crumbs, spills, pet hair, your dog's leftovers, dead bugs, or your lost earring. So, once you notice your kiddies' socks or cat's paws sticking to your floor, it's a clear sign that it's time to clean them. This doesn't mean that you need to get on your hands and knees unless you're a sucker for punishment—just grab a pillow to keep your knees comfy. I would also suggest that you consider seeing a therapist to find out why you wouldn't opt for the manicure-friendly cleanups that follow.

ONE-STEP MOP 'N' GOS

What you'll need:
1. Swiffer WetJet system or Clorox ReadyMop Mopping System
2. iRobot Scooba Floor Washing Robot

What you'll do:

1. Simply read the instructions, which are close to idiot-proof, pull the trigger to release some suds, and let it rip—I mean wash! No wringing, washing, or waiting till dry.
2. This robotic floor washer is another accidental housewifely personal fave of mine and my son's since he loves to program it and watch it glide across the floor, which means I don't have to do a thing! Check it out at www.irobot .com.

CHILD'S PLAY! Let your kiddies remove their own heel marks from the floor—just give them a pencil eraser, which will do the trick!

For those who are still in conflict with your inner older-fashioned housewife self and your newer need to get it done with minimal effort, the following offers you a good compromise.

Please Note: For ceramic, marble, granite, and tile: Do not use white vinegar, since it can break down the sealants on stone flooring.

TWO-STEP MOP 'N' GOS

What you'll need:
- Dishwashing liquid, store-bought floor cleaner, or white vinegar
- Bucket
- Microfiber mop with machine-washable mop head

What you'll do:
- Prepare one of the following solutions in a clean bucket:
  - ¼ cup dishwashing liquid with water
  - 1:1 ratio of water with vinegar; or
  - store-bought cleaner according to package directions
- Mop floor with solution and let dry

LARGE APPLIANCES

Unlike the bathroom, where we do a variety of personal activities (showering, shaving, pooping, brushing, personal grooming, and so on) the kitchen is generally a "meet, greet, and eat" place. That means there aren't as many opportunities to blend general cleaning tasks into your everyday routines. It's also got some really big items (your fridge, freezer, oven, stove, and dishwasher) that you need to clean often enough to keep them in working order, which is what you'll learn how to do next.

FRIDGE AND FREEZER

Your fridge and freezer are probably the two most used appliances in your kitchen, unless you're Martha Stewart and in that case it would be your oven and stove. That means they need to be cleaned fairly regularly:

- Fridge: every two weeks
- Freezer: every four to six weeks

Here are a few simple ways to keep your fridge clean enough:

What you'll need to clean the inside:
- Store-bought multipurpose spray or vinegar
- Paper towels and/or microfiber cloth

What you'll do:
- Empty all the items and discard anything that smells, or has expired, turned color, or changed consistency.
- Wipe bottles, jars, containers, and any other items that are touched frequently or your hand sticks to with a disinfecting multipurpose, multisurface cleaning spray or undiluted white vinegar.
- Next, remove the shelves and bins and wash them in the sink in hot sudsy water.

Seven Scent-Sational Kitchen Odor Eaters

1. Dried coffee grounds in fridge
2. Fabric dryer sheets in kitchen drawers
3. Newspapers on bottom of garbage
4. Vanilla extract–seeped cotton balls placed in small bowls, scattered around house
5. Vinegar in small bowls
6. Freshly baked batch of refrigerated ready-to-bake cookie dough
7. Baking soda: Keep an open box outside the fridge—it'll work there too!

Be sure to dry them thoroughly with paper towels or a dry microfiber cloth to prevent mold from finding a new moist place to form colonies. See "Dealing with the Fungus Among Us" on page 9.

- Don't forget to clean the rubber seals with the same disinfecting options used above and dry them thoroughly to deter our mold buds from spawning.

What you'll need to clean the outside:
- Disinfecting wipes
- White vinegar
- Paper towels, newspaper, or microfiber cloth

What you'll do:
- Clean door handles thoroughly with a disinfecting wipe or a microfiber cloth dampened with white vinegar.
- Clean fridge door with a microfiber cloth dampened with water—the microfiber won't smear or scratch the surface.

DOWN UNDER

What you'll need to clean underneath:
- Lint roller adhesive sheets or masking tape
- Yardstick or wire hanger unwound

What you'll do:
- Attach a sheet of disposable lint removal tape or wrap masking tape to a yardstick or wire hanger.
- Swish around under fridge until the sheet or tape is relatively clean.

You Know It's Time to Defrost When . . .

1. You can write your name clearly in the frost.

2. The frost is thicker than a thumbprint (approx. ½" thick).

3. Your freezer looks like an ice-crystal museum.

Homeschooling: How to Snuff Out Smells That Just Won't Quit

Have you ever wondered why you smell that yummy leftover garlicky scampi dish you brought home from the restaurant and put in your freezer? Well, unless you cover or put those pungent leftovers in a seal-proof container, they'll stink up your freezer—and fridge!—for days since the fridge and freezer share one air flow system. As I often say, *Who'd have thunk?*

Here's a way to de-stink your fridge and freezer:

What you'll need:

- Loaf of fresh bread
- Vinegar
- Baking sheet or tin foil

What you'll do:

- Saturate the loaf in vinegar and put it on a baking sheet or piece of aluminum foil.

- Leave in your fridge or freezer for two to three days

- If your child's lunch box smells you can use this technique as well, only use one slice of vinegar-soaked bread and leave it in overnight.

CHIP OFF THE OL' BLOCK

Fortunately, with the exception of the occasional spill, leak, or drip from leftovers or ice cream, the freezer doesn't get too dirty. Still, it should be cleaned every few months.

What you'll need:
- Ice scraper
- Dampened microfiber cloth (use warm water)

What you'll do:
- Use the ice scraper to gently loosen built-up ice or yuk that's frozen from a leak, spill, or drippy ice cream.
- Rub with the microfiber cloth.

Beauty and the Feast: Kitchen Multitaskers

Your kitchen cupboard and fridge hold many items that you can use to fix or soothe everything from highlights to bug bites! Here are a few of your kitchen's best:

(Note: Results may vary so use at own risk!)

- MAYONNAISE—massage in hair as a conditioner

- SUGAR—put it on the tip of a burned tongue

- APPLE CIDER VINEGAR—take a swig to relieve hiccups

- LEMON—squeeze it on a strand or two and heat with a blow dryer to highlight hair

- PEANUT BUTTER—rub a spoonful to remove gum from hair

- COOLED WET TEA BAGS or CUCUMBERS—lay a bag or slice on eyes to depuff them

- RAW ONION—put a slice on mosquito bites to relieve itch

- FLAT BEER: My beauty bud Mickey says a great way to get super-shiny strands and give them more body is to rinse them with flat beer that is room temp or warm. Leave it in your hair for a few minutes and then rinse. As for the smell, keep rinsing!

- VODKA (hey, I keep it in my freezer and that's in the kitchen): Forget the Botox! Give a shot to your facial pores to tighten them, and drink one to make those pores and wrinkles look better before gazing at yourself in the mirror!

OVENS, STOVES, COOKTOPS, AND RANGES (OR A COMBO THEREOF!)

For those like me who are usually talking on the phone, helping children with their homework (or yelling at them to please do it!), or letting your dog out back to do his business while cooking, reheating, or microwaving leftovers, you are probably more than familiar with:

- pasta water boiling over
- premade sauces splattering
- meat juices sizzling and spritzing all over

So my friends, these cleaning tips are just for you!

Self-Cleaning and Continuous-Cleaning Ovens

LOOK MA, NO HANDS!
1. *SELF-CLEANING:* Unless you check your manual and it says otherwise, it's a good idea to remove racks before you start cleaning to avoid discoloration and affecting the finish. It is a major no-no to use oven cleaners on a self-cleaning oven so *do not use them!* I did mention one earlier in this section that I have had success with, Easy-Off Fume Free Max Oven Cleaner, which you can use. But to be on the safe side check your manual, with your manufacturer or salesperson first.
2. *CONTINUOUS-CLEANING:* My fave, since it's always working! Again, it's a no-no to use store-bought oven cleaners unless your manual recommends a specific kind. You don't want to affect the potency of the oven's self-cleaning agents that make food splatters and spills go bye-bye without your lifting a finger.

Old-Fashioned Clean It Yourself Ovens
For those who *do not* have a self- or continuous-cleaning oven, here are a few ways to clean them.

RACKS
RACK 'EM UP! (Recommended as an outside activity)

What you'll need:
- Newspaper or garbage bags
- Store-bought oven cleaner
- Paper towels or dry rags

What you'll do:
Wait until they're cool enough to handle before removing.

- Lay racks on newspaper or garbage bags.
- Spray with store-bought oven cleaner of choice and leave overnight.
- Rinse thoroughly in the morning and dry.

SPLISH SPLASH! (Inside activity)

What you'll need:
- Bathtub
- Dishwashing liquid
- Soft brush or microfiber cloth
- Rubber duckie (optional)

What you'll do:
- Fill the bathtub with enough hot water to cover the racks.
- As the bath is filling add ¼ cup dishwashing liquid.
- Let the racks soak for forty-five minutes to an hour and play with the duckie, if you like.

A Word of Warning

I use fairly nontoxic and natural stuff and most of the ideas I suggest shouldn't cause any damage. But, to be safe, check your owner's manual before trying any of the simple cleaning solutions in this section, and please remember:

- Always let your appliance cool "just enough" that you don't burn yourself but not not so much that stuff becomes a second skin.

- Wear rubber gloves.

- Know if your oven, stove, range, or cooktop is either:

   1. Gas—you can tell it's gas if it has a pilot light. If it does, it's connected to a gas supply line so you need to be careful as to what you use to clean it so that you don't blow your home up!

   2. Electric—identified by coils that heat up.

- Use a soft brush or cloth to get rid of any leftover yuk.
- Rinse the racks with water and dry.

FLOOR AND SIDES
SHAKE 'N' BAKE

What you'll need:
- Box of baking soda
- Water
- Spatula
- Expired credit card (or overused one that you should destroy before applying for bankruptcy)
- Damp cloth

What you'll do:
- Make sure the oven is turned off. When it's cool to the touch, remove the racks.
- Mix 3 parts baking soda to one part water to make a pastelike mixture.
- Use a spatula or your hands to spread it all around oven floor and sides.
- Let it "bake" naturally overnight—do not turn the oven on!
- Remove gunk with a spatula or credit card.
- Wipe with a damp cloth and use a handheld vac to suck up remaining hardened soda crumbs.

OVERFLOWS: SHAKE IT UP
Shake some salt onto any drips or spills as soon as you see them. This will help keep your cleaning to a minimum and firemen from showing up due to the smoke that those drips and spills may cause.

EXTERIOR OF OVEN DOORS

What you'll need:
- White vinegar
- Water
- Dry microfiber cloth or streak-free disinfecting wipe

What you'll do:
- Use a mixture of vinegar and water and wipe with a microfiber cloth.

HOODS

What you'll need:
- Dishwashing detergent or streak-free disinfecting wipe
- Microfiber cloth

What you'll do:
- Wipe the outside of the hood with hot, sudsy water or cleaning wipe. Buff with a dry microfiber cloth to reduce smudging.

For filters: Check the manual to see if you can clean them in your dishwasher—keep your fingers crossed that you can.

COOKTOPS

IMMEDIATE CLEANUPS

What you'll need:
- Dishwashing liquid or multisurface, nonabrasive cleaner
- Microfiber cloth or paper towels

What you'll do:
- Wipe up as much of the spill as you can without burning yourself.
- Let the surface cool and then wipe with sudsy water (use nonabrasive stuff like dishwashing liquid or a store-bought multisurface cleaner so you don't scratch anything).

SUGARY CLEANUP

What you'll need:
- Salt
- Spatula or overextended credit card

What you'll do:
- Sprinkle salt immediately onto the overflow and let it "bake to a crisp." When done and cool enough to the touch, remove "crisp" with a spatula or credit card.

LEFTOVER CLEANUPS

What you'll need:
- Boiling water
- Spatula or overextended credit card
- White vinegar
- Dry microfiber cloth or paper towels

What you'll do:
- Pour boiling water onto spills that have hardened.
- Let it sit before scraping off the spills with a spatula.
- Wipe dry with paper towels or a microfiber cloth.
- If you care about any water spots that remain, use some white vinegar to erase them. Vinegar will also help cut the grease residue.
- Optional: Use a streak-free wipe to finish.

CHILD'S PLAY

What you'll need:
- Baking soda
- Water
- Small plastic bowl
- Spoon
- Spatula
- Timer

What they'll do:
1. Mix up enough paste (3 parts baking soda to 1 part water) to cover the entire area.
   After it's cooled completely:
2. Have kids spread it on with a spatula or use their fingers to finger paint.
3. Set the timer for ten minutes and when it ringy-dingys tell them to wipe it up with a damp microfiber cloth or paper towels.

KNOBS

What you'll need:
- Dishwashing liquid
- Microfiber cloth

What you'll do:
- Turn the knobs to the off position and pull them off.
- Fill the sink with warm water and dishwashing liquid and let them soak. Wipe them with a microfiber cloth.
- Dry and replace the knobs. Be sure they're firmly reattached so you don't under- or overcook your next stovetop stuffing!

DRIP PANS

What you'll need:
- Dishwasher
- Foil

What you'll do:
- Put them in the dishwasher—revolutionary, I know, but very manicure-friendly!
- When clean, line with foil to make future cleanups easy.

BARBECUE GRATES

First, check the manual to see if it's okay to use store-bought oven cleaner, then take them outside so you don't inhale fumes.

What you'll need:
- Old newspaper
- Oven cleaner
- Large trash bags
- Dish detergent

What you'll do:
- Lay them on newspaper and spray with store-bought oven cleaner.
- Put them in a large garbage bag and leave them overnight.
- Wash them off with water and detergent.
- Rinse and dry.

DISHWASHERS

Now we're talking! Clearly we want to keep this most useful appliance in good working condition, since it means less work for Mama and more days of life for our manicures! So put on those fashionable rubber gloves and clean this machine!

What you'll need:
- Paper towels
- White vinegar

What you'll do:
- Gunk in the bottom of your dishwasher can cause your dishes to still look dirty after the wash. Check the strainer on the bottom or back and remove any debris that's there. Keep damp paper towels handy to help remove it.
- Pour one cup of white vinegar into the strainer to break up any gunk and then put another cup in during the rinse cycle. The vinegar will clean the gunk you can't see, and deodorize the dishwasher too. Double duty—love that!

THE TOUGH STUFF—RUST

A high iron content in your water will cause your dishwasher to form rust and could even put an orangey cast on the door. Don't worry—it's easy enough to clean.

What you'll need to remove the rust:
- Tang or Kool-Aid (unsweetened lemonade)

What you'll do:
- Place a few tablespoons of Tang or unsweetened lemonade Kool-Aid in your washer's soap dispenser and run it through one full cycle. The citric acid will eliminate the rust.

SMALL TO MIDSIZE APPLIANCES AND GADGETS

The kitchen has lots and lots of stuff to clean, so before you start reading this you might want to take a look at the items cluttering your counters and give away any that you haven't used in months to minimize your cleanup. Then do the follow before getting to the task at hand to help keep you and yours from an unexpected trip to the emergency room.

1. Unplug.
2. Let cool.
3. Don't let any water or liquid touch electrical stuff. Do not submerge appliances in water unless directions say otherwise.

Do the Bundy Tang-O!

Remember the Bundys from Fox TV's hit sitcom *Married with Children*? They were that happy-go-lucky dysfunctional family who lived in Chicago and attracted millions of viewers for ten years *way back*, from 1987 to 1997. The Bundy clan included:

- Peggy—an uneducated housewife who looked like a sixties throwback sporting a red bouffant, heels that were too high, and clothes that were too tight

- Al—her dim-witted husband, who sold women's shoes unsuccessfully (Hmmm, were shoes Peggy's attraction?)

- Kelly—their sex-crazed, equally dim-witted daughter

- Bud—their son, who was unpopular, girl crazy, and the only Bundy who ever went to college

The Bundys' dysfunction was played out in lots of ways and one of them revolved around Peggy's culinary skills—or lack thereof—which leads us to this "As Seen on TV." In one episode we learned that the Bundys were big Tang fans and hated to let one little granule go to waste. In fact, they loved the stuff so much that they would make Tang sandwiches. Well, one day there wasn't enough Tang for a whole sandwich, so they just took a slice of bread and swiped the sides of the Tang container to create what they lovingly called a *Tang Wipe*. If only the Bundys had been around back in 1965, NASA and the *Gemini* crew could have celebrated the Bundys' spaciness and this yummy recipe!

MICROWAVE

The microwave is an accidental housewife's best cooking bud, or at least mine. It's also one of the most overworked appliances in our household, since everyone knows how to use it. Here's a cleaning tip that's easy and that you can blend into an everyday activity such as making yourself a cup of tea.

TEA TIME!

What you'll need:
- Microwavable mug
- Water
- Damp microfiber cloth or paper towel
- Favorite tea (bag variety)
- Optional: Lemon wedge

What you'll do:
- Fill the mug ⅔ of the way up with water and microwave until it boils (times vary according to microwave, but figure three to five minutes).
- The mug may be hot to the touch, so carefully remove it when time's up or use a potholder.
- Put your tea bag into your freshly boiled water and while it's brewing wipe the inside yuk with a damp microfiber cloth or paper towel.
  - *Optional:* Freshen the scent of your family's favorite cooking appliance by squeezing the lemon into the water before zapping.

Alternatively: Forgive the pun, but if the preceding isn't your cup of tea, try using a cup of white vinegar and follow the steps as above, without the optional lemon zest.

For big messes use a small microwaveable glass bowl filled ⅔ with water. Squeeze in a whole lemon and put both halves into the bowl. Mirowave for 5 minutes. Follow as above.

COFFEE BREAK

Coffee's a great odor absorber, so if your microwave smells as a result of those microwaveable fish sticks your kiddie zapped up, try this recipe.

What you'll need:
- 2 tablespoons freshly ground coffee
- ½ cup water
- Microwaveable coffee mug
- Microwaveable bowl big enough to place mug inside

What you'll do:
- Put coffee into the mug and fill it halfway with water.
- Place the mug in the microwaveable bowl (this is for your cleaning protection, since the water will boil and overflow).
- Zap for two minutes.

TOASTER OVEN

Some of the folks who make toasters have realized that cleaning a toaster's interior is difficult. So if you're in the market for a new toaster oven look for one that enables you to remove and machine-wash the inner shell and/or has a nonstick, dishwasher-safe tray. Speaking of which, yours probably has some kind of "catch tray," crumb tray, or toasting tray that you should line with foil that you change regularly to limit cleaning.

INTERIOR

- *SPILLS:* They're the easiest to clean if you can get to them quickly without burning yourself. So let the oven cool enough for you to touch and use a dry microfiber cloth to suck up the spill. Same thing applies if something spills on the coils—as always, unplug it first, then let it cool and wipe with a damp microfiber cloth. If stuff hardens or you notice yuk from a while ago, sprinkle some baking soda on a damp microfiber cloth and wipe.
- *CRUMBS:* Take out the tray and shake it over your garbage can. Wipe the crumb tray with a damp cloth or put it in the dishwasher. Cover the tray with foil so you don't have to wash it next time.

EXTERIOR

- *MELTED PLASTIC:* Left that packaged bread a little too close while you were toasting a piece? Let your toaster cool and then get your nail polish remover. Put some on a paper towel or soft cloth and gently rub to remove the melted plastic. While you're at it, this would be a good time to finally take that chipped nail polish off your index finger, too!
- *SHINE:* Put some vodka or vinegar directly on a microfiber cloth to reduce smearing and wipe. Any multipurpose, multisurface store-bought spray will work. Apply it directly to the cloth.
- *FINGERMARKS:* Wipe with a little bit of baby oil followed by a splash of club soda, then dry with a microfiber cloth or paper towel. Vodka and vinegar will also work—though no club soda is necessary, just swipe with a dry microfiber cloth.

AUTO-DRIP COFFEEMAKER

Our morning godsend needs some extra TLC every now and then to ensure its ability to brew a robust carafe of coffee which helps get us through our hectic mornings or late-night feedings. My first tip is to buy a coffeemaker that comes with a dishwasher-safe carafe. Put the carafe on the top rack to avoid the possibility of melting the handle. My second tip is to brew a pot of coffee for yourself and sip a cup of your morning brewsky before trying one of the following solutions.

TWO BREWS FOR YOU

Brew 1: What you'll need (for an average ten- to twelve-cup coffeemaker):
- 2 cups white vinegar
- 2 cups water

What you'll do:
- Empty remaining coffee and rinse the carafe. You might want to save a cup that you can reheat later since it may take repeating one or both of the following steps, depending upon how long it's been (if ever) since you cleaned it.
- Fill the carafe with equal parts of white vinegar and water. Don't worry if you can't decide how big your carafe is since the vinegar isn't going to hurt it. Just don't put more liquid in than your carafe can hold.
- Once filled, run it through the brewing cycle.
- Empty the carafe and run a carafe of water through a normal brew cycle to get rid of any vinegar smell or residue.

Brew 2: What you'll need:
- Hot water (enough to fill carafe)
- Two effervescent denture or tummy tablets

Double Dripping Tip!

As I've said ad nauseam, I'm all about blending my housewifely tasks into my activities, so here's another mindless way to clean your sink's garbage disposal while you're drinking your coffee: Pour the "brewed vinegar" from this tip down ye ol' drain. Feel free to add a little bit of baking soda for a total clean!

What you'll do:
- Fill your coffeemaker's water reservoir up with hot water.
- Drop in two denture or tummy tablets. Let them fizz, and then turn on to brew.
- Empty contents and run a carafe of water through one brewing cycle.

COFFEE BEAN GRINDER

UNCLE BEN'S BEST

What you'll need:
- Handful of uncooked white rice
- Toothbrush (used)

Who Would Have Thunk!! Five Fab Uses for Coffee Filters

(Eco-friendly Tip: Use Recycled Filters vs. Regular)

1. DEGREASER: Put that egg roll or batch of fries on a filter and let it absorb the grease.

2. DE-SERVER: Forget the dessert dishes—use filters to serve cookies, cupcakes, candy, or cake. It's a great way to portion control mindlessly, too!

3. DECANTER: Cork crack while you were pulling it out? Then use a filter to catch the cork by pouring the wine into a clear carafe or pitcher. Tip: Next time buy a wine with a screw top!

4. DE-LINTER: Use a filter instead of paper towels to clean your windows. FYI—paper towels leave lint, unlike these little wonders.

5. DIFFUSER: Use one over your camera's flash to soften the brightness and diffuse the dark circles under your eyes.

What you'll do:
- Put rice in the grinder and grind away for a minute (it is Uncle Ben's after all!).
- Use the toothbrush to clean crevices and remaining residue.

    FYI: The rice will also sharpen the blade so be aware that your next batch of coffee may have you buzzing a bit more! By the way, a friend of mine loves a product she gets online aptly called the Urnex Grind Home Cleaner that you can check out at www.espressoparts.com/product/urnx _grindz_hm.

BLENDER

The blender gives us a wonderful opportunity to "blend" our everyday activities into cleaning. We'll start by getting it dirty and whipping up a frozen margarita!!! *Olé!*

What you'll need:
- Margarita mix
- Tequila
- Ice
- Salt, lime wedges for garnish
- Liquid dishwashing soap
- Warm water

What you'll do:
- Pour mix and tequila shots into blender according to directions, number of people, and/or your alcohol tolerance.
- Add ice according to quantity; cover; and mix, frappe, or crush away until relatively smooth.
- Wet the rims of margarita glasses or plastic cups (my choice, since there'll be no dishes!!!) and dip them into salt. Pour margaritas into the glasses, and garnish with a lime wedge, if you like.
- If the blender's pitcher isn't dishwasher-safe, squirt a few drops of dishwashing liquid into it and fill with warm water.
- Cover, blend, and drink away as it cleans away, *olé!*
- Rinse thoroughly with warm water until no soap remains.

Electric Can Opener

FLOSS 'N' BRUSH

What you'll need:
- Dental floss (unflavored)
- Old toothbrush
- White vinegar

What you'll do:
- Use dental floss to remove debris around blade.
- Loosen remaining yuk with an old toothbrush. Spritz or wipe with vinegar to shine and deodorize.

Cheese Grater

TWO EASY CHEESY CLEANING TIPS

1. What you'll need:
- Nongel, nonwhitening toothpaste
- Toothbrush (old)

What you'll do:
- Put regular, nongel, nonwhitening toothpaste on toothbrush and brush.
- Rinse off with warm water.

2. What you'll need:
- Cooking spray (plain unless you prefer some garlic zest on your cheese!)

What you'll do:
- Before using, spray with your favorite cooking spray to avoid cheese sticking.

Chapter 4

The Kitchen

My next house will have no cupboards, just vending machines. —Unknown

Way back in the bathroom section of this guide, I shared that organizing is a great way to disguise some of the dirt lurking about and provide a temporary respite from dealing with it. The same holds true in the kitchen, where we continue to indulge our need for the latest and greatest kitchen gadget or juice maker and rarely discard or evaluate what we already have, need, or use.

In fact, according to an interesting statistic I discovered:

The average household uses only 20 percent of our kitchen-related tools 80 percent of the time.

TRANSLATION: Time to cut the fat!

Organizing Enough

It is this 20 percent household uses statistic that drives the simple organizing solutions that follow and will help you learn to let go just as you did in the bathroom:

- *LIVE THE 20:80 RULE:* Keep reminding yourself that you only use 20 percent of your kitchen stuff 80 percent of the time. So go through all your pots, pans, small appliances, utensils, cutting boards, dishes, flatware, glasses, miscellaneous gourmet tool "must-haves," and wedding, anniversary, and housewarming gifts and multiples of any of the preceding.* Then "rule" out the excess.

- *IF IT'S BROKE, DON'T FIX IT!* Get rid of broken items or those that have needed repair for more than three months. The likelihood is if you haven't repaired it yet, your need for it is nil and qualifies as the 80 percent of your unused items.
- *LET GO WITHOUT GUILT:* I know it's hard to part with some items that loved ones or close friends may have given to you. Or maybe you have momentary dreams of Martha-like entertaining. I do too. Then I look in the mirror and remind myself who I really am!
- *BE CHARITABLE!* Once you've cut the fat, do a good deed and donate the things that are in relatively good shape to a college student, local school, first-time apartment owner, or a charity. Be sure to get an itemized deduction receipt or something from the charity or organization you donate to since your charitable act will most likely provide you with a tax deduction.
- *SPREAD THE GLOVE—RE-GIFT!* It's a great way to spread the organizing glove. Just be sure to give the re-gifted item to a person other than the one who gave it to you. That or let them know how much you appreciated their thinking you could cook, but that's not the case and you thought they'd put it to better use than you!

*PLEASE NOTE: Experience has taught me to keep at least two sets of serving pieces, dishes, glasses, and flatware. Chances are dishes and glasses will break "accidentally" and if you're like me, you may unintentionally throw out silverware while scrap-

Can't Part With . . .

That pitcher from Aunt Molly?

Repurpose it! Use it to store wooden spoons and other cooking utensils

All those Mother's Day mugs you've collected over the years?

Repurpose it! Collect change in it

That ten-year-old never-used wok from your bridal shower?

Repurpose it: Put it on your counter and use it for dish-towels and potholders.

ing off plates. I find this happens frequently when I use paper plates since I tend to mindlessly toss everything out—then again, maybe it's intentional and my way of avoiding any further cleanup!

How to Keep Your Clutter in Check:

Now that you've learned some simple ways to let go, you're ready to organize your home's hub. The fact is that it's really a very personal task and varies according to your household's routines. That's why I'm going to give you three simple tips that will help you keep clutter in check according to your individual needs:

1. *IDENTIFY BUSIEST KITCHEN ACTIVITY AREAS*
   These may include:
   - Prepping
   - Cooking
   - Serving
   - Cleaning
   - Ordering-in!
2. *PRACTICE GROUP THERAPY*—Put like things together according to their activity area and where they're easy to access. We're not talking brain surgery here but about using common sense. For example:

Short on Counter Space?

Get *on board!* Open a drawer and lay a cutting board across it.

Go vertical! Get hanging baskets, stackable containers, or cascading hooks to hold potholders, dishtowels, pots, pans, and all else you deem worthy.

Bag it! Hang a shoe-bag over a cupboard or on the back of a nearby door to hold wooden spoons, measuring spoons, pasta tongs, ladles, spatulas, small mixing tools, or petite gadgets with no sharp edges.

Under play! Replace small appliances that sit on your counters such as can openers, toasters, and coffee makers with under-the-counter models.

- *Prepping:* Keep cutting boards, knives, measuring spoons, measuring cups, and mixing bowls and cocktails (!) within reach.
- *Cooking:*
  - Pots and pans: Store them under the cooktop or on a hanging rack above the cooking area.
  - Wooden mixing spoons, pasta tongs, ladles, spatulas: Keep them in decorative crocks or flower pots.
  - Spices: Buy pre-stocked containers or put on Lazy Susan.
  - Pot holders: Place them in hanging baskets, on nearby knobs, or on hanging racks or connecting cascading hooks above the cooking area.
- *Serving:* Keep dishes, flatware, glasses, serving bowls, and utensils near your sink and dishwasher—this makes loading and unloading a lot more convenient!
- *Cleaning:* Put everything you need to wash dishes; to clean sinks, appliances, or countertops and trash cans under, on, or near your sink.

Note: Group items like aluminum foil, plastic wrap, wax paper, and storage bags together in one drawer.

3. *MAKE SURE THINGS ARE VISIBLE*—This goes hand in hand with accessible. If you can't see it, chances are you'll forget you have it and it will be categorized as part of the 80 percent that goes unused.

Here are some easy ways to keep them within view:

- *Knives:* Buy a knife block, which will also save you from accidentally slicing your finger when reaching for a knife as you talk on the phone.
- *Spices:* Buy pre-stocked standing unit or lazy Susan.
- *Sugar, flour, etc.:* Use stackable glass, plastic, or Tupperware type containers and label them to avoid confusion!
- *Small utensils, wooden spoons, ladles, etc.:* Keep them in decorative crocks, flowerpots, hanging cooking utensil racks, or cascading hooks near cooking areas.

I think you get the gist. Trust me—(I know that sounds like something Tricky Dicky Nixon asked his fellow Americans to do back when I was in diapers, but I really mean it!) if you set up these areas and group like stuff together where you can easily reach and see it, your kitchen will look organized and cleaner. And, if you hardly ever cook, it may even stay that way!

PART **2**

THE NOT-SO-TOXIC ZONES

Chapter 5

Living Spaces

JUST ENOUGH CLEANING

I had a linguistics professor who said that it's man's ability to use language that makes him the dominant species on the planet. That may be. But I think there's one other thing that separates us from animals. We aren't afraid of vacuum cleaners. —Jeff Stilson

It's time for you to get up close and personal with those cutesy dust bunnies that share your general living spaces and bedrooms. These not-so-toxic zones are generally places where you and yours chill so the sanity-saving tips, tools, and solutions that follow are far less onerous than those in the toxic zones section. After all, clutter is clutter and dust is dust whether it's in your common living spaces or bedroom, with one exception—those not-so-cutesy dust mites which you'll meet, greet, and try to defeat beginning on page 125. But hey you've learned how to conquer our M & M (mold & mildew) and bacteria buds so squashing these varmints will seem like a walk in the park.

By the way, in this chapter whenever I refer to Living Spaces, I'm including areas like the family room, dining room, living room, and sometimes entranceways. Basically, any space where you and yours may greet people, socialize, enjoy a flick or TV while eating take-out food, or simply chill.

Cleaning

Unlike the bathroom and kitchen, where I divided and conquered by location, hot spot, or appliance, your living spaces and bedrooms are broken down by the frequency with which you need to clean them—that is, daily, weekly, monthly, and seasonally. And, since these areas generally don't get that dirty or house things that reproduce or smell, I've created a new category of cleaning called Quickies to keep these spaces clean enough. That means I've also eliminated the "what you'll need" and "what you'll do" breakdowns in the hope that the words *dust, wipe, sweep, vacuum, spray,* and *straighten* are self-explanatory. Defensive cleaning tips are included. However, offensive ones are not separated out as not too many terrible mishaps occur in these rooms other than some fairly easy-to-clean accidental spills, drips, pees, or scribbles gone astray. Thus, unless your mother-in-law is coming over wearing her white gloves, cleaning these areas will be a breeze.

DEFENSIVE CLEANING

- *USE MATS:* Place absorbent doormats inside and outside all entranceways to limit the tracking of dirt and moisture through your house. You should consider purchasing a wonderfully decorative mat that will get the job done and benefits breast cancer research in the U.S. and Canada during Breast Cancer Awareness month (October) as well as in November and December. For more info visit www.carpetone.com.
- *GO SHOELESS:* Keep a basket or decorative bin at key entranceways for all household members to toss their shoes into. If you're having guests over have everyone take their shoes off and give them a pair of inexpensive flip-flops, slippers, or socks to wear. If they refuse, just tell them they'll have to walk on their hands and knees!
- *GET DUST BUSTERS:* Put door sweeps and weather strips on your doors and windows to close up any gaps. You'd be surprised how much pollen, dirt, bugs, and other yucky stuff those gaps can let in. It'll also help reduce heating or cooling bills, since you'll stop the hot or cold air from escaping to the outside.
- *CLOSE WINDOWS:* If you don't have screens (and may I suggest you consider buying them to both help keep your home clean and keep bugs at bay), keep windows closed to keep dirt and dust from entering! I love keeping my screened windows open particularly in the warmer months, not only to let the fresh air in, but because on very windy days it's an eco-friendly, hands-free way to dust!
- *WAX AWAY:* Use furniture polish or wax to keep dust at bay. Plus if you spill something it'll just bubble up instead of running like a river all over your wood furniture. Check labels so you use the right wax for the right surface.
- *KEEP DECORATIVE DUMPSTERS NEARBY:* If it doesn't create a total eyesore or tripping hazard, strategically place bins and baskets for household members so they can mindlessly toss shoes, boots, toys, and so on.
- *DIM LIGHTS:* Dim lights, draw curtains, and/or close blinds to keep people

from noticing the dust and dirt! I've also found that serving guests an alcoholic beverage upon arrival is a good way to "dim" the focus on dusty tables and floors. And what more perfect cocktail to serve than The Accidental Housewife Dirty Martini, whose recipe can be found on page 66.

- *USE DECORATING DECOYS:* Another way to dim the focus when you're having guests is by buying fresh flowers, lighting scented candles, and putting out photos of family and friends to divert and catch their attention.

QUICKIE CLEANING JUST ENOUGH

If God wanted us to bend over he'd have put diamonds on the floor. —Joan Rivers

Here are four simple tips to insure that you don't do more than you need or want to:

1. *CLEAN ONLY WHAT'S DIRTY*
2. *KEEP SUPPLIES NEARBY SO YOU CAN CLEAN ON A WHIM*
3. *DO ANYTHING THAT CREATES OR DISTURBS DUST OR DIRT* such as:
- Fluffing pillows
- Shaking out throws
- Straightening magazines and books
- Opening or closing blinds, curtains, or windows
4. *SPRAY DIRECT*—Whenever you use any kind of spray, spray it directly onto the cloths unless instructions advise otherwise to avoid schmearing, seeping, or discoloration of mirrors, artwork, photos, and furniture.

YOUR MULTITASKING MANICURE-FRIENDLY SHOPPING LIST

As always, you should have your fashionable and functional rubber gloves on hand (forgive the pun!) and your schlep vehicle filled and ready to go. Since these Quickies are fairly painless, I find that I generally do one living space at a time from start to finish. That and I can blend them easily into other activities I enjoy such as chatting on the phone, singing, or simply dancing with those dust bunnies.

TRADITIONAL MANICURE-FRIENDLY CLEANING PRODUCTS

FOR DUSTING
- Microfiber:
  - Machine-washable cloths
  - Mini duster with machine-washable bonnet

- Dust mops with extendable handles so you can reach cobwebs and ceiling fans, with hooks or holes on their ends to hang them
- Genuine feather duster
- Array of disposables
  - Multipurpose, multisurface cloths and sprays for dusting, cleaning mirrors, and waxing.

FOR FLOORS

- A lobby set: This is a broom with a dust pan attached—pretty much eliminates a need for a whisk broom
- Disposable floor and carpet sweeper (like the Swiffer)
- Angled broom (for tight spaces and corners)
- Microfiber mop with detachable, machine-washable mop head
- Hand or stick vacuum (Dirt Devil and Dyson have some attractive, major sucking-up models)
- Canister or upright vacuum with multiple attachments (lots to choose from but I love one from Hoover that floats and another from Electrolux that has the suction to pick up eight bowling balls but is compact and easy to store, making it great for small spaces)
- Robotic vacuum (I'm a big fan of iRobot Roomba Scheduler since you can program it to do the work for you!)
- A child five or older (indulge their love for vacuuming before they figure out it's a chore that bores!)

THE ACCIDENTAL ENVIRO-KEEPER'S CLEANERS

FOR DUSTING:

- *LINT BRUSH*—with disposable sheets—these are great for lampshades and plant leaves
- *BLOW DRYER*—for hard-to-reach areas
- *SOFT BRISTLE PAINT BRUSH*—terrific for cleaning mirrors, lampshades, paintings. A basting brush is also good for smaller items, but many of you accidental housewives may not own one of these since that might also indicate that you cook!
- *WHITE VINEGAR*—for glass-top furniture—Shines without schmearing when applied directly to microfiber cloth prior to wiping. It will also shine your wood furniture, as you'll see shortly.
- *GOLF CLUB*—Attach a sock dampened with multisurface, multipurpose cleaner

to clean high spots of dust and spiderwebs. A broom or an umbrella works well too!

FOR FLOORS:
- *CHILD* five years of age or older

MISCELLANEOUS
- *COOKIE DOUGH:* Buy some of the Dough Boy's ready-to-bake cookie dough and let your kiddies bake up a batch before guests arrive to create a wonderful homey scent and aromatic distraction!

My Quickie Cleaning Tool Belt
When I do Quickie cleanups I wear my handy-dandy tool belt, which is my portable schlep vehicle of choice, and stock it with the following:

- Genuine ostrich feather duster (chicken or synthetic don't hold the dust as well)
- Disposable disinfecting, multisurface, multipurpose cleaning wipes
- Microfiber dust cloth
- Disinfecting air freshening spray
- BlackBerry or iPhone
- iPod
- Water bottle

Should you choose to adopt the tool belt as your portable schlep vehicle of choice when cleaning the other rooms in your home simply add or swap out those items that work best for you and the chore at hand. Don't forget to wear your gloves!

The Daily Quickie
If you're in the mood, on a daily or every-other-day basis you can keep your living spaces looking reasonably neat and clean simply by:

- Straightening magazines, newspapers, books, and DVDs
- Fluffing pillows
- Folding throws
- Tossing toys in bins
- Putting remotes and eyeglasses in boxes or baskets (decorative, of course!)
- Spraying with an aromatic disinfecting spray

White-Glove Test

Before I wrote this guide I thought that the expression "white-glove test" referred to a 1950s mother-in-law who wore white gloves every time she visited her son and daughter-in-law's home. Her goal: to humiliate the new woman in her precious little boy's life.

I have since discovered that this phrase has its roots in the military. Seems back in the day NCOs or noncommissioned officers (who are enlisted folks who have been given authority by their COs or commissioned officers) would put on a pair of white cotton gloves and run their fingers along every surface in a barrack searching for the littlest speck of dirt or dust. The rationale behind this was to build character and see if they could break a new recruit. Sort of like scenes from the 1982 movie *An Officer and a Gentleman* where the always-good-to-look-at Richard Gere is continually harassed by his attending officer played by Louis Gossett Jr. All I can say is I'd love for an officer who looked like Richard Gere to do his white-glove test in my home unannounced, anytime!

The Weekly or Bi-Weekly Quickie

In addition to your daily or every-other-day Quickie cleanup you should try to do the following every week, though every two weeks is good enough depending upon how often you have company or your mother over:

- Chuck old newspapers
- Dust furniture and windowsills
- Wipe TV screens, phones, remotes, doorknobs, and switch plates with disinfecting wipes, fabric softener sheets, or baby wipes
- Vacuum (make it mindless and consider buying the Roomba Scheduler which you can program to vacuum for you!)

The Monthly Quickie

If you're in the mood and have the time, these are tasks you should try to do monthly. You can stretch it to six weeks, give or take, so long as you're keeping up with your daily and weekly Quickie cleanups:

- Dust baseboards and wall hangings
- Use a feather duster to clean blinds
- Vacuum carpets and/or mop hardwood floors

Men Are Messy

I Love Lucy was must-see TV from the moment it debuted on October 15, 1951. For those of you who were born a bit later or have never seen an episode on TV Land, the series was a hysterical and human take on being a housewife and trying to balance home, career, and friendship. *Sound familiar*? Its main characters were:

- Lucy McGillicuddy Ricardo (Lucille Ball)—a truly accidental housewife and showbiz wannabe with a real talent for getting herself into trouble while trying to improve her life.

- Ricky Ricardo—Lucy's Cuban husband who was a singer and the bandleader at a New York City nightclub. Ricky was known for always saying; "Ai-yai-ai-yai-yai" in response to Lucy's escapades.

- Ethel and Fred Mertz—Lucy and Ricky's best buds, neighbors, and landlords.

In one episode called "Men Are Messy," Lucy decides to teach Ricky a lesson since she's tired of him constantly messing up their living room. She starts by dividing their apartment into his messy half and her neat half. Then Lucy takes it a step further by turning their home into a real pigsty. What she doesn't know is that Ricky is bringing home a photographer from *LOOK* magazine to do a feature story about their home and them. Insanity ensued: Ricky and the photographer enter their home to discover clotheslines hanging in the living room, chickens flying around, and garbage everywhere. Not exactly *House Beautiful*! And, to top it off, Lucy and Ethel are dressed in flannel shirts and overalls preparing to go "hunting" for a black bear that's in Lucy's bedroom. Well, the photographer took pictures of all this and one made *LOOK's* cover. Unfortunately, it was a shot of Lucy with her bear. So much for teaching Ricky a lesson about neatness. I guess the moral of this story is: Men are messy so you have to "bear" with them!

- Vacuum upholstered furniture if you have pets or people who shed
- Wash throw rugs and entranceway mats—check labels to be sure they're machine washable

THE SEASONAL QUICKIE (QUARTERLY, OR AT LEAST FOR FALL AND SPRING)
- *Look up!* Remove cobwebs and dust ceiling fans.
- *Work out!* Move couches and other heavy furniture, then vacuum under, on, and

behind them. You should remove and vacuum the cushions too. Be forewarned: You may find some very yucky stuff there.

- *Suck it up:* Use your vacuum to clean out debris and dirt in your air filters and vents.
- *Open up:* Open blinds and drapes and clean them using your vacuum's brush attachment.
- *Wash windows:* Self-explanatory, I hope!

Occasional and Accidentally Inspired Quickies

In addition to the daily, weekly, monthly, and seasonal cleanups, here are a few more cleaning targets that require regular cleaning. Accidental cleanups are also included, such as when your pooch's bladder can't hold it in any longer or you spill that third glass of red wine.

SWITCH PLATES
Switch it out!

Use one of the following:

- Disinfecting wipes
- Microfiber cloth and dishwashing liquid or antibacterial cleaning spray—spray onto cloth
- Baking soda on dampened micofiber cloth

CEILING FANS
Sock it to them!

- Turn fan off.
- Put a sock on a golf club.
- Spray sock with all-purpose cleaner and swing gently. An extendable microfiber duster will work well too.

FINGERMARKS ON WALL
Rub them out!

Use one of the following to remove them:

- Mr. Clean Magic Eraser or Scotch-Brite Easy Erasing Pad
- White vinegar and water on microfiber cloth or paper towel

Handy Sports Stuff Helpers

You probably have many sports items cluttering your home which aren't being used for their intended purpose. Here are some ideas to give them a new lease on life:

- **BASEBALL BAT:** Wrap a microfiber cloth sprayed with your fave dusting stuff around the bat. Secure with coated elastic bands, then roll the bat under your couch to pick up God knows what!

- **FRISBEES:** Use as a Dumpster for coins, keys, and glasses. If you have mini-Frisbees, use them under furniture legs to prevent scratches.

- **GOLF CLUBS:** Put a sock on the head and spray with your fave multitasking cleaner for hard-to-reach places. You may need to call FORE! when all the dirt or that gigantic spider comes falling down from these spots, since it's probably been a while since they were cleaned, if ever.

- **TENNIS BALLS:** Slit one and cover your hammer's head to ensure you put in a nail without breaking one of yours and to hang that picture quietly!

- **TENNIS RACQUETS:** Use them as a fly swatter or attach some tape to dust under narrow, hard-to-reach spaces below and between.

COMMON CARPET STAINS
Out, Out, Damn Spot!

Remember always blot, blot that spot, spot—never rub, rub unless otherwise told, told!

- *SPILLS:*
    - Blot immediately with white paper towels or a microfiber cloth
    - Mix a little clear dishwashing liquid with water and blot
    - Rinse with water and let dry
- *RED WINE:*
    - Blot excess with microfiber cloth, paper towel(s), or a sponge
    - Put a bit of cold water on it mixed with baking soda—3 parts baking soda to 1 part water. You'll have to figure out just how much to mix depending on if

you've spilled a glass or the entire bottle—and may I say, what a waste that would be!
- Let it sit overnight, then vacuum.
- *GREASE:*

Three options:

1. Saturate with foam shaving cream, and let sit for a few hours or overnight. Use a blow dryer to dry it.
2. Sop up with the microfiber cloth, rag, or paper towels, then gently rub baby powder or cornstarch into stain, let sit overnight, and vacuum.
3. You can also use our fave 3 parts baking soda and 1 part water cleaner-upper. Let it sit overnight and then vacuum.

PET PEES
Blot as much of it as you can with paper towels, then:

- Wash with liquid dishwashing soap.
- Rinse with 1/2 cup white vinegar and cover with paper towels.
- Leave overnight and let dry completely.

I'm a big fan of Nature's Miracle Stain & Odor Remover, which you can find at pet stores as well as on amazon.com and other online sites.

TABLE MARKS—WOOD

LIQUIDS/WATER RINGS
The first tip is to keep coasters with felt bottoms or absorbent liners handy to use under drink glasses and vases. If the damage is done:

BRING OUT THE MAYO!
- Spread a generous amount of mayonnaise on the ring and let it sit for 4 to 6 hours. If you forget to remove it, it's okay to leave it on longer or overnight.
- Wipe off the mayo and buff with microfiber cloth.

CANDLE DRIPS
Here are four manicure-friendly ways to deal immediately with candle drips:

1. *IRON IT:*
   - Put a piece of newspaper or a paper towel over the wax.

- Set iron on warm setting and put on top of paper. Don't move the iron around unless you want to spread the wax.
- Pick up the iron—hopefully all the wax is on the paper. If not, repeat until it's all gone.

2. *ICE IT*
- Freeze the freshly melted wax by putting an ice cube on top.
- Lift it with an expired or overextended credit card or spatula.

3. *BLOW IT OUT*
- Set your blow dryer on high to soften the wax.
- Gently wipe it off with a paper towel and continue blowing until it's all gone. Polish with a mix of vinegar and water.

4. *BUY DRIPLESS*—Clearly the accidental housewifely way!

FOR SHINING WOOD FURNITURE AFTER A SPILL AND IN GENERAL

CHILD'S PLAY (Yes, it's what you'll need and do to make it easy for your kiddie!)

MAKE SOME DRESSING!

What they'll need:
(it's a 3:1 mix like with our baking soda paste so you'll have to see how much you'll need depending on how much shining you're doing!)

- 3 parts olive oil
- 1 part white vinegar
- Small bowl
- Microfiber cloth

What they'll do:
- Mix together the olive oil and vinegar.
- Dampen the cloth with the mix.
- Wipe and buff with the dry side of the cloth.
  Color-compatible shoe polish will also work if that's all you've got. Apply and buff!

Smelly Carpets
- Sprinkle with baking soda, cornstarch, or baby powder
- Let sit for twenty to thirty minutes, then suck it up with your vacuum

Pet Peeves

Forget the ammonia! A friend of mine who has a cat told me she doesn't use any ammonia-based products to clean up her cat's pee since peepee contains ammonia. Cats, like most animals, are attracted to their own pee smell and as a result they will continually snuff it out and pee again in the same area. Your answer: Nature's Miracle Stain & Odor Remover, available at amazon.com.

Call in the Guard! If you have an older dog or a puppy who needs a diaper or one who hasn't met a place on your carpet that he didn't like, you probably have given up and called in your handy-dandy carpet cleaning man. For extra protection, ask him about applying a Scotchgard type coating to your carpets. Better late than never!

Pickups: Unless you give your pet a buzz cut, here are some simple ways to deal with their shedding on your carpet, couch, or clothing:
- Use a disposable lint brush roller
- Rub with a fabric dryer sheet

WALL STAINS

COLORED MARKERS: (YES, THIS EVEN WORKS ON PERMANENT-MARKER SCRIBBLES!)
1. Spray with hairspray and immediately wipe before it can drip down your walls. Not recommended for enamel-base painted walls.

CRAYONS: TWO OPTIONS:
1. Put a dab of toothpaste on a toothbrush and gently brush or wipe it out.
2. Rub softly with a dampened microfiber cloth and baking soda.

If your little Picasso has shown his artistic creativity on wallpaper: Squirt a dollop of foam shaving cream onto his rendering and gently rub with a microfiber cloth.

Chapter 6

Living Spaces

JUST ENOUGH ORGANIZING

I am a marvelous housekeeper. Every time I leave a man I keep his house. **—Zsa Zsa Gabor**

No bells, no whistles, and no long intros this time, since you're going to use some of the same offensive clutter cutters and organizing sanity savers you've used before. So if you're like me and lack an ironclad memory, read on.

Offensive Organizing

- *LET GO:* Look at all the stuff you have lying around: remotes, video players, eyeglasses, and so on, and chuck anything that you haven't used in the last month or has been replaced by the latest electronic wonder.
- *CHECK PUBLICATION DATES:* Unless you're hoping that the May 2007 issue of your fave magazine is going to be worth something someday, chuck and recycle.
  - **Alternatively:** Build a few end tables by stacking old magazines or larger books. If using paperbacks, think about stability since you don't want to rest that glass of wine down only to have it fall, causing you stress and a mess. The table's height will be dependent upon where you position them for easy reach.

- *BE CHARITABLE!* Once you've figured out which books, DVDs, old eyeglasses,* sunglasses, and electronic equipment you can part with, give them away! Again, be sure to get an itemized deduction receipt from the charity or organization you donate to since your charitable act should result in a nice little tax deduction from Uncle Sam!
- *AVOID FLEA MARKETS, GARAGE SALES, AND RESALE SHOPS:* The last thing you need is to be tempted to buy another dust-collecting, kitschy lamp, vintage rug, or poster, even if the price is too good to pass up. In fact, you might want to consider holding your own garage sale and letting others enjoy your excesses as you put a little moola back in your own pocket!

Organizing It Just Enough

REMEMBER LOCATION, LOCATION, LOCATION

If you want to stay organized, you have to put your clutter cutters where they're needed most and can be clearly seen, and easily accessed. I refer to these organizers as Dumpsters since they enable everyone to mindlessly "dump" their stuff somewhere where it's contained and gives the appearance of controlled chaos—is that a double negative making it a positive?

ENTRANCEWAY DUMPSTERS
- Put out small decorative bowls and baskets to toss small like items into, such as keys, change, and sunglasses (toss gently—you don't want to break them).
- Use baskets or attractive plastic buckets for shoes and boots. Give each household member a "shoe dump" and personalize it with his or her picture.
- Buy a coat rack, hooks, or use an old golf bag to keep umbrellas, backpacks, scarves, coats, leashes, and keys.

FAMILY ROOM, LIVING ROOM, AND GREAT ROOM DUMPSTERS
- Use decorative boxes on end and cocktail tables for things like remotes, glasses, cell phones, pens, and paperbacks.

---

*There are lots of charities that collect glasses for the elderly and poor in the United States and around the world. A few you may want to check out include www.neweyesfortheneedy.com, www.lionsclub.org, and www.uniteforsite.org.

- Skirt a table (cover it) with a machine-washable tablecloth, throw, or some kind of attractive fabric covering and store things like current magazines, DVDs, videos, and books under it.
- Hang a bold poster or painting over shelves stacked with books and mags to distract the eye from the clutter below.
- Use a wine rack to store magazines—just roll and fill.

Hmmmmmm Almost Dunnnnnn!

Breathe in, then out, repeat, and feel the stress and tension leave your body. Okay, who am I kidding! Hopefully you're feeling some sense of calm since you're close to completing our not-so-toxic housekeeping tour. But, if breathing isn't helping you chill, go to our next stop—our bedrooms—and take a short siesta.

Chapter 7

The Bedroom

JUST ENOUGH CLEANING

No one ever died from sleeping in an unmade bed. I have known mothers who remake the bed after their children do it because there's a wrinkle in the spread or the blanket is on crooked. This is sick. —Erma Bombeck

U nless you're newly married, oversexed, sleep all day, have lots of pajama parties, or live in the Taj Mahal with crystal chandeliers hanging everywhere, your bedrooms shouldn't get too dirty, disorganized, or have much call for repairs. That's why dealing with the chores that bore in this zone shouldn't take you more than fifteen to thirty minutes. The other good news is that this section of the guide is probably the shortest, so you'll be out of here before it's bedtime.

I will warn you that I am going to gross you out *one last time*, since the bedroom is home to one last house pest, the dust mite, and their doo is pretty much everywhere.

Cleaning

Oscar Wilde said that man (and woman) were made for something better then disturbing dirt and when it comes to your bedrooms this will be your cleaning mantra. Just as you did for your living spaces, you'll keep your sleeping chambers clean enough with Quickie daily, weekly, monthly, and seasonal cleanups. But before you get to these it's time to learn about our last little pesty pal: the dust mite. And disturb them you must so that you and yours can sleep alone by choice. *Have I gotten your attention?*

OFFENSIVE CLEANING: DO YOU KNOW WHO YOU'RE SLEEPING WITH?

You and I have lots of company when we go to sleep at night. And though I wish it were your husband, your child's teddy bear, or in my dreams Brad Pitt, it's not. Instead you and I are snoozing with tens of thousands of microscopic little bugs known as dust mites and their doo.

Here's the poop on these prehistoric poopers:

- They've been around for more than 23 million years, which means that our prehistoric ancestors slept with them too. That's actually good news since it clearly shows they won't cause the end of civilization, just the end of your favorite pillow, mattress, or stuffed animal!
- They take up residence in dark, warm, and humid places, which is why they love sleeping with us. Since we spend a third of our lives in our bedrooms, which is their favorite hangout, we're going to focus on their presence there, but be aware they also live in our couches, vacuums, and carpets.
- Their favorite foods are dead human and pet skin cells, otherwise known as dander, which by the way is where the word dandruff has its roots.
- They also like to feast on their own doo—appetizing thought, eh!
- One mite poops about twenty times a day.
- And it is their doo that causes us allergy and health problems such as sneezing, coughing, irritated eyes, and so on!

And now to really gross you out:

- An average mattress can have anywhere from 100,000 to 10 million mites inside of it—you *doo* the math!
- A two-year-old pillow can weigh 10 percent more than a new one due to the presence of mites and their doo.

What You Can Do to Minimize Mites

I don't want to gross you out any further, so here are manicure-friendly and sanity-saving ways you can limit these mites from forming colonies, co-ops, condos, and all else in between.

A Few Facts About Mites

- They don't fly.
- They don't bite.
- They don't cohabit with dust bunnies.
- They like dark, warm areas and not wide open spaces.

- *BI-WEEKLY*
  - WASH AND DRY SHEETS AND PILLOWCASES ON HOT CYCLE
  - If you or your kiddies are also sleeping with stuffed animals, you should wash them regularly as well. Read care labels first so your favorite Teddy's eyes don't melt! If you do wash them, place them in a zippered pillowcase that you can close and remove batteries if present.
- *MONTHLY*
  - WASH AND DRY MATTRESS COVERS AND BLANKETS ON HOT CYCLE
  - VACUUM MATTRESSES AND YOUR BED'S BASEBOARDS
    - Be sure to lift and vacuum under your mattresses and in all the corners of your bed
    - Only use HEPA bags (High Efficiency Particulate Air filter vacuum bags), which can trap these mighty mites, unlike regular bags or bagless vacuums from which they can escape.
- *SEASONALLY*
  - WASH AND DRY COMFORTERS ON HOT CYCLES
- *BLOCK THEM OUT*
  - Buy dust-mite-proof encasings for your pillows, beds, and boxsprings.
  - Invest in a dehumidifier or move to Arizona
- *EVERY 1 to 3 YEARS, BUY NEW PILLOWS*
- *EVERY 5 to 7 YEARS, BUY NEW MATTRESSES*

If you're still not grossed out enough or would like more info on ways to minimize these mighty mites you can visit www.natlallergy.com. Wallet-size pictures of them may be available there should you want to show others who you're sleeping with.

DEFENSIVE CLEANING

You've been here and done this before so I'm not going to give you a long-winded intro or explanation on basic things you can do to minimize cleaning:

- *CLEAR CLUTTER PRONTO:*
  - Hang stuff up before it becomes a carpet for your hardwood floors or an area rug on your existing carpeting.
  - *Child's Play:* Put laundry in hamper and toys in bins or under bed
- *DON'T SHAKE!*—The more you lift and shake out sheets, comforters, and pillows the more dust you'll make, so keep your shaking and straightening to a minimum.
- *PULL, FLUFF, AND PUFF*—Even though Erma pointed out that no one ever died from sleeping in an unmade bed, they're your room's focal point, so if you make them your room will look neat. That doesn't mean you have to make it with perfect hospital corners, just:
  - Straighten and pull up your blankets/comforters, sheets, and/or bedspreads
  - Gently puff and fluff pillows
  - Keep visitors away from your night tables and dressers so they don't see the dust!
- *DO NOT DISTURB.* If guests are coming, close the doors to all the bedrooms and direct them to the LIVING SPACES or, better yet, direct them outside.

HOW TO QUICKIE CLEAN JUST ENOUGH

YOUR MULTITASKING MANICURE-FRIENDLY SHOPPING LIST
In addition to your schlep vehicle of choice and fashionable and functional rubber gloves, here's a complete list of stuff that you can choose to use or lose. If it looks familiar, it is because many of the items are those I've already shared for our LIVING SPACES:

FOR DUSTING
- Genuine ostrich feather duster
- Microfiber:
  - Cloths or mini duster with machine washable bonnet
  - Dust mops with extendable handles and hooks to hang them. These are great for cleaning cobwebs and ceiling fans.

- Array of disposables
  - Multipurpose, multisurface cloths and sprays for dusting and cleaning mirrors.
- Soft bristle paint brush. They're terrific for cleaning mirrors, lampshades, photos, and paintings. Again, if you have one handy (and again, who are we kidding!) a basting brush is a good tool, particularly for smaller items.
- Golf club. Attach a sock dampened with multisurface, multipurpose cleaner to clean high spots of dust and spiderwebs. An old broom works well too!

FOR FLOORS
- Disposable floor and carpet sweepers (such as Swiffer)
- Stick vacuum (Dirt Devil's got some terrific ones)
- Canister or upright vacuum with multiple attachments (Electrolux and Hoover have some space-saving ones you should check out on their Web sites)
- Child five years of age or older
- Robotic floor vacuum (check out www.irobot.com)

MISCELLANEOUS
- Disinfecting air fresheners

My Quickie Cleaning Tool Belt
Using a Quickie tool belt for all your basics works in the bedroom too! Keep your thoughts clean, please. Again, feel free to swap out items that you like to use, and don't forget to wear your gloves!

- Genuine feather duster
- Disposable multisurface, multipurpose cleaning wipes,
- Disinfecting wipes
- Microfiber dust cloth
- Disinfecting, air freshening spray
- BlackBerry
- iPod
- Water bottle

THE DAILY QUICKIE

Daily or every other day is fine, too.

- Pick up stuff on floors and hang or toss in laundry or bins immediately.
- Put items lying on night table or dresser into decorative containers.
- Make the bed without too much shaking of sheets, pillows, and blankets.
- Spray with aromatic disinfecting spray.

THE WEEKLY QUICKIE

You have to deal with dust mites on a regular basis to keep them from permanently cuddling up with you and yours while snoozing, which is why they're your first and most important weekly or bi-weekly Quickie. If you skipped over that section feel free to flip back to "Do You Know Who You're Sleeping With?" on page 125.

- Mite Maintenance:
  - Wash sheets and pillowcases.
- Straighten books and magazines.
- Dust dressers and night tables.
- Wipe switchplates and doorknobs.
- Vacuum carpets and/or mop floors.
- Straighten shoes in closet.
- Empty wastebasket.

THE MONTHLY QUICKIE

If you're doing your daily and bi-weekly Quickies fairly consistently you can probably stretch this to every six to eight weeks with the exception of the Mite Maintenance, but you'll have to be the judge of that.

- Mite Maintenance:
  - Wash comforters and mattress pad.
  - Vacuum mattress and bed frame.
- Dust baseboards, photos, knickknacks, windows, and blinds.
- Clean ceiling fan.
- Wipe mirrors and wall hangings.
- Vacuum under bed, night tables, and dressers.
- Vacuum/mop closet floors.

THE SEASONAL QUICKIE
- Clean off scratch marks on walls.
- Wash windows.
- Vacuum drapes.
- Organize closets.
- Dust closet shelves, shoes, and vacuum entire closet.

Chapter 8

The Bedroom

JUST ENOUGH ORGANIZING

Family: A social unit where the father is concerned with parking space, the children with outer space, and the mother with closet space. —Evan Esar

The same basic organizing tips that you used in other rooms in your home apply to your bedrooms. Once again, it is led by the fact that if you do just enough organizing you'll give the illusion that you have both neat and clean bedrooms. And, if you focus only on organizing the key clutter areas listed below, this chore that bores me more than any other won't wear you out:

- Night tables (eyeglasses, remotes, books)
- Dresser tops (jewelry, cell phones, change)
- Closets (clothes, shoes, laundry)
- Floors (toys, clothes)

So take another breath, let it out, and let's get to it.

How to Organize It Just Enough

I think I've shared that I'm not a very organized soul. The Chinese art of feng shui (which refers to keeping the flow of energy in one's home uncluttered to achieve harmony and balance) is *no way* a part of my life. That's why in my bedroom, a place I consider my personal space and one rarely visited by strangers, I spend little time fretting over my disorganization. Instead, I have several offensive tactics that make organizing and staying organized flow naturally or, as I like to say, mindlessly. (Give or take my biannual need to crank it up a notch and reorganize my closet so I can find my summer clothes and shoes before winter arrives.) That is why this section is not separated into "Offensive and Defensive Organizing." They flow together to achieve harmony and balance *my* way.

NIGHT TABLES AND DRESSERS

- *DISH IT OUT:* Keep a decorative bowl, box, or a piggy bank on your dresser for change. I also keep one in my closet, since change is always falling out of my jeans when I hang, fold, or toss them on the floor.
- *BOX IT:* Buy decorative boxes (straw, laminated, jewelry, or other) that you can place on the top of your night table and dressers for all the junk that you deposit there, such as glasses, remotes, jewelry, sexual enhancing drugs, and condoms.
  - *Detangling tip:* Use straws for link jewelry to keep them tangle-free. Just cut a straw to size, drop your chain down, and clasp. Cheap and easy!

CLOSETS

- *FORGET THE MAGIC MIRROR:* I know it's hard to part with certain items like clothing, hats, ties, handbags, and shoes that bring back fond memories or inspire you to lose weight, since they no longer fit, but part with them we must! Just a friendly reminder: You're not Sleeping Beauty's evil stepmother and your mirror won't lie, so sort and discard!
  - *USE THE 20/80 RULE:* Keep the stuff you use most and chuck the rest—that is, give it away. Clearly this doesn't apply to seasonal items, including linens or blankets, that you may use at different times of the year.
- *BAG IT:* I collect and store shopping bags in my closet the way Carrie Bradshaw collected Manolo Blahnik shoes (though I wish the reverse were the case!). Clearly, they hold no real value, but for some reason I suffer separation anxiety every time I consider tossing them. But I realized that I needed intervention, so I came up with ways to slowly part with my shopping bags and repurpose them. So for those like me who share this inexplicable attachment to Neiman Marcus, Macy's, or Target bags, here are some sanity-saving ways to help you let them go:

Mommie Dearest

Mommie Dearest was a 1981 movie about the legendary actress Joan Crawford. The movie was based on a book written by Crawford's daughter, Christina, who endured a lifetime of parental abuse from the star. The kicker was that while she tortured poor Christina, the rest of the world saw Crawford as a glamorous star and perfect mother. There's one scene in the movie where Crawford (played by Faye Dunaway) goes into Christina's room while she is sleeping to admire her neat closet—that alone is a sign she was nuts. Anyway, she discovers that Christina has used a wire hanger instead of the "nice ones" she had told her to use. Well, Crawford makes a scene, torments her daughter, and screams out "No wire hangers, ever!" Can you imagine! At any rate, the scene and her outcry actually became a cult call to arms for neat freaks. It even led folks to show up at the movie with wire hangers. Guess, as the saying goes, truth is stranger than fiction. All I know is that I'm glad she wasn't my mom 'cause I'd have hung her out to cry!

- *Discard on a whim:* Simply line up a few shopping bags in your closet where you can see them. Then next time you put on a pair of pants that are too big (wishful thinking) or you notice your platform shoes have pointy toes instead of rounded ones or your tie is about two inches too thick, just bag it. When the bag's full, take it to the nearest charity dropoff, school, or house of worship.
- *Gift wrap:* One of the reasons I find it hard to part with my bags is because they're pretty, so I began using them as a quick and often last-minute gift-wrapping option. Hey, you might even fool those you're giving the gift to into believing it's from Neiman Marcus rather than your local dollar store!
- *Stop drafts:* Use them to stop drafts under your vanity or by your kitchen sink, dishwasher, or A/C unit.
- *DIAL UP:* Be totally offensive and hire a pro! Check local listings or go to www.napo.net.

FLOORS
- *GO BELOW:* Buy storage bins that have wheels and easy-to-open tops that fit under a bed or in a closet. Then push and pull them out and about so you and

your kiddies can toss in toys or laundry or fill them with anything else that's lying around.

Yippee! Your work here is done. Next it's time to Lighten the Load. But first go enjoy your favorite local cuisine, a libation, get messy, and get ready to deal with our country's red, white, and goo!

PART **3**

LAUNDRY: LIGHTENING THE LOAD

Chapter 9

Just Enough Laundry Basics

As a housewife, I feel that if the kids are still alive when my husband gets home from work, then hey, I've done my job. —Roseanne Barr

Forgive me, but I'm truly going to lighten the load in your laundry room in respect to cleaning and organizing it. I realize that many of us spend half our lives there and that some have turned it into an entertainment center complete with flat-screen TVs and sound systems, but for most of us it's the one room that few visitors see unless you're buying or selling your home. And, other than the yuk we bring in that has been deposited on our undergarments, there's nothing that multiplies or smells. So in our continued homage to Erma and her philosophy . . . *who cares!*

How to Clean It Just Enough

Here are five manicure-friendly things you can do monthly to keep your laundry room clean enough. As always, your fashionable and functional rubber gloves are recommended.

1. *WIPE:* Use a disinfecting or baby wipe to clean the outside of the washing machine and dryer. Do the inside rims, too!
2. *RINSE:* Run a hot wash cycle with a gallon of white vinegar to remove soap scum and hard water deposits, which will help prevent clogs!
3. *DE-LINT:* Remove your dryer's lint screen (which I know you clean after every load!) and vacuum the lint trap.

4. *VACUUM:* Twist off the exhaust hose located at the back of your dryer and vacuum it to prevent lint from accumulating, which can cause clogs and create a lovely lint carpeting all over your house. While you're at it, also vacuum the floors surrounding your washer and dryer.

5. *SPRAY:* Spritz your favorite disinfecting air freshener from time to time to kill any M & M and camouflage any musty smells since the laundry room usually has limited ventilation.

How to Organize It Just Enough

Here are several simple tips to whip your laundry room into a functional and organized-enough space:

- *ARM'S REACH:* Put all your detergents, bleaches, softeners, pretreaters, and dryer sheets on a shelf above your washing machine or in a crate or basket near your washer and dryer.

- *PLAIN SIGHT:* You might also want to put up a Fabric Care Guide on a wall or cabinet to help you make a quick decision on washing and drying a garment to avoid ruining it. Check out www.tide.com for a downloadable version.

- *HANG SPACE:* If you don't have room for a folding rack, put up hanging rods. If that's not an option, consider putting up a retractable clothesline, which is easy to install and great for fine washables.

- *WORK SPACE:* You need a flat area for sorting and folding, which any of the following can serve as:
  - the top of your washer or dryer
  - an ironing board, which you can use for triple duty. I recommend using one that you can either hang over your door or mount on a wall, since they're great space-saving options.
  - a small collapsible table that can be easily stored in your space.

- *SEE THE LIGHT*
  - Be sure you have lighting that enables you to clearly see stains, so they don't become blaring distractions after you've washed, dried, and allowed them to set.

- *FUND RAISE*
  - Keep a jar, bowl, or piggy bank to deposit accidentally laundered money, which you can use later to indulge yourself.

- *TAKE OUT THE GARBAGE*
  - Keep a trash can nearby to empty lint from the dryer and goodies found in pockets prior to washing.

Lightening the Load Just Enough

Some of us find doing laundry calming, while others would like to send out every last sock to fluff and fold. My sister-in-law Gayle loves doing it and misses the days when both her sons were home blocking passageways with all their stuff. I, on the other hand, find it a chore that bores but also fairly simple to blend into my everyday routines. Takes all kinds! Still, few of us have the luxury of avoiding laundry altogether, so we better get used to the basics of sorting, pretreating, washing, drying, and sometimes ironing, because your favorite outfit is a terrible thing to waste.

SORTING:

- *DIVIDE AND CONQUER:* Set up different hampers by color or label for whites, darks, lights, fine washables, and towels.
- *CHILD'S PLAY:* have your kiddies sort laundry into darks, lights, whites, fine washables, and towels. Don't forget a pile for dry cleaning as well, though you may have to sort that.
- *EMPTY:* Check pockets for money, pens, gum, iPods, et cetera.

PRETREATING

- *DO IT PRONTO:* Never let a stain set or throw it in the dryer after treating it if you can still see the stain. Putting it in the dryer will ensure it becomes a permanent embellishment.
- *NEVER RUB:* Blot, dab, scrape, or spray to avoid working the stain farther into your garment or linen.
- *LOAD UP ON STORE-BOUGHT PRETREATERS:* This is the easiest and safest way to go if you don't have time to read the other stain-removal solutions that begin on page 145.
  - For whites: Clorox Bleach Pen
  - For colors: Spray 'n Wash or Shout
  - For wine: Wine Away
  - For everything: Your dry cleaner
- *IMPORTANT NOTE:* Always launder immediately after pretreating.

WASHING

- *CHECK CARE LABELS:* This is one instance where we veer from Erma's philosophy of who cares. I learned this the hard way by assuming that my son's

How to Deal with Memory Loss

In case a portable electronic gadget or memory stick takes an unexpected spin in your wash cycle, here's an easy way to try to preserve its memory.

What you'll need:
- Blow dryer

- Uncooked rice (amount will depend upon size of item washed)

- Bowl

- Pastry brush or toothbrush

- Chinese take-out menu

What you'll do:
- Take the battery and memory chip out of the gadget if there is one.

- Use your blow dryer (put it on a cool setting) to get rid of any moisture on chip, battery and device, or stick

- Place your device or stick in a cup or bowl filled with uncooked rice. Be sure the rice covers it.

- Let it sit for at least three days. If you have memory loss and leave it in longer it won't harm anything, since the rice acts as a sponge absorbing the moisture from your soaked stick or gadget.

- Use a pastry brush and/or blow dryer to blow away any debris.

- Cook up the rice and order in Chinese food.

favorite Tiger Woods red golf shirt could be washed with and dried like his others. Nope! It bled, or rather hemorrhaged, all over his other favorite red-and-white-striped golf shirt and when I took it out of the dryer it had become pint size, so he uses it now as a head cover for his not-so-favorite driver.

So the moral of this story is, care, and read the little label that is located somewhere on the inside corner or seam of your garment! If you're like me and need help deciphering those sticklike pictures, you can go to www.tide.com. You might also want to print it out and hang it somewhere close to your washing machine for easy reference. In case you're too lazy to heed this advice, here are some basic water temp guides:

- Whites: hot or warm
- Lights and darks: warm or cool
- Permanent press: cold
- Delicates: cold
- Wool: cold

- *DON'T MIX:* Wash sorted loads separately. That is whites, darks, lights, and so on.
- *DON'T OVERLOAD:* Load per machine capacity so all your clothes get washed properly.
- *TIME IT:* Set a timer so you don't forget that you threw in a load. It will also help:
  - Reduce the chance for our M & M buds to get busy.
  - Minimize wrinkling and therefore your need to iron.

HAND WASHING

Like it or not your fine washables generally have care labels that read: HAND WASH ONLY, which is why you might want to consider reading all labels before you buy. But if that sexy little negligee has your name written all over it (and I'm jealous if you have reason to buy one and/or fit in one), here are a few ways to care for them just enough:

- *PUT THE WOOL OVER THEM:* Use a gentle hand-wash product such as Woolite, which has been around forever. It even comes in an HE (high efficiency) version, which is what front-load washers require. Just be safe and read the directions in case you've bought a leather S & M–type nightie, which Woolite is not formulated to handle.
- *SOAK DUDS IN SUDS:* Use a mild detergent and lukewarm water. Let your fine washables sit for about five minutes, then gently work the suds through. Do not rub. Rinse thoroughly with cool water. Avoid the urge to wring them out when you're done.
- *HANG THEM OUT TO DRY:* The best way to keep your fine washables in shape after you wash them is to let them line dry, as long as their wet weight

doesn't cause them to stretch. If you live in an apartment, this may have neighbors talking, so use a plastic hanger and hang them out to dry in your shower or lay them on a towel on a flat surface to maintain shape.

- *GIVE YOUR BOOBS BALLS:* Bras in general should never be machine-washed, since they can shape shift, metal can melt, and they can attach to other items. But if you are simply too lazy to hand wash them, there's a product called BraBall that may be your bras' savior. You can find it at www.braballs.com. FYI: You will still need to dry your bras the old-fashioned way, unless you wish to purchase new bras for your boobs more frequently.

DRYING

- *DON'T OVERLOAD:* Check your machine's capacity so that you know how much you can put in at once. Though it may be tempting to stuff your dryer to the brim, if you exceed its limit your clothes won't dry and you'll need to repeat.
- *DON'T DO PARTIAL LOADS:* Simply put, it's an energy abuser, so do your part and wait until you can do a full load per your dryer's capacity.
- *GIVE A SHEET:* I like using dryer sheets instead of adding fabric softening liquid during the rinse. Sheets help reduce static cling, wrinkling, and drying time. It also helps eliminate my chance of "accidentally" spilling some fabric softener and making a mess.
- *HAVE A BALL:* You have a couple of options:
  - *Fabric dryer balls:* Toss them in to help soften fabrics and reduce lint, wrinkles, and ironing. I'm a big fan of Nellie's Dryerballs, which are nontoxic and allergy free (very eco-friendly!). You can find them at Target or at www .nellieslaundryproducts.com. My son also likes using them as mini footballs and my dog as chew toys so you may want to buy an extra set, just in case your kids or pets find them fun to play with.
  - *Tennis balls:* Lob one or two new ones in and you'll fight static cling and put some poof in your quilts and pillows.
- *THROW IN THE TOWEL:* If lightweight items such as T-shirts or linens are wrinkled, simply throw in a damp towel and voilà, wrinkles be gone!
- *SCREEN SAVER:* Be sure to remove and clean the lint screen after every load so your dryer can work efficiently and save you money on your energy bill.

IRONING

Here's how to minimize and perhaps avoid ironing altogether, which will also be saving energy. Way to go, accidental enviro-keeper!

- *EXITO:* Remove items from the dryer immediately.
- *TOWEL DRY:* Throw wrinkled stuff that's been sitting in your drawer into the dryer with a damp towel to remove wrinkles.
- *SPRAY 'N' BUY:* Use store-bought, spray-on wrinkle releasers (not from Olay but from companies like Downy). For really deep wrinkles, spray items directly and put them in the dryer on low for a few minutes.
- *FRESHEN UP:* Check out the Fabric Freshener from Whirlpool. It's compact and within minutes it will relax wrinkles and remove odors—which, by the way, is why 75 percent of people take their clothes to the dry cleaner. Plus it uses water instead of chemicals, so it's eco-friendly! Check it out at www.whirlpool.com and type in *fabric freshener.*
- *BUY WRINKLE-FREE:* Lots of companies have realized that ironing is not only a chore that bores but one you often don't have time for, so they've developed wrinkle-free clothing. Many items also have stain repellants, which may make garments a bit stiffer but it's worth the little bit of discomfort. The Gap, Dockers, Eddie Bauer, and Brooks Brothers are among the many who have seen the light.
- *DO CRUNCHES:* Before you buy certain everyday basics (T-shirts, shorts, golf shirts, et cetera) crunch them up in your hand at the store to see their "wrinkle tolerance"—if they come out a mess, do not buy! Tip: Do this out of sight of the sales help or they may want to crunch you up in a ball as well!
- *GO NATURAL:* Consider becoming a nudist—at least at home!

If you need or decide to iron here are some simple tips to a wrinkle-free result:

- *CHECK CARE LABELS:* Make sure you check the care label to put your iron on the right setting.
- *GO STRAIGHT:* Keep your ironing motion up and down versus side to side to avoid stretching the item.
- *WATER THEM:* Spray water on deep wrinkles before ironing.
- *FLATTEN THEM:* If traveling, use your flat iron as a mini press and hold it on the wrinkle for a few seconds. Shorter is better, since you don't want to inadvertently add a new opening to your shirt.

Chapter 10

United Stains of America

Now they show you how detergents take out bloodstains, a pretty violent image there. I think if you've got a T-shirt with a bloodstain all over it, maybe laundry isn't your biggest problem. Maybe you should get rid of the body before you do the wash. —Jerry Seinfeld

L egend has it that Russians have the secret for getting rid of borscht stains, that Indians know how to get out that spot of turmeric, and that Scots understand the way to stop haggis from ruining their best kilts. Good for them. But here in the good ol' U.S. of A., we have a wide variety of stains to deal with—a variety, I might add, that reflects our rich heritage—and you need a broader approach, which is just what I'm offering here in this patriotic, geographic, new and simplified guide to Stains Across America. So read on. From Arkansas to New York to Texas to Wyoming, from gumbo to gravy, from salsa to mint julep, there's a stain removal for however big or small a slob you and yours may be.

The Main Stains

Like the five major food groups (or has that changed again?), stains are also divided into five major groups: protein, tannin, dye, oil, and combo—fascinating, I know! I share this riveting info with you, since, if you have the time or inclination to read the pages that follow, you'll have a shot at getting out those stains that result when your loved ones miss their mouths as they eat. *Shot at* are the operative words, since most stains have several stain components. That's why after many months of trying a variety of what I often refer to as PMS (pretty manageable stain) removals, I found that most stains can be gotten out or at least barely seen if you focus on the key ingredient in *the main stain*. That's what you'll find in the stain removal solutions that follow. Please note that results will vary, depending upon how serious a stain it is, your commitment to getting it out, and how soon—or if at all—you choose to deal with it.

The Main Stain Groups

The five main stain groups—protein, tannin, dye, oil, and combo—are further divided into two groups as they relate to the types of stain-removing solutions that work:

1. Water-soluble stains
2. Non-water-soluble stains

Simple enough, and in this case their names pretty much say it all.

PLEASE REMEMBER THAT ALL THE PMS REMOVAL TIPS IN THIS GUIDE ARE FOR WASHABLE ITEMS ONLY! They are not for stuff like wool, cashmere, angora, silk, suede, and leather, unless your care label says anything goes!

WATER-SOLUBLE STAIN GROUPS

Stains that *may* be removed with water-based cleaning solutions—please note the word *may*. These include:

PROTEIN STAINS

Included in this group are baby food, milk, baby formula, blood, snot, cheese sauce, mud, cream, ice cream, pudding, egg, urine, poop, vomit, gelatin, white glue, and school paste.

GENERAL TIP: Never use hot water to flush out or to soak a stain, since hot water will set the majority of protein-based stains.

- Scrape off with plastic spoon or knife (no dishwashing this way!) or blot up the excess with white paper towels or a cloth.
- Flush immediately in cold water.
- Soak in a liquid enzyme laundry product for thirty minutes or, if you have the time and baby Sarah has really outdone herself, soak for several hours.
- If the stain remains, use color-appropriate bleaching agent applied with an eyedropper or a sponge as follows, unless otherwise noted on care label:

- Whites only
  - Chlorine bleach: dilute with equal parts water.
- Whites and colors
  - Oxygen bleach
  - White vinegar
  - 3 percent hydrogen peroxide (1:3 ratio of peroxide to water)
  - Isopropyl alcohol (Remember, rubbing alcohol is not as strong but you can use it if that's what you have handy. Then, when you're done, have your significant other put a little on as he or she gives you a well-deserved PMS rubdown!)
- Machine wash in the hottest water that the care label allows.

Tannin Stains

These include alcoholic beverages, red wine, beer, fruits and their juices (peaches, grapefruit, apple, lime, and orange), coffee, tea, soy sauce, soft drinks, tomato juice, perfume, felt-tip pen, and washable ink.

GENERAL TIP: Never use regular bar soap to remove these kinds of stains since, according to the gurus and my personal mistakes, it makes them virtually impossible to remove.

- Gently scrape off with a butter knife or spoon or blot up excess using white paper towels or a cloth.
- Run cool water or club soda through the back of the stain.
- Rub with dishwashing detergent or liquid enzyme detergent. Let sit for five minutes and blot dry.
- If the stain remains, use color-appropriate bleaching agent applied with an eyedropper or a sponge as follows, unless otherwise noted on care label:
  - Whites only
    - Chlorine bleach: dilute with equal parts water
  - Whites and colors
    - Oxygen bleach
    - White vinegar
    - 3 percent hydrogen peroxide—1:3 ratio of peroxide to water
    - Isopropyl alcohol
- Launder according to garment instructions in warmest water that the care label allows.

Dye Stains

These include cherry, blueberry, blackberry, strawberry, cranberry, grape, watermelon (and all their juices); spices (curry); Kool-Aid; Tabasco; mustard; and grass.

GENERAL TIP: Avoid letting these stains dry or heating them since this will cause them to set—it's sort of like getting your hair colored and although the color fades and your gray starts to show, the color still hangs on to your ends—or is that until *the* end?

- Immediately scrape off as much as you can without mushing any into fabric.*
- Flush thoroughly with cool water.
- Use an eyedropper filled with the strongest color-appropriate bleaching agent your fabric can handle and drip it onto the stain as follows, unless care label indicates otherwise.
  - Whites only
    - Chlorine bleach: dilute with equal parts water
  - Whites and colors
    - Oxygen bleach
    - White vinegar
    - 3 percent hydrogen peroxide (1:3 ratio of peroxide to water)
    - Isopropyl alcohol
- Machine wash with liquid enzyme detergent in the hottest water the fabric's care label allows.

FOR THOSE WHO "DYE" FOR HEIGHTS

- Gently scrape off any excess—do not mush as you remove.
- Flush thoroughly with cold water.
- Stretch the fabric over the sink, stand on a step stool, and pour boiling water onto the stain (you should be at least a foot or more higher than the item). Be careful! Please do not attempt this if you've been drinking! Let it sit for a couple of minutes.
- If the stain remains, use color-appropriate bleaching agent applied with an eyedropper or a sponge as follows, unless otherwise noted on care label:
  - Whites only
    - Chlorine bleach: dilute with equal parts water
  - Whites and colors

---

*For little stains, after you remove any excess, try hitting them with aerosol hairspray before trying any of the other steps.

- Oxygen bleach
- White vinegar
- 3 percent hydrogen peroxide (1:3 ratio of peroxide to water)
- Isopropyl alcohol
- Launder with enzyme detergent in the hottest water the garment's care label allows.

NON-WATER-SOLUBLE STAIN GROUPS

These are near impossible stains that I take to the dry cleaner since they generally require more effort to remove but it's worth giving them a try.

Oil-Based Stains

These include bacon fat, butter, margarine, mayonnaise, salad dressing, cooking fats and oils, sweat (ring around the collar), and face cream.

GENERAL TIP: Any time you have an oil-based stain you should immediately sprinkle cornstarch, talcum, or baby powder onto it and let it sit to absorb the yuk.

- Scrape off with plastic spoon or knife or blot up the excess with white paper towels or a cloth.
- Sprinkle thoroughly with cornstarch, talcum, or baby powder to absorb. Leave on for fifteen minutes and gently scrape off.
- If the stain remains, soak in enzyme detergent for five minutes in warm water and use an eyedropper to apply some dry-cleaning solvent directly to the stain.
- Launder in the hottest water that the care label allows.

Combo Stains

These include barbecue sauce, ketchup, tomato sauce, chili, curry sauce, gravy, chocolate, ice cream, coffee with cream, candle wax, mascara, lipstick, and calamine lotion.

I call them PIA (pain in the ass) stains since they have lots of different ingredients that may need our attention to get out. I, however, cannot be bothered with figuring out each and neither should you. So what I've done throughout is focus on one of the key ingredients in each stain and given the PMS removal solution that hopefully will work for all. If it doesn't, take it to your handy-dandy dry cleaner.

GENERAL TIP: This one's too complicated to have a general tip other than take it to the dry cleaner and make your life easy.

- Scrape off with plastic spoon or knife (you know why by now!) or sop up the excess with white paper towels or a cloth.
- Run cool water through the back of the stain.
- Soak with liquid enzyme detergent and let sit for five minutes, then rinse. Feel free to gently rub while soaking.
- If the stain remains, unless care label notes otherwise use color-appropriate bleaching agent applied with an eyedropper or a sponge as follows:
  - Whites only
    - Chlorine bleach: dilute with equal parts water
  - Whites and colors
    - Oxygen bleach
    - White vinegar
    - 3 percent hydrogen peroxide (1:3 ratio of peroxide to water)
    - Isopropyl alcohol
- Machine wash with enzyme detergent in the hottest water allowed by your care label.

Offensive Stain Removal

Sex is a bad thing because it rumples (and can stain) the clothes. —Jacqueline Kennedy Onassis

Okeydokey, we're almost ready to defend against our selves since all removals are defense acts, but first, here are some simple offensive measures:

- Check pockets before you do laundry. Pens, crayons, gum, and tissues make a huge mess if you end up washing them by mistake—not to mention the stains pens and crayons can make!
- Never put the stained item into the dryer until the stain is out or it will set the stain.
- Buy stain-resistant clothing and linens.
- Scotchgard all fabric furniture.
- Put your household on a clear liquid diet.
- Wrap everyone in plastic.
- In homage to Jackie's words of wisdom, avoid spontaneous sex if fully clothed.

Now we're *really* ready to begin our United Stains of America Tour

Life's a Bleach

'm sure you've spent many a restless night wondering what the difference is betwixt chlorine bleach and oxygen bleach. Well, sleep again you will, because here's the load down (sorry, I'm in my laundry-speak mode!):

CHLORINE BLEACH: Good old-fashioned chlorine bleach is a chemical that removes or lightens colors, so it should be used only on whites. Bleach also kills bacteria and lifts stains, which helps maintain your clothing's whiteness.

OXYGEN BLEACH: This is the kinder, gentler bleach. It has no chlorine or harsh chemicals and can be used on whites and colors (though you should always check care labels to be sure). It is also very eco-friendly since it's biodegradable (that means it breaks down into a natural soda ash after the oxygen is released, which helps to break down the stain).

NOTE: Even though oxygen bleach can be effective on whites, chlorine bleach is still the best one to use on them, particularly when dealing with dye stains.

Now you know—sweet dreams!

PMS REMOVAL MULTITASKING SHOPPING LIST

Just as you had a list of items to help you with your other chores that bore, the same holds true when conquering our pretty manageable stains. But before I share this list, a brief word or two on one of your most important stain-removal pals.

BASIC STAIN REMOVERS AND TOOLS (These include both traditional and enviro-friendly products and tools. The enviro-friendly ones are indicated with an asterisk.)
- Chlorine bleach
- Oxygen bleach*
- Enzyme detergents (liquid or powder; I prefer liquid)*
- Laundry detergents (liquid or powder; again, I prefer liquid)
- 3 percent hydrogen peroxide
- Isopropyl alcohol* (Rubbing alcohol is not as strong but you can use it if that's what you have handy.)

- White vinegar*
- Cornstarch, talcum powder, or baby powder*
- Sunshine*
- Liquid hand sanitizer
- Sponge
- Eyedropper
- Electric toothbrush
- White paper towels or microfiber cloth

PRETREATERS
- Clorox Bleach Pen (for whites only)
- Dryel
- Dry Cleaner's Secret—great for oil-based stains
- Shout
- Spray 'n Wash
- Wine Away (works on blood, grape, cranberry, tomato-based stains, chili, ketchup, salsa, and red wine)
- Yellow Out
- Zout

TO GO STAIN REMOVERS (TAKE THEM ON VACATION OR IN THE CAR)
- Clorox Bleach Pen
- Madame Paulette's Professional Stain Removal Kit (www.madamepaulette.com)
- OxiClean Spray-A-Way
- Shout Wipes
- Spray 'n Wash Stain Stick
- Tide to Go
- Hand sanitizer

Seven Stain Removal Tips

I spilled spot remover on my dog and now he's gone. —Steven Wright

Before we take off on our United Stains of America Tour I'm going to share seven things you should try to remember when a stain occurs.

Homeschooling : The Breakdown on Enzymes

Enzymes are proteins that are found in all living organisms, including accidental housewives, animals, plants, and microorganisms. They're also found in most detergents, since some very smart people figured out how to use them to break down a variety of our main stains. And if that doesn't get your blood rushing, it's also another mindless way to be eco-friendly, since they don't need hot water or a long wash cycle to work well and because they're "living" they're biodegradable.

Here are some of the stains they love to break down and digest:

- Blood
- Vomit
- Oil
- Poop
- Grease
- Dairy foods, such as milk and ice cream
- Sweat
- Grass

1. *SHOW YOU CARE*

Always read your stained item's care label first so that your garment doesn't meet a fate similar to Steven Wright's dog—then pray that they all say DRY CLEAN ONLY!

2. *WORK IT PRONTO*

The quicker you attack a stain the more of a chance you'll have to get it out. So put down your cup of coffee and start working it out as follows:

- Blot, dab, sop, or gently scrape off as much of the excess as possible using recycled or white paper towels or a white cloth.
- *If an oily stain:* Sprinkle cornstarch, talcum, or baby powder on the stain and let sit for fifteen minutes, then gently scrape off.
- *If a liquid stain:* Rinse in cool water to wash out as much of the stain as possible.

3. *PRETREAT IT*

First try using a store-bought pretreating stain remover, since that is the simplest and most mindless thing you can do. However, if you do and the stain is staring back at you after you launder it, DO NOT PUT IT IN THE DRYER—IT WILL SET THE STAIN. It is then that you will need to try one of the solutions that follow in the next section or take it directly to your dry cleaner. If neither option works for you, you can always use the permanently stained garment as a cover-up or bib to protect other clothing from meeting the same fate.

4. *COOL IT*
Unless informed otherwise on the label or in the solutions that follow, use cool water when you're removing stains since hot water can set certain kinds of stains. Never iron or put your spotted item in the dryer until you've removed the stain entirely. If you do, it can bake and set the stain and you'll be sporting that lovely red wine blotch forever, as well as letting everyone know that you're a slob and a wino.

5. *DO YOUR BACKUP*
- It's best to remove stains from behind to prevent them from spreading. Turn the item inside out or over and place it on a clean white cloth.
- First test the stain remover on the inside of your garment or somewhere it won't be seen in case it will cause discoloration.

6. *NEVER MIX*
- Never mix bleach and ammonia together—they cause toxic fumes.
- If using dry-cleaning solvents be sure to dry the item thoroughly since they are potent chemicals and can be a fire hazard in both your washer and dryer.

7. *SEND YOUR DRY CLEANER TO FLORIDA*
If all removal tactics fail, you're not in the mood to deal with it, or your label didn't say DRY CLEAN ONLY, here's your pass to take it to the dry cleaner and keep him happy. Of course, should you prefer to save the money for your own trip to Florida, here are two options to hide the stain:

- *If on the front:* Cover the stain with a decorative pin.
- *If on a cuff:* Take out your cutting shears and cut off the stained cuff to turn your long-sleeved blouse into a short-sleeved one!

Born in the USA
Stains are as American as apple pie, egg creams, and Elvis Presley. . . . So, my fellow Americans and accidental housewives, here are many of the stains that bind us from

coast to coast, meal to meal, and spot to spot. The Oh Say Can You See United Stains of America Tour begins—time to chow down, drink up, and get messy as I share a few more thoughts!

- *DÉJÀ VU:* Though I have tried to share as many innovative PMS removal tips as I could, many of them work for a variety of our nation's hot spots so I repeat them.
- *CSI I'M NOT:* Most of our nation's favorite foods are made up of a combination of proteins, oils, tannins, and dyes and I'm not a CSI professional; that means I'm not going to analyze every ingredient to determine who our *number-one* stain criminal is. Instead, through trial and error I've focused on what I consider to be the stain that may remain if not treated pronto.
- *TAKE FIVE OR TAKE A DRIVE:* All the solutions that follow are no more than five steps. If after you've tried them the stain remains, you have two options:
  - Get your butt in the car and drop the stained garment off at your dry cleaner.
  - Wear it like a badge of courage with others who share your talent for being a slob!

ALABAMA

Pecan Pie: Combo Stain

PMS REMOVAL OF MAIN STAIN: PECAN FILLING
- Use a dull knife or spoon to remove any excess—feel free to lick it off if you're still hungry!
- Rinse well with cold water.
- Gently rub some liquid detergent into the stain and let it sit for a few minutes. Feel free to enjoy another piece of pie while you wait—just don't miss your mouth this time. Rinse in hot water, letting it run through the stain.
- If the stain remains, stretch the fabric over a sink, stand on a step stool, and pour boiling water over the stain. Please be sure you haven't been drinking anything alcoholic.
- Machine wash with enzyme detergent and color-appropriate bleach according to care label.

Pecan Perfection

Although the first pecan tree was planted on Long Island in 1772, it was Alabama that became its *numero uno* producer due to its soil. So next time you come to Alabama with a banjo on your knee, be sure to leave with a bag of pecans in your hand! By the way, the word *pecan* comes from Native Americans, who used it to describe "all nuts requiring a stone to crack"—good to know I'm not a pecan!

ALASKA

SALMON WITH DILL SAUCE: OIL STAIN

PMS REMOVAL OF MAIN STAIN: DILL SAUCE
- Remove excess sauce with a butter knife or lick it off.
- Sprinkle thoroughly with cornstarch, talcum, or baby powder to absorb. Leave on for fifteen minutes and gently scrape off.
- Gently rub liquid enzyme detergent into stain and let it sit for fifteen minutes. Go rub noses with your significant other while you wait.
- Machine wash in the hottest water care instructions allow.

The Thingamajig State

I'd love to live in a place where the word *thingamajig* is an accepted way to describe something—it sort of feels Mary Poppins–ish! As it turns out, the word *thingamajig* is the English equivalent for the word *chimichanga*. And, Tucsonans consider this "thank God for Lipitor" dish their signature food. In fact, its origins are "accidental" and date back to 1922. Apparently it was in Arizona at one of their oldest Mexican restaurants, El Charro Cafés, that Monica Flin cursed and "accidentally" flipped a burrito into a fryer and thus the chimichanga was born—or the thingamajig, which is my new favorite word.

ARIZONA

C HIMICHANGA: C OMBO S TAIN

PMS REMOVAL OF MAIN STAIN: SALSA

- Gently spoon off any excess or dip a chip and scoop off without mushing it into fabric.
- Working from the back of the garment, flush the stain with cold water.
- Sponge with hydrogen peroxide or white vinegar and rinse with cool water. If the fabric is white, use a chlorine bleach product. Repeat until the stain is gone.
  If the stain still remains after rinsing, you didn't put enough tequila in your margarita to blur your vision, so consider adding another shot and try the following:
- Gently rub with a liquid enzyme laundry detergent and soak in warm water for up to thirty minutes. This is a good time to finish your margarita or have a fresh one.
- Machine wash with enzyme detergent and fabric-appropriate bleach in the hottest water the care label allows.

If this fails, give up eating chimichangas or dye your garment red or black.

ARKANSAS

S PINACH: D YE S TAIN

PMS REMOVAL

- Spoon off excess spinach.*
- Flush stain thoroughly with cool water.
- Place fabric stain side down on a cloth and sponge the back with rubbing alcohol. If it's a colored garment test the fabric first.
- If the stain remains, use color-appropriate bleach applied with an eyedropper or a sponge as follows:
  - Whites only
    - Chlorine bleach: dilute with equal parts water
  - Whites and colors
    - Oxygen bleach
    - White vinegar

---

*After you remove any excess, you can also try hitting the stain with aerosol hairspray.

I Can What I Can!

According to folks who live in Alma, Alabama, their town is the spinach capital of the world. Seems two of its residents were sipping coffee one day back in 1987 and trying to figure out how to put their town on the map. Then, as the caffeine kicked in, they realized that the Allen Canning Company exported and canned more than 50 percent of all the spinach in the United States, which at the time was about 60 million pounds plus per year! That led them to think, if we're the spinach capital of the United States, why not the world? Well, it didn't end there. The story goes that a writer from a paper in Crystal City, Texas, took issue with these two fellows. He claimed that his Texas town had been the spinach capital since 1937 and that their position was confirmed by the presence of a Del Monte cannery. No one knows exactly why, but eventually the Texan let it go, and Alma is the "can, what I can and that's all I can" spinach capital of the world and perhaps the universe. By the way, both towns have a statue of our bud Popeye smack in their centers. Alma's even painted their water tower to look like a can of spinach along with the words *World's Largest Can of Spinach* to prove it—and they say only Texans think big.

- 3 percent hydrogen peroxide (1:3 ratio of peroxide to water)
- Isopropyl alcohol
  Repeat if necessary and rinse in between.
- Machine wash with liquid enzyme detergent according to the fabric care label.

CALIFORNIA

FRENCH DIP SANDWICH: COMBO STAIN

PMS REMOVAL OF MAIN STAIN: ROAST BEEF GREASE
- If you accidentally drip some grease on your clothes when you're out, gently rub liquid hand sanitizer into the stain.
- If eating and dipping leisurely at home, do the following pronto:
  - Scrape off with spoon or knife and sop or blot up the excess with white paper towels or a cloth.
  - Saturate with liquid enzyme detergent and let sit for five minutes.
  - If the stain remains, put a white cloth behind to catch the stain and douse a sponge with dry-cleaning solvent, which you can buy online (try Afta

Law and Order

The story goes that the French Dip sandwich was "accidentally" created in Los Angeles in 1918 by a shop owner named Philippe Mathieu. It seems that Philippe was making a roast beef sandwich for a policeman when he dropped half the French roll into a pan of roast beef drippings. Well, I guess the policeman had crooks to catch so Philippe didn't have time to make a new sandwich and the policeman ate his fallen lunch. The next day, the policeman ordered another and thus the French Dip sandwich was born.

Cleaning Fluid). Please wear your rubber gloves and open a window when you use it, since it's toxic. Blot or let dry naturally.
- Machine wash with enzyme detergent in the hottest water the care label allows. *You can also try using foam shaving cream. Lather the stain and let it sit overnight, then rinse in cold water before laundering per above.*

RED WINE: TANNIN STAIN

PMS REMOVAL
- Sop up any excess with a white paper towel or cloth and flush the stain with cool water or club soda. (FYI: If you spill white wine this should be all you need to get it out.)
- If the stain remains, sprinkle some salt on it and pour white wine vinegar or white

Pop Culture

Leave it to a kid to invent something like the Popsicle, which is exactly what happened way back in 1905 when eleven-year-old Frank Epperson, a San Francisco native, "accidentally" left a soft drink with a stirrer in it outside overnight. And, yup, it froze. He originally called it the Eppsicle and patented his "frozen ice on a stick" in 1923. I'm not sure exactly how the name changed, but it became the Popsicle after he had become a "pop" himself—that is, a father. Frankie eventually sold his rights to the Popsicle but he is credited for inspiring other tasty "icles" like the twin Popsicle (so kids of all ages could share), the Fudgsicle, the Creamsicle, and the Dreamsicle.

vinegar on the stain. (I prefer using *regular* white wine versus white wine vinegar so that I can sip a bit as it sits for a few minutes!) Rinse thoroughly.
- Machine wash with enzyme detergent and color-safe bleach in the hottest water the care label allows. Resume drinking clear libations only!

COLORADO

ROCKY MOUNTAIN RAINBOW TROUT WITH BUTTER DRESSING: OIL STAIN

PMS REMOVAL OF MAIN STAIN: BUTTER DRESSING
- Scrape off any excess with a butter knife (duh!) and put it on a piece of bread (kidding!).
- Sprinkle the stain thoroughly with cornstarch, baby powder, or talcum powder to absorb. Leave on for fifteen minutes and then gently scrape off.
- If the stain remains, soak it with liquid enzyme detergent for five minutes in cool water.
- Launder with enzyme detergent in the hottest water that the care label allows.

A Whale of a Tasty Tale

It seems chowder's been around since our great country was settled. And, though Boston is credited with its first mention, it quickly became a New England thing that anyone living in Connecticut and the Northeast pronounced "chowdah." Chowdah was so much a part of the New England diet that the famous American novelist Herman Melville wrote of its splendors in his masterpiece *Moby-Dick:*

> However, a warm savory steam from the kitchen served to belie the apparently cheerless prospect before us. But when that smoking chowder came in, the mystery was delightfully explained. Oh, sweet friends! harken to me. It was made of small juicy clams, scarcely bigger than hazel nuts, mixed with pounded ship biscuit, and salted pork cut up into little flakes; the whole enriched with butter, and plentifully seasoned with pepper and salt. Our appetites being sharpened by the frosty voyage, and in particular, Queequeg seeing his favourite fishing food before him, and the chowder being surpassingly excellent, we dispatched it with great expedition.

CONNECTICUT

NEW ENGLAND CLAM CHOWDER: COMBO STAIN

PMS REMOVAL OF MAIN STAIN: DAIRY
- Sop up or scrape off any excess.
- Soak the stain in cold water for five minutes and gently agitate. You can also sponge it with club soda. Enjoy another bowl while wearing a bib in between agitating.
- If the stain remains, gently soak it with liquid enzyme detergent in tepid water for up to thirty minutes. Rub a dub from time to time.
- Machine wash in cool water with color-appropriate bleach and enzyme detergent. As always, check care labels first.

DELAWARE

CRAB PUFFS: OIL STAIN

PMS REMOVAL
- Lick and blot off any excess without taxing yourself in the process.
- Sprinkle the spot with talcum powder, baby powder, or cornstarch to absorb. Leave on for fifteen minutes and then gently scrape off.
- If the stain remains, soak it with enzyme detergent for five minutes in warm water.
- Launder with enzyme detergent in the hottest water that the care label allows.

FLORIDA

ORANGES, GRAPEFRUITS, AND LIMES: TANNIN STAINS

PMS REMOVAL
- Blot as much of the excess off as you can with white paper towels or a white cloth. Then douse the stain with cold water.
  - If the stain has set, gently rub it with glycerin soap—which you can find in any supermarket—before treating.

The Key to the Lime

As the saying goes, necessity is the mother of invention and so it was with key lime pie. As you might imagine, Florida and the Keys in general don't lend themselves to cows sunbathing or grazing in the grass. Fresh milk was not a ready option when making pies back in the late 1800s, which is why the invention in 1856 of sweetened condensed milk saved the day for those wanting to make key lime pie. A truly sweet and "moo-ving" story, I'd say!

By the way, Florida is the largest grower of limes, like most things citrus, coming in with 90 percent of the U.S. crop! As for key limes, most of the trees were ruined during a hurricane in 1926, so they're a rarity to find. But if you do, they look like lemons in lime denial sporting both a yellow and greenish skin and sometimes they have brown blotches.

- If the stain remains, sponge it with white vinegar and then rinse in cool water.
- Machine wash with a liquid enzyme detergent in the hottest water that the care label allows.

Cuban Sandwich: Combo Stain

PMS REMOVAL OF MAIN STAIN: CHEESE AND MUSTARD
- Scrape off any excess.
- Soak the stain with liquid enzyme detergent in cool water for fifteen to thirty minutes.
- Machine wash with enzyme detergent and fabric-appropriate bleach in the hottest water that the care label allows.

See "PMS Removal: Mustard" on page 180.

Key Lime Pie: Combo Stain

PMS REMOVAL OF MAIN STAIN: KEY LIME FILLING
- Scrape or lick off any excess.
- Flush the stain in cool water.

- Soak it in an enzyme laundry product for thirty minutes or, if necessary, several hours. Use cool water.
- Machine wash with enzyme laundry detergent in the hottest water that the care label allows.

GEORGIA

Peach Pie: Tannin Stain

PMS REMOVAL OF MAIN STAIN: PEACHY FILLING
- Lick off the excess immediately.
  - If you want to finish your pie before treating the stain, sprinkle it with salt and then rinse with cold water.
- Gently rub laundry detergent into the stain—do not use soap because it can set the stain.
- If the stain remains, use color-appropriate bleaching agent applied with an eyedropper or a sponge as follows:
  - Whites only
    - Chlorine bleach: dilute with equal parts water
  - Whites and colors
    - Oxygen bleach
    - White vinegar
    - 3 percent hydrogen peroxide (1:3 ratio of peroxide to water)
    - Isopropyl alcohol
- Machine wash with enzyme detergent in the hottest water that the care label allows.

HAWAII

Pineapple: Tannin Stain

PMS REMOVAL
- Scrape off any excess and flush the stain under cold water.
- Machine wash with fabric-appropriate bleach in the hottest water that the care label allows.
- While the item is washing, have kids create a new home for SpongeBob.

Spud Away the Mud

Next time your kiddie gets some mud on his or her duds take a spud, cut it in half, and gently rub the mud away. Then let the garment soak in cool water and throw it in with your next load. Feel free to zap up the other half of the potato and enjoy it as a midday snack!

IDAHO

Baked or Mashed Potato with Sour Cream: Protein Stain

PMS REMOVAL OF MAIN STAIN: SOUR CREAM OR MILK
- Scrape off any excess.
- Flush the stain with cold water to loosen it.
- Wash in liquid enzyme detergent using the hottest water that the care label allows.

ILLINOIS

Chicago Deep Dish Pizza: Combo Stain

PMS REMOVAL OF MAIN STAIN: PIZZA SAUCE
- Scrape off any excess and run cool water through the back of the stain.
- Soak the stain with liquid enzyme detergent and let sit for five minutes, then rinse well in cool water.
  Feel free to gently rub while soaking and have another slice, but stand so no more drips onto your lap!
- If the stain remains, use color-appropriate bleaching agent applied with an eyedropper or a sponge as follows:
  - Whites only
    - Chlorine bleach: dilute with equal parts water
  - Whites and colors—use one of the following:
    - Oxygen bleach
    - White vinegar
    - 3 percent hydrogen peroxide (1:3 ratio of peroxide to water)
    - Isopropyl alcohol

Fast Food Lingo

LOCO MOCO: This is considered Hawaii's original fast food. It's a hamburger patty served on a bed of white rice topped with a fried egg that is served sunny-side up and smothered in gravy. Sounds like a dish that will have your arteries begging for mercy! By the way, I tried to find a literal translation for *Loco Moco* and didn't have much luck. I asked my thirteen-year-old-son, who takes Spanish, to help figure it out and for what it's worth (and it's not very appetizing) *loco* means "crazy" and *moco* means "snot" or "booger" in Spanish. Too bad we can't change "booger" to "burger," since that would make it a Crazy Burger versus a Crazy Booger!!

PIZZA: According to the folks at whatscookingamerica.net, no one knows exactly where the word *pizza* came from, though they think it may be from an old Italian word meaning "point." In time, the word became *pizzicare*, which is Italian for "to pinch or to pluck," which may refer to being "plucked" from a hot oven.

SLYDER: No, I'm not talking about a pitch in baseball but the original Slyder that White Castle invented back in 1942. It seems even back then folks were worried about tainted meat so it was no "accident" that the owners picked the name White Castle to suggest a clean and safe place to eat. Now back to the Slyder—what made the Slyder "safer" was that they were mini square-shaped burgers with five holes in them. The holes allowed them to cook more evenly and thoroughly and not be flipped over—which I guess meant they could "slyde" off the grill.

- Machine wash with enzyme detergent in the hottest water that the care label allows.

INDIANA

Hoosier Pie: Protein Stain

PMS REMOVAL OF MAIN STAIN: CREAM FILLING
- Scrape off the excess.
- Soak the stain with an enzyme detergent in cold water for thirty minutes.
- Shoot some hoops while soaking.
- Machine wash in the hottest water that the fabric care label allows.

IOWA

CORN ON THE COB WITH BUTTER: OIL STAIN

PMS REMOVAL OF MAIN STAIN: BUTTER
- Shuck off and/or blot up the excess with white paper towels or a cloth.
- Sprinkle the stain thoroughly with cornstarch, baby powder, or talcum powder to absorb. Leave on for fifteen minutes and gently scrape off.
- If the stain remains, soak it with enzyme detergent in warm water for five minutes.
- Launder in the hottest water that the care label allows.

KANSAS

KANSAS CITY BBQ RIBS: COMBO STAIN

PMS REMOVAL OF MAIN STAIN: BARBECUE SAUCE
- Lick off any excess and run cool water through the back of the stain.
- Soak it with liquid enzyme detergent, let sit for five minutes, and rinse in cool water.
  - Feel free to gently rub while soaking.
- If the stain remains, use color-appropriate bleaching agent applied with an eyedropper or a sponge as follows:
  - Whites only
    - Chlorine bleach: dilute with equal parts water
  - Whites and colors
    - Oxygen bleach
    - White vinegar
    - 3 percent hydrogen peroxide (1:3 ratio of peroxide to water)
    - Isopropyl alcohol
- Machine wash with enzyme detergent in the hottest water that the care label allows.

Wake Up and Smell the Julep

Though most of us have come to think of the mint julep as the official drink of the Kentucky Derby, its history goes further back. It seems farmers in the southeast and east would chug down this tasty cocktail rather than a cup of coffee to help them "get out of the gate" first thing in the morning. I don't know about you, but the idea of walking into a Starbucks and ordering a mint julep instead of my usual latte has a certain appeal given *my race* to get everything done after dropping my son off at school! I do believe it may be time to wake up and smell the mint julep!

By the way, the "wake up" ingredient in a mint julep is bourbon, which is America's only native spirit. And, according to the Kentucky Distillers' Association, 95 percent of it is produced in Kentucky.

KENTUCKY

MINT JULEP: TANNIN

PMS REMOVAL OF MAIN STAIN: BOOZE, AS IN BOURBON
- Run cold water or club soda through the back of the stain.
- Gently rub the stain with dishwashing detergent or liquid enzyme detergent. (Remember: *Do not use bar soap* because it can set the stain and make it a permanent embellishment, documenting your overindulgence or need to imbibe after your horse lost the Derby!)
- Machine wash according to fabric care instructions.

KENTUCKY FRIED CHICKEN: OIL STAIN

PMS REMOVAL
- Gently remove any "fried" stuff.
- Sprinkle the stain thoroughly with talcum powder or cornstarch to absorb. Leave on for fifteen minutes and then gently scrape off.
- Soak with enzyme detergent in warm water for five minutes.
- If the stain remains, use an eyedropper filled with dry-cleaning solvent or isopropyl alcohol. Blot and let dry naturally.
- Launder in the hottest water that the care label allows and go back to finishing the Colonel's finger-lickin' chicken with a bib and napkin on your lap.

LOUISIANA

GUMBO: COMBO STAIN

PMS REMOVAL OF MAIN STAINS: ROUX (WHICH, TO WE NON-CREOLE-SPEAKERS, IS A MIX OF BUTTER OR OIL AND FLOUR)

- Spoon and/or blot off excess with white paper towels or a cloth.
- Soak the stain with liquid enzyme detergent and let sit for five minutes, then rinse in cool water.
  - Feel free to gently rub while soaking.
- If the stain remains, use color-appropriate bleaching agent applied with an eyedropper or a sponge as follows:
  - Whites only
    - Chlorine bleach: dilute with equal parts water
  - Whites and colors
    - Oxygen bleach
    - White vinegar
    - 3 percent hydrogen peroxide (1:3 ratio of peroxide to water)
    - Isopropyl alcohol

Repeat if necessary and rinse in between.
- Machine wash with enzyme detergent in the hottest water that the care label allows.

PRALINES: COMBO STAIN

PMS REMOVAL OF MAIN STAIN: CARAMEL

- Use a dull knife or spoon to remove excess and rinse well with cold water.
- Gently rub liquid detergent into the stain and let it sit for five minutes.
- Machine wash in warm water with fabric-appropriate bleach.

MAINE

LOBSTER WITH MELTED BUTTER: OIL STAIN

PMS REMOVAL OF MAIN STAIN: MELTED BUTTER

- Scrape off with plastic spoon or knife or blot up the excess with white paper towels or a cloth.

- Sprinkle the stain thoroughly with cornstarch, baby powder, or talcum powder to absorb. Leave on for fifteen minutes and then gently scrape off.
- Rub the stain with baby shampoo (change of pace!) and rinse in cold water.
- Machine wash with enzyme detergent in the hottest water that the care label allows.

While the item is washing, rent the movie *Annie Hall* and look for the kitchen lobster race scene betwixt Woody Allen and Diane Keaton, which may either inspire or retire your desire to eat lobsters ever again!

MARYLAND

CRAB CAKES: COMBO STAIN

PMS REMOVAL OF MAIN STAIN: TARTAR SAUCE
(If a piece of crab has landed in your lap without the sauce, it's an oil stain, so go to page 148.)

- Remove the excess.
- Gently rub liquid enzyme detergent into the stain and let it sit for fifteen minutes.
- Machine wash in the hottest water that the care label allows.

MASSACHUSETTS

BAKED BEANS: COMBO STAIN

PMS REMOVAL OF MAIN STAIN: MOLASSES
- Scoop off or sop up any excess with white paper towels or a cloth.
- Douse the back of the stain with cold water. (It is recommended that you do this in the privacy of another room to prevent sharing with friends or family any gas emissions that may emanate from your body after eating said beans.)
- Soak with liquid enzyme detergent and let sit for five minutes before rinsing in cool water.
  - Feel free to gently rub while soaking.
- If stain remains use color-appropriate bleaching agent applied with an eyedropper or a sponge with one of the following:

- Whites only
  - Chlorine bleach: dilute with equal parts water
- Whites and colors
  - Oxygen bleach
  - White vinegar
  - 3 percent hydrogen peroxide (1:3 ratio of peroxide to water)
  - Isopropyl alcohol
  - Machine wash with enzyme detergent in the hottest water that the care label allows.

CRANBERRIES: DYE STAIN

PMS REMOVAL

- Remove any excess and flush the stain with cold water.
- Let it soak for thirty minutes in cool water after you gently rub in some liquid enzyme detergent and fabric-safe bleach. Rinse in cool water.
- If the stain remains, get that step stool out, and start boiling water. Then stretch out fabric and pour the water over and through stain. Repeat if necessary and rinse in between.
- Machine wash with enzyme detergent in the hottest water that the fabric care label recommends.

MICHIGAN

CHERRIES: DYE STAIN

PMS REMOVAL

- Gently scrape off any excess immediately—do not mush into fabric as you remove.
- Use an eyedropper filled with the strongest color-appropriate bleach your stuff can handle and drip it onto the stain.
- Machine wash with liquid enzyme detergent according to the fabric care label.

You can also try hitting the stain with aerosol hairspray after you remove any excess.

NOTE: If you're so inclined, feel free to refer to "For Those Who 'Dye' for Heights" on page 147.

SPAM I Am

The origins of the name SPAM are a bit fuzzy, but here's what I've learned. This canned phenomenon, which has been celebrated in song on Broadway in *SPAMalot,* was created in 1937 by Jay Hormel, who thought it would be a tasty way to package pork shoulder meat. Hard for me to think of pork shoulder and tasty in the same thought, but I digress. In need of a name for this foie gras of pork shoulder, Jay held a nationwide contest, which a guy named Ken won. Ken received $100 and a lifetime supply of his newly named SPAM. (Actually, I'm not sure of the latter, but it seems like an appropriate part of the prize!) There is some speculation that the name came from combining the words *spiced* and *ham* to form SPAM, but no one I reached out to would confirm this. Should you like more info on its roots, you can go to www.spam.com.

MINNESOTA

SPAM: Protein Stain

PMS REMOVAL
- Scrape off excess and feed it to Fido.
- Machine wash with enzyme detergent according to fabric care label.

Wild Berries: Dye Stain

PMS REMOVAL
- Immediately scrape off as much as you can without mushing it further into fabric and then flush thoroughly with cool water.
- Use an eyedropper filled with the strongest color-appropriate bleach your stuff can handle and drip it onto the stain.
- Machine wash with liquid enzyme detergent according to the fabric care label.

MISSISSIPPI

MUD PIE: COMBO STAIN

PMS REMOVAL OF MAIN STAIN: CHOCOLATE
- Gently scrape off excess chocolate—avoid licking it off, since that could mush it into the fabric.
- Soak with liquid enzyme detergent and water for about twenty minutes.
- If the stain remains, use a sponge or an eyedropper to apply fabric-safe bleach.
- Machine wash with enzyme detergent in the hottest water that the care label allows.

This will work on any chocolate stain you have.

MISSOURI

PEANUT BUTTER: PROTEIN STAIN

PMS REMOVAL
- Scrape off excess and put it on a fresh piece of bread or a cracker.
- Gently rub the stain with liquid enzyme detergent and let sit for five minutes.
- Machine wash in the hottest water that the fabric care label allows.

In Search of Peanut Butter's Papa

George W. Carver may be known as the father of the peanut, but the person often cited as the father of peanut butter was a St. Louis physician whose name remains a mystery. At any rate, it seems our Missouri mystery doc felt peanut butter would be an excellent and easy protein for his elderly patients and those with bad teeth (or none I suppose!) to digest. Little did he know that someday it would also become a kids' fave and a way for us moms to get our kids to eat something other than Cheerios and pasta. Here's to our mystery doc and the inspiration for PB & J sandwiches!

Kool Hair

You may recall that I'm a fan of using Kool-Aid to clean our toilets. Well, here's another nontraditional way to enjoy this sugary packet—use it to dye your hair! It seems if you mix a packet with a spoonful of cornstarch and a little bit of water you can be sporting a new color do—of course, it will be red or green, but hey, you could feel like a rock star. Apparently Kurt Cobain of the band Nirvana did just that before one of his appearances on *Saturday Night Live.* On second thought, Kurt's not with us anymore so perhaps this is not such a Kool idea.

MONTANA

Forgive me, Montana, you have the sole distinction of being the only stain-free state. Thank you for giving us a break!

NEBRASKA

KOOL-AID: DYE STAIN

PMS REMOVAL
- Immediately sponge or blot off excess with cool water.
- Soak for at least thirty minutes in cool water and enzyme detergent. Every now and then, gently rub some of the detergent into the stain. Depending on how big a mess it is, you may need to soak overnight.
- If the stain remains, use fabric-appropriate bleaching agent.
- Machine wash in enzyme detergent per the care label.

Who'd Have Thunk!

- *AVOCADO* means "testicle" in Spanish.
- TOMATOES are fruits, not veggies.
- WATERMELONS are berries on steroids (kidding about the steroids!).

Cool Cooler

Next time avoid the stains altogether and do as the early explorers did: Use a watermelon as a canteen. Of course, you could also "explore" using it as a vodka cooler, which is what my buds and I did in college!

STEAKS/BEEF: COMBO STAIN

PMS REMOVAL OF MAIN STAIN: STEAK SAUCE
- Scrape off excess with plastic spoon or knife or sop it up with white paper towels or a cloth.
- Run cool to cold water through the back of the stain.
- Soak with liquid enzyme detergent and let sit for five minutes, then rinse. Feel free to gently rub while soaking.
- If the stain remains, use color-appropriate bleaching agent applied with an eyedropper or a sponge with one of the following:
  - Whites only
    - Chlorine bleach: dilute with equal parts water
  - Whites and colors
    - Oxygen bleach
    - White vinegar
    - 3 percent hydrogen peroxide (1:3 ratio of peroxide to water)
    - Isopropyl alcohol
- Machine wash with enzyme detergent according to care label

WATERMELON: DYE STAIN

PMS REMOVAL
- Immediately scrape off as much as you can without mushing it into the fabric* and flush the stain thoroughly with cool water.
- Use an eyedropper filled with the strongest color-appropriate bleach your stuff can handle and drip it onto the stain.

---

*You can also try hitting the stain with aerosol hairspray after you remove any excess.

- Machine wash with liquid enzyme detergent according to the fabric care label.

NEVADA

Eggs: Protein Stain

I thought I'd give you some removal tips for eggs, which Nevada cowboys, or buckaroos, as they're called, often whip up while on the frontier, or, as they like to say, at home on the range.

PMS REMOVAL
- Gently scrape or blot off any excess and rinse the stain in cold water.
- Apply some enzyme detergent to the stain and soak in warm water for thirty minutes. Every now and then rub gently.
- If the stain remains, crack open and use color-appropriate bleach. Let it sit for fifteen minutes.
- Machine wash with enzyme detergent according to the care instructions.

If serving your eggs with some bacon and it gets on your chaps—forgive me, I meant laps—go to oil stain removal on page 148.

NEW HAMPSHIRE

Corn Chowder: Combo Stain

PMS REMOVAL OF MAIN STAIN: MILK
- Spoon off or blot any excess with a white paper towel or cloth.
- Soak in enzyme laundry detergent for about fifteen minutes and gently rub the stain while it's soaking.
- Machine wash with enzyme detergent according to the fabric care label.

NEW JERSEY (MY HOME SWEET HOME STATE!)

Blueberries: Dye Stain

PMS REMOVAL
- Gently scrape off any excess pronto—do not mush into fabric as you remove.
- Stretch the fabric over the sink, stand on a step stool, and pour boiling water

onto the stain (you should be at least a foot higher than the item). Be careful! Let it sit for a couple of minutes.
- If the stain remains, use color-appropriate bleaching agent applied with an eyedropper or a sponge with one of the following. Repeat if necessary and rinse in between.
  - Whites only
    - Chlorine bleach diluted with water
  - Whites and colors
    - Oxygen bleach
    - 3 percent hydrogen peroxide (1:3 ratio of peroxide to water)
    - Isopropyl alcohol
    - Launder with liquid enzyme detergent and color-appropriate bleach.

After you remove any excess, you can also try hitting the stain with aerosol hairspray.

New Jersey is also famous for its delicious tomatoes, so if you bite into one and it drips, the PMS removal is on page 146. FYI: It's a tannin stain!

NEW MEXICO

CHILE RELLENOS: COMBO STAIN

PMS REMOVAL OF MAIN STAIN: FRIED CHILE PEPPER
- Scrape off excess with a butter knife.
- Sprinkle with constarch, talcum, or baby powder to absorb grease. Leave on for fifteen minutes and gently scrape off.
- Gently rub liquid enzyme detergent into the stain and let it sit for a few minutes.
- Soak in cold water for ten minutes. Feel free to rub between your fingers every now and then.
- Rinse thoroughly and machine wash according to the care label.

NEW YORK

BEER: TANNIN STAIN

PMS REMOVAL
- Sop (don't sip!) or blot up excess using white paper towels or a cloth.
- Run cool water or club soda through the back of the stain.

- Blot with dishwashing detergent or liquid enzyme detergent and let sit for five minutes. Rinse.
- If the stain remains, sponge with a mix of $1/3$ cup white vinegar and $2/3$ cup water. Rinse and blot dry.
- Machine wash in enzyme detergent per the care label. Cut your guest or self off and or "tap" into a clear-colored libation next.

JELL-O: DYE STAIN

PMS REMOVAL

- Immediately scrape off as much as you can* and flush the stain thoroughly with cool water.
- As your kiddie wiggles and shakes, use an eyedropper filled with the strongest color-appropriate bleach your stuff can handle and drip it onto the stain.
- Machine wash with liquid enzyme detergent according to the fabric care label.

NORTH CAROLINA

PULLED PORK: COMBO STAIN

PMS REMOVAL OF MAIN STAIN: BARBECUE SAUCE

- Scrape off any excess and run cool water through the back of the stain.
- Soak with liquid enzyme detergent, let sit for five minutes, and rinse in cool water. Feel free to gently rub while soaking.
- If the stain remains, use color-appropriate bleaching agent applied with an eyedropper or a sponge with one of the following:
  - Whites only
    - Chlorine bleach: dilute with equal parts water
  - Whites and colors
    - Oxygen bleach
    - White vinegar

---

*After you remove any excess, you can also try hitting the stain with aerosol hairspray.

- 3 percent hydrogen peroxide (1:3 ratio of peroxide to water)
- Isopropyl alcohol
  Repeat if necessary and rinse in between.
- Machine wash with enzyme detergent in the hottest water that the care label allows before returning to the Tar Heels or Blue Devils game.

NORTH DAKOTA

CREAM OF WHEAT: PROTEIN STAIN

PMS REMOVAL
- Remove any excess.
- Flush the stain under cold running water.
- If the stain remains and/or you had also added honey, gently work in a liquid enzyme detergent and let sit for five minutes, then rapidly flush the stain with hot water.
- Machine wash with enzyme detergent and color-safe bleach in the hottest water that the care label allows.

OHIO

CINCINNATI CHILI: COMBO STAIN

PMS REMOVAL
- Scrape off with a plastic spoon or a knife or sop up the excess with white paper towels or a cloth.
- Run cool to cold water through the back of the stain.
- Soak with liquid enzyme detergent and let sit for five minutes, then rinse. Feel free to gently rub while soaking.
- If the stain remains, use color-appropriate bleaching agent applied with an eyedropper or a sponge with one of the following:
  - Whites only
    - Chlorine bleach: dilute with equal parts water
  - Whites and colors
    - Oxygen bleach
    - White vinegar

- 3 percent hydrogen peroxide (1:3 ratio of peroxide to water)
- Isopropyl alcohol

Machine wash with enzyme detergent in the hottest water that the care label allows.

OKLAHOMA

SAUSAGE AND GRAVY: COMBO STAIN

PMS REMOVAL OF MAIN STAIN: GRAVY
- Gently scrape, lick, sop up, or blot off any excess with white paper towels or a cloth—allow Fido to eat any scraps!
- Sprinkle the stain thoroughly with cornstarch, talcum powder, or baby powder to absorb. Leave on for fifteen minutes and then gently scrape off.
- Soak with enzyme detergent in warm water for five minutes.
- Launder in the hottest water that the care label allows.

STRAWBERRIES: DYE STAIN

PMS REMOVAL
- Scrape off as much as you can immediately without mushing into fabric.*
- Flush the stain thoroughly with cool water.

Overbaked

The hard pretzel was "accidentally" invented in Pennsylvania sometime in the seventeenth century when a baker's helper fell asleep as the pretzels were baking. When he awoke, the flames in the oven had petered out and he thought the pretzels needed to bake longer. He rekindled the fire, continued to bake them, and I suspect took another snooze. When he awoke and took them out they had hardened. Fortunately, the master baker decided to try one before throwing them away and firing his helper. Not only did he like the way they tasted, but being a shrewd businessman, he realized that these hard pretzels would stay fresher longer since all the moisture was baked out—no one would know if they were fresh or stale; forgive the pun, but this turned out to be a truly well-baked idea.

---

*After you remove any excess, you can also try hitting the stain with aerosol hairspray.

- Use an eyedropper filled with the strongest color-appropriate bleach your stuff can handle and drip it onto the stain.
- Machine wash with liquid enzyme detergent in the hottest water that the care label allows.

OREGON

BLACKBERRIES: DYE STAIN

PMS REMOVAL
(I feel like I'm having dye-ja vu since we just did this one for strawberries!)

- Immediately scrape off as much as you can.*
- Flush the stain thoroughly with cool water.
- Use an eyedropper filled with the strongest color-appropriate bleach your stuff can handle and drip it onto the stain.
- Machine wash with liquid enzyme detergent in the hottest water that the care label allows.

PENNSYLVANIA

CHEESESTEAK: COMBO

PMS REMOVAL OF MAIN STAIN: CHEEZ WHIZ
- Gently scrape, lick, sop up, or blot off any excess with white or recycled paper towels or a cloth.
- Douse the stain pronto with cold water.
- Soak with enzyme detergent in cold water for thirty minutes.
- If the stain remains, use color-appropriate bleaching agent applied with an eyedropper or a sponge as follows:
  - Whites only
    - Chlorine bleach: dilute with equal parts water
  - Whites and colors
    - Oxygen bleach
    - White vinegar

---

*After you remove any excess, you can also try hitting the stain with aerosol hairspray.

- 3 percent hydrogen peroxide (1:3 ratio of peroxide to water)
- Isopropyl alcohol
- Launder in the hottest water that the care label allows and take a whiz.

PRETZELS WITH MUSTARD: DYE STAIN

PMS REMOVAL: MUSTARD
- Scrape off excess mustard and put it back on remaining pretzel—joking!
- Gently rub glycerin soap into the stain with your fingers—make sure you wipe them first to remove any remaining mustard. Let sit for a few minutes, then rinse with cold water. You can also try flushing it with white vinegar—just test to make sure it doesn't affect color.
- Machine wash using the hottest water that the care instructions allow. Finish eating the pretzel plain, without mustard.

HERSHEY'S CHOCOLATE: COMBO STAIN

I know I've shared how to remove this before, but Hershey's and Pennsylvania are like love and marriage, so I felt it bears repeating!

PMS REMOVAL
- Gently scrape off excess chocolate—avoid licking it off, since that could mush it in, and keep it away from Fido.
- Soak with liquid enzyme detergent in cool water for about twenty minutes.
- If the stain remains, use an eyedropper or a sponge to apply fabric-safe bleach.
- Machine wash with enzyme detergent in the hottest water that the care label allows.

RHODE ISLAND

COFFEE MILK: PROTEIN STAIN
- Sop up or blot off excess using white paper towels or a cloth.
- Run cool water or club soda through the back of the stain.
- Soak in liquid enzyme detergent for thirty minutes.
- Machine wash with color-appropriate bleach and enzyme detergent according to care label.

SOUTH CAROLINA

Sweet Tea: Tannin Stain

PMS REMOVAL
- Gently sop up or blot off excess using white paper towels or a cloth.
- Soak in cool water with enzyme detergent and white vinegar and let it sit for twenty to thirty minutes. Blot dry. Remember, *do not use bar soap* because it will set the stain.
- If the stain remains, use color-appropriate bleaching agent applied with an eyedropper or a sponge as follows unless care label notes otherwise:
  - Whites only
    - Chlorine bleach: dilute with equal parts water
  - Whites and colors
    - Oxygen bleach
    - White vinegar
    - 3 percent hydrogen peroxide (1:3 ratio of peroxide to water)
    - Isopropyl alcohol
- Launder according to garment instructions in warmest water allowed.

Chitlins: Oil Stain

PMS REMOVAL
- Gently remove any fried stuff.
- Sprinkle the stain thoroughly with cornstarch or talcum or baby powder to absorb. Leave on for fifteen minutes and then gently scrape off.
- Soak with enzyme detergent in warm water for five minutes.
- If the stain remains, use an eyedropper filled with dry-cleaning solvent or isopropyl alcohol. Blot and let dry naturally.
- Launder in the hottest water that the care label allows.

SOUTH DAKOTA

Custard Kuchen*: Protein Stain

PMS REMOVAL OF MAIN STAIN: CUSTARD
- Scrape off excess with your fork or a butter knife.†
- Flush the stain immediately in cold water.
- Soak in enzyme detergent for fifteen minutes.
- Machine wash in the hottest water that the care label allows. (If it's made with peaches use color-appropriate bleach when machine washing.)

TENNESSEE

Blackberry Jam Cake: Combo Stain

PMS REMOVAL OF MAIN STAIN: JAM
- Scrape off as much as you can immediately.**
- Douse the stain thoroughly with cool water.
- Use an eyedropper filled with the strongest color-appropriate bleach your stuff can handle and drip it onto the stain.
- Machine wash with liquid enzyme detergent in the hottest water that the fabric care label allows.

TEXAS

Chili: Combo Stain

PMS REMOVAL OF MAIN STAIN: TOMATOES
- Scrape off any excess and run cool water through the back of the stain.
- Soak with liquid enzyme detergent and let sit for twenty minutes, then rinse well

---

Kuchen is the German word for cake.
†If crust lands on you instead of the custardy filling scrape off excess, then use cornstarch, talcum powder, or baby powder to absorb the oil. Let sit for fifteen minutes, then drip some dry-cleaning solvent onto the stain and machine wash in enzyme detergent as above.
**After you remove any excess, you can also try hitting the stain with aerosol hairspray or try the "For Those Who 'Dye' for Heights" removal on page 147.

in cool water. Feel free to gently rub while soaking and have another bowl—just put a bib on!
- If the stain remains, use color-appropriate bleaching agent applied with an eyedropper or a sponge as follows:
  - Whites only
    - Chlorine bleach: dilute with equal parts water
  - Whites and colors
    - Oxygen bleach
    - White vinegar
    - 3 percent hydrogen peroxide (1:3 ratio of peroxide to water)
    - Isopropyl alcohol
- Machine wash with enzyme detergent in hottest water care label allows.

UTAH:

H O N E Y : T A N N I N S T A I N

PMS REMOVAL
- Scrape off any excess and flush the stain under cold water to loosen the sticky stuff.
- Machine wash with enzyme detergent and color-appropriate bleach in the hottest water that the care label allows. Then go give your honey a hug!

VERMONT

M A P L E S Y R U P : T A N N I N S T A I N

PMS REMOVAL
- Use a butter knife or a spoon to wipe off any excess and then rinse the stain thoroughly with cold water.
- Rub the stain gently with enzyme detergent and let sit for several minutes. Rub tenderly (change of pace!) every now and then.
- Rinse the back of the stain with hot water.
- If the stain remains, use color-appropriate bleaching agent applied with an eyedropper or a sponge as follows:
  - Whites only
    - Chlorine bleach: dilute with equal parts water
  - Whites and colors

Coffee to Go Drip Tips

Whether you're gulping down a cup at home or in your car, accidents happen, so:

- If you like your coffee with milk or cream, drip a few drops of dry-cleaning solution onto the stain with an eyedropper. Rinse thoroughly with cool water and then machine wash with enzyme detergent per above.

- If you're drinking your cup of java from hours ago while driving your kiddies to school and hit a bump, gently rub some hand sanitizer into the coffee stain. Resume drinking, but make it bottled water.

- - Oxygen bleach
  - White vinegar
  - 3 percent hydrogen peroxide (1:3 ratio of peroxide to water)
  - Isopropyl alcohol
- Machine wash with enzyme detergent in the hottest water that the care label allows.

VIRGINIA

GRITS: PROTEIN STAIN

PMS REMOVAL OF MAIN STAIN: MILK
- Remove any excess with your spoon pronto.
- Sponge the stain with a small amount of dry-cleaning solvent.
- If the stain remains, mix some enzyme detergent and hydrogen peroxide or white vinegar together with lukewarm water. Blot.
- Machine wash with enzyme detergent according to the care label.

WASHINGTON

Coffee: Tannin Stain

PMS REMOVAL
- Gently sop up or blot off excess using white paper towels or a cloth.
- Run cool water or club soda through the back of the stain.
- Rub the stain with dishwashing detergent or liquid enzyme detergent and let sit for five minutes, then blot dry. Remember, *do not use bar soap!*
- If the stain remains, use color-appropriate bleach applied with a sponge.
- Launder according to garment instructions in the warmest water allowed.

WASHINGTON, D.C.

Senate Bean Soup: Combo Stain

PMS REMOVAL OF MAIN STAIN: BEANS
- Spoon, blot off, sop up, or "vote" off any excess soup using white paper towels or a cloth.
- Run cool water through the back of the stain.
- Soak in liquid enzyme detergent for five to ten minutes, then rinse. Feel free to gently rub while soaking.
- If the stain remains, use an eyedropper to apply some dry-cleaning solvent directly to the stain.
- Machine wash in the hottest water possible that care label allows. Then, veto any further eating of soup for the future.

WEST VIRGINIA

Apple Butter: Combo Stain

PMS REMOVAL OF MAIN STAIN: APPLESAUCE
- Scrape off excess with a spoon or a butter knife.
- Flush the stain under cold water.
- Machine wash with enzyme detergent in the warmest water that the care label allows.

Gas in the House

Believe it or not, there's an archive in the Senate records dating back to 1903 that declares Senate Bean Soup be a mandatory item on the Senate's menu. Except for during 1943, when there was a bad navy bean crop, so it has been. This led me to wonder if that's another reason why there are only 100 senators vs. 435 representatives. Is it possible that those who have visited the Senate prior to running for the office discover that their civic duty and credentials must include not only strong minds and character but strong digestive tracts? I vote to amend the menu and not pass the gas.

WISCONSIN

CHEESE: PROTEIN STAIN
Since we've dealt with removing cheese stains from clothing, I thought I'd share how to remove it from suedes and leathers.

PMS REMOVAL
- Gently scrape off any excess with a butter knife—be careful not to smush it in any more.
- Sprinkle the stain thoroughly with cornstarch, talcum powder, or baby powder to absorb. Leave on for thirty minutes and then gently brush it off with a toothbrush. Repeat if necessary.
- If the stain remains, say "cheese" and take it directly to the professionals—your dry cleaner.

You can also try buffing it out with an emery board or applying foam shaving cream and then gently sponging it off after a few minutes. Test first on the inside. Blot dry.

WYOMING

JACKSON HOLE HAMBURGERS: COMBO STAIN

PMS REMOVAL OF MAIN STAIN: KETCHUP
(If you dropped some burger, check out "French Dip Sandwich" on page 157.)

- Gently lift off any excess, being careful not to mush any into the fabric.
- Run cold water through the back of the stain.
- Soak in white vinegar and water.
- Machine wash with liquid enzyme detergent in the hottest water that the care label allows.

Conquering Condiment PMS

These are some of the most common stains that you'll deal with thanks to the variety of to-go and take-out food alternatives that you and I have come to rely on to keep our families from starving.

KETCHUP: COMBO STAIN

- Gently lift off any excess, being careful not to mush any into the fabric. Replace on your hamburger or fries.
- Run cold water through the back of the stain.
- Soak in white vinegar and water.
- Machine wash with liquid enzyme detergent in the hottest water that the care label allows.

MAYONNAISE: OIL STAIN

- Gently scrape off any excess.
- Bring out the best and sprinkle some cornstarch, baby powder, or talcum powder on the stain and let sit for fifteen minutes to absorb. Then gently scrape off.
- Work in enzyme detergent with a little warm water and let soak.
- Machine wash in enzyme detergent according to the fabric care label.

MUSTARD: DYE STAIN

- Scrape off excess and put it back on your hot dog or pretzel.
- Gently rub glycerin soap into the stain with your fingers—make sure you wipe them first to remove any remaining mustard or relish! Let sit for fifteen minutes. You can also try flushing it with white vinegar.
- Rinse with cold water.
- Machine wash using enzyme detergent and fabric-appropriate bleach in the hottest water that the care label allows.

SOY SAUCE: TANNIN STAIN

- Immediately flush it out by running cold water through the back of the stain.
- If the stain remains, fill an eyedropper with hydrogen peroxide—or, if it's a white item, use regular bleach—and drip it directly onto the stain.
- Machine wash with enzyme detergent and fabric-appropriate bleach according to the care label.

TABASCO SAUCE: DYE STAIN

- Wash out as much of the stain as you can with cold water.
- Soak in liquid enzyme detergent and cold water for thirty minutes. Before soaking add a dash or two of salt directly to stain.
- If the stain remains, apply color-appropriate bleaching agent with an eyedropper as follows, unless otherwise noted on care label.
  - Whites only
    - Chlorine bleach: dilute with equal parts water
  - Whites and colors
    - Oxygen bleach
    - White vinegar
    - 3 percent hydrogen peroxide (1:3 ratio of peroxide to water)
    - Isopropyl alcohol
- Machine wash with enzyme detergent in the hottest water that the care label allows.

PART **4**

FIX IT, DON'T FORGET IT

Chapter 11

A Repair to Remember

I have too many fantasies to be a housewife. I guess I am a fantasy. —Marilyn Monroe

Like everything else in this guide, what follows are a variety of manicure-friendly repairs, ways to help avoid catastrophes, and riveting info that will give you just enough know-how to deal with or identify the most common household fix-its. From clogs, leaks, and cracks to creaks, wobbles, and a variety of other everyday breakdowns there's a repair to remember should you choose to do so.

Please note: Home repairs are a new frontier for yours truly. I preferred hitting the speed-dial button on my phone to reach my personal Mr. Fix-It, since I was intimidated and grossed out by things like a toilet overflowing or a clogged sink. But what I realized as I took on these challenges was that without much effort or even breaking a nail or a sweat I could do many more repairs than I thought. And the look on my significant other's face when I fixed something was more than worth the gook that splattered on my jeans or T-shirt.

You may or may not enjoy the same sense of pride and accomplishment with each or any repair, but you will enjoy the money you'll save by not calling your local Mr. Fix-It. Of course, if he looks like Ty Pennington don't bother reading the pages that follow and make that call pronto! But if not, doing repairs is upon us, or rather knowing what to do is, so put on those rubber gloves and let's plunge into it. Again, please remember: None of these repairs is difficult and they do not require you to have any previous knowledge or experience. Obviously, an increasing number of steps usually indicates that the problem needs a bit more TLC, but do not give up; these repairs are simple enough for *any* accidental housewife to do.

General Living Space Repairs

We'll ease into home repairs by starting with areas in your home that don't require you to have an electrician's license or wear a biohazard suit.

LIVING ROOM, DINING ROOM, AND FAMILY ROOM

OFFENSIVE REPAIRS TO REMEMBER

- *GO WITH A NEW FLOW:* If your heating and cooling systems or units are more then ten years old, it's time to consider an Energy Star–approved one. Not only will it save you the expense of fixing them, it will also save you money on your energy bill. If you'd like to learn more about this go to www.energystar.gov. And flip to the next chapter, "A Convenient Truth," which begins on page 243.
  - VAC VENTS: Regularly vacuum your heating and air-conditioning filters and vents to minimize the crud that can clog them up and cause them to run inefficiently or break down.
- *SKIM THE RIM:* Next time you replace your lightbulb with an energy-efficient compact fluorescent one, or CFL (hint hint), put a thin coating of Vaseline around the rim to prevent you from breaking any bulbs (or nails) the next time you change them!
- *GET FELT UP:* Put self-adhesive felt pads or rubber disks on the bottoms of the legs of chairs, couches, cocktail tables, or anything else that may scratch your floors when you move them "seasonally" to clean under them. TIP: Rather then drag furniture you should try to lift it—think of it as a way to build up your arms and pecs!
- *STOP THE DENTS:* Install doorstops to prevent wall dents that are courtesy of your little darlings slamming doors open.
- *DRAW THE BLINDS:* Keep blinds and draperies closed during sunny days to preventing fading and burning. You should also check into treating your windows with a film coating to block the UV rays and protect all your furnishings and drapes.
- *BE PREPARED:* In case of an emergency or accident, you should have a few things handy.
  - Band-Aids—if you cut your finger changing a lightbulb
  - Flashlight to find the circuit breaker when a switch "trips"
  - Fresh batteries for all remotes
  - Nail file in case you break or chip a nail

How to Repair It Just Enough

LIGHTING

PROBLEM: DARKNESS (NO TV, LIGHTS, ETC.)

FLIP-FLOP

The first and simplest thing you should do when your light doesn't turn on is to check if the bulb blew. If that's not the answer and you also notice that your television isn't working, it could mean that your circuit breaker has flipped a switch. Knowing how to do this fix-it may also help you fix a similar problem with other items in your home that use electricity (for example your refrigerator and blow dryer).

What you'll do:
- Go to your circuit breaker panel (See "Homeschooling: Day Tripping— Circuit Breakers" on page 194).
- Look for any switch that is in the OFF position.
- Flip the tripped switch all the way to the OFF position and then flip it all the way back to the ON position. Let there be light and *Grey's Anatomy*!

PROBLEM: BROKEN BULBS
Sometimes a lightbulb can get stuck in the socket and can crack when you try to remove it, leaving you with its base in place. Help is only a spud away.

ONE POTATO, TWO POTATOES

What you'll need:
- Half a raw potato

What you'll do:
- Turn the lamp off and unplug it.
- Push the non-skin side of the spud into the broken glass and twist it until you can lift the bulb out of the socket.
- Chuck the debris, put a new CFL bulb in, and bake or microwave the other half of the potato for a "light" snack!

Homeschooling: Day Tripping—Circuit Breakers

A circuit breaker is an automatic switch that stops the flow of electricity when suddenly overloaded or otherwise abnormally stressed. It can easily be reset without fear of breaking a nail. As an accidental housewife, I think of the words *circuit breaker* a bit more personally: I define it as the point at which we accidental housewives have had enough of our normal day-to-day stress and although over-loaded have little opportunity to "reset." But, I digress.

Some homes may have a fuse box instead of a circuit breaker, but regardless of which one you have, they both take care of the same stuff.

A circuit breaker box is silver and hangs on a wall in your basement, garage, or utility room. It is filled with a variety of switches that stop and start the flow of electricity to different zones and items such as lights, electronics, or appliances. When a circuit turns off by itself it is referred to as having "tripped."

Some breakers show something red when they've tripped, which will help you ID which one it is. Once you've located the tripped switch, simply press it all the way to OFF and then press it all the way back to the ON position. Easy enough! If you're fortunate enough to have an anal household member, he or she may have labeled the switches by room as well. This will enable you to easily locate the right switch for the right job and not accidentally short-circuit your home.

If you have a fuse box, the fuse "blows" instead of trips. You can tell it's blown if its glass top or the glass itself looks smoky. Unlike a circuit breaker switch, which you flip to fix, you'll need to replace the blown fuse with a new one. Make sure to turn off the main switch first and the "blown" appliances, electronics, or lights.

A note of caution: If you feel any heat other than your own body heat when you're checking the circuit breaker, call your electrician pronto. The problem may be beyond our accidental housewifely ability and may require a "trip" from a pro. Also, if it keeps tripping you may have a short, which means you may have overloaded a specific circuit, have a loose connection, or there is some other problem that someone in the know should deal with.

CENTRAL HEATING AND A/C

PROBLEM: No Heat or No A/C

K.I.S.S. IT

Here are a few Keep It Simple Stupid tips to try before you call for help:

- Check that your thermostat is in the heat or A/C mode and set it to the temp desired.
- Adjust the heat or A/C up or down a few degrees to see if the system clicks on or off.
- Visit your circuit breaker or fuse box to see if it's taken a "trip" or "blown."
- *If feeling ambitious:* Check to see if your furnace's pilot light is out. If so, relight it carefully with a long fireplace matchstick to avoid burning yourself! Do not use a Bic or any other small, handheld lighter to relight it.

CEILING FANS

PROBLEM: Wobbles

BROTHER, CAN YOU SPARE A DIME?

What you'll need:
- Penny, dime, or quarter
- Scotch tape
- Step-ladder
- Optional: someone tall, dark, and handsome nearby to catch you if you wobble

What you'll do:
- Turn the fan off.
- Step onto the ladder and tape your coin of choice to the top of one blade.
- Turn the fan on. If you still see it wobbling or it looks unbalanced, try another blade until you find the source.

If still imbalanced (your fan, not you!) it may be time to either replace the fan or call in your handy-dandy repairman.

FLOORS

PROBLEM: SQUEAKS

CHILD'S PLAY: SPRINKLE, SPRINKLE

What you'll need:
- Child (five or older)
- Baby powder
- Broom

What your kiddie will do:
- Sprinkle the powder over the floor and then sweep so it gets into the cracks and fills them.

DOORS

PROBLEM: GAPS

CHILD'S PLAY: STICK IT!

What you'll need:
- Child (five or older)
- Dollar bill

What your kiddie will do:
- Let your kiddie do the good ol' dollar bill gap test like you can do to check your fridge seal (see page 246).
- Place "George" in the door and if he or she can pull it out it's time to spend a few bucks on buying new weatherstripping. Installing it is your call, since there are several ways to go depending on eye appeal, durability, and your desire to fix it or have a pro do the job. Just in case you're one of the few of us who choose to try your hand at it, here's an easy fix-it option. PLEASE NOTE: THIS IS NOT A CHILD'S PLAY ACTIVITY! *Sorry!*
- SELF-STICK FOAM: The name sort of says it all—you can generally find it at

your local hardware store or at retailers like Home Depot and Lowe's. There'll be instructions on the package but if you're too lazy to read it you'll need a tape measure and a knife or shears. Then cut and stick it on. Be warned: This is a quick fix-it and not the most durable replacement, but it's good enough for an accidental housewife!

SHOOT IT!

If you're feeling ambitious or have had one of those days when you feel like shooting someone but don't want to spend the rest of your life in jail, here's a less offensive alternative and a good gap fixer.

What you'll need:
- Caulking gun
- Ladder (optional)

What you'll do:
- Take your caulking gun and stroll around the inside and outside of your house "shooting" in the holes or leaks everywhere you see them (for example, windows and doors). Be sure to buy a caulking gun that is dripless since you don't want to create more work for yourself.

PROBLEM: CREAKS

Here are two simple ways to keep you from becoming unhinged every time that creaky cabinet or family room door opens.

TAKE AIM

What you'll need:
- Nonstick cooking spray

What you'll do:
- Spray directly into the top and sides of each hinge on your door.
- Sop up any excess with a paper towel.
- Repeat until the squeaks are silenced. Note: You can also try this solution if your key or door lock is sticking.

PUCKER UP!

What you'll need:
- Lip balm

What you'll do:
- Rub some lip balm where the hinges meet and move the door back and forth until you have peace and quiet.

WALLS

PROBLEM: CRACKS

We get lines as we get older; houses get cracks. (Actually, the cracks are from the house settling.) Regardless of how or why these things happen, I believe that's why God invented Botox and spackle. It's also why I figured you were ready for a slightly more challenging fix-it, since we can all relate to the notion of "no pain no gain," particularly when it comes to preserving ourselves and, oh yeah, our homes. If you can't, hand over this fix-it to your preteen or older Picasso that you deem worthy and capable of this work.

CHILD'S PLAY: GET PLASTERED

What you'll need:
- Child (twelve or older)
- Spreading knife or emery board
- Vacuum
- Paintbrush or sponge
- Water
- Premixed spackle (Adults: Please read packages to be sure of any safety issues.)

What they'll do:
- Gently chip off loose plaster with a knife or use the rough side of an emery board.
- Use the upholstery attachment on your vacuum to suck out any dust in the crack.

- Use a clean paintbrush or sponge dampened with water to lightly wet the crack.
- Use the knife to fill up the crack with the premixed spackle.
- Smooth it out and let dry.
- Eliminate any roughness with your emery board.
- GROWN-UP FRIENDLY REMINDER: Look for shrinkage. If you find any, try some Viagra—oops, wrong problem—I meant to say you'll need to have your preteen Picasso do it again!

TABLES

PROBLEM: DENTS AND SCRATCHES

GO NUTS!

What you'll need:
- Pecans or walnuts
- Nutcracker
- Soft cloth
- Bottle of your favorite brew

What you'll do:
- Gently rub the nuts into the scratch and buff with cloth.
- Grab a bottle of beer to enjoy with the remaining nuts.

COFFEE BREAK
(This is a great fix-it for darker wood furniture.)

What you'll need:
- 1 tablespoon instant coffee (regular or decaf—it's your call!)
- 1 teaspoon water
- Soft cloth
- Mug

What you'll do:
- Mix up the coffee and water to make a paste (it's a 3:1 ratio, similar to the one you used for the baking soda and water paste).

- Using the cloth, rub the coffee paste into the scratch. *Do not add milk or sugar!*
- Let sit a couple of minutes and gently buff away the excess.
- Now take a coffee break!

CHILD'S PLAY: COLOR BY NUMBER

What you'll need:
- Child (five or older)
- Wood touch-up pens, wax sticks (available at local hardware stores), or your kiddie's crayons
- Blow dryer
- Soft cloth

What they'll do:
- Find the closest color touch-up pen, wax stick, or crayon.
- Color in the scratches.
- If the area isn't smooth, use a blow dryer to soften the crayon or wax and buff with a soft cloth.

PROBLEM: BURNS

NAIL IT

What you'll need:
- Nail polish remover
- Soft cloth
- Clear nail polish

What you'll do:
- Use a soft cloth dampened with nail polish remover and rub lightly. Fill in with clear polish to even out the hole.

Alternatively: You can also try coloring it in using a color-coordinated marker.

VACUUM

PROBLEM: CLOGGED VACUUM HOSE

GET YOUR AUGER-ACHIEVER!

Use your drain auger—that's the one you will use to fix bathroom clogs—to clear it out. Just place it at the mouth and let her rip! A brush handle may also help shove the yuk out.

For more riverting auger info see page 227.

PROBLEM: SUCKY ODOR

PERK IT UP!

If your vacuum's got a musky smell, perk it up with some coffee. Just sprinkle some fresh grounds on the floor and let it sip it up!

Bedroom Repairs

Bedrooms are truly your dream room when it comes to the repairs they need, so you'll be saying night-night soon enough. The repairs are also about as manicure-friendly and easy as they come—especially the final fix-it! If you're in need of more details or solutions regarding creaks, wobbles, gaps, and leaks feel free to flip back to "General Living Space Repairs" on page 192, since many of the same repairs may apply to your sleeping chambers.

OFFENSIVE REPAIRS TO REMEMBER

- *CLOGGING:* Vacuum filters and vents regularly to prevent clogs in your air conditioners and heating units.
- *WOBBLING:* Attach a coin of choice with tape to a blade to prevent your ceiling fan from shaking and wobbling.
- *WEARING:* Put throw rugs over the most trafficked spots, such as near the sides of the bed and in entranceways, to prevent scratches and wear and tear on carpets and floors.
- *SCARRING:* Cover dressers and night tables with fabric or decorative placemats to preserve the finish, so tossing stuff on them or spills from a nighty-nightcap won't harm them.
- *ROCKING:* Limit your sexual activity to maintain the sturdiness of the bed

frame and to keep the headboard from cracking or breaking—or forget the headboard and footboard and use just a mattress and box spring!

- *PRESERVING:* Keep these items handy, in case you need them.
  - Band-Aids—in case you cut your finger changing a lightbulb
  - Flashlight—to find the circuit breaker if a switch "trips"
  - Fresh batteries—for all remotes
  - Morning-after pill

How to Repair It Just Enough

BEDS

PROBLEM: CREAKY WOODEN BED

One solution might be to take a break and use it for what it was intended for— sleep—but try telling your kids or significant partner that unless you've been married ten years or longer.

BABY SOFT

What you'll need:
- Baby powder

What you'll do:
- Sprinkle powder into all the joints so they don't rub and make noise.

DRESSERS/NIGHT TABLES

PROBLEM: DRAWERS STICK

What you'll need:
- Candle or lip balm

What you'll do:
- Rub the candle or lip balm on the top and bottom interior edges of the drawer and/or track.
- Open and close. Repeat if it still sticks.

WALLPAPER

PROBLEM: TEAR

What you'll need:
- Piece of matching wallpaper
- Painters' tape
- Sponge

What you'll do:
Make sure the design and size of the piece of wallpaper matches what you're fixing.
- Tape the piece on top of the torn piece.
- Cut the new piece to create a patch that fits.
- Dip the sponge in hot water and dampen the torn area to unstick it.
- Wash off any yuk or glue that remains on the wall and let dry.
- Wet the patch and stick to the wall per instructions.
- If that fails, hang a picture or your child's artwork over the torn area.

PAINTED WALLS

PROBLEM: CRACKS, CHIPS, PEELING (WALLS, NOT CEILINGS)

What you'll need:
- Framed photos or other artwork

What you'll do:
- Hang photo over crack, chip, or peel.

I told you this last one was a no-brainer! Okay, if you want a "real" fix-it, turn to "Child's Play: Get Plastered" on page 198.

Laundry Room Repairs

Laundry room repairs are another one of my favorites because there aren't a lot of them that we accidental housewives can do without overloading. So what follows are just enough offensive tips followed by just enough simple fix-its to lighten the repair load.

OFFENSIVE REPAIRS TO REMEMBER

- *BE A STAR:* If your washing machine and dryer are more than ten years old, consider buying new ones before either starts to break down. Look for an Energy Star model since they use up to 50 percent less energy and will use less of your hard-earned money! Dryers don't sport the label since they all use about the same amount of energy. For more eco-saving tips flip to "A Convenient Truth" on page 243.
- *DE-LINT DE DRYER A LOT:* Every time you finish drying, be sure to clean out the filter so lint doesn't accumulate, because it can clog up your dryer's vents and exhaust hoses, which will minimize its ability to dry your wash thoroughly.
- *TAKE A VINEGAR SPIN:* Next time you're tossing your salad with some white vinegar pour a gallon of it into the washing machine and run it on a hot wash cycle without clothes. It will remove soap scum and hard water deposits, which in turn will prevent clogs!
- *SUCK IT OUT:* Twist off the exhaust hose located at the back of your dryer and vacuum both the hose and the vent to prevent lint from accumulating. And guess what else? Clogs!

How to Repair It Just Enough

WASHING MACHINES

PROBLEM: LEAKS OR OVERFLOW

ROW, ROW, ROW YOUR BOAT!

What you'll need:
- Your hands
- Telephone
- Life raft

What you'll do:
- Turn off the water supply valves located behind your washing machine.
- Call your plumber pronto as you and your household get into your dinghy.

PROBLEM: IT'S TIPSY, NOISY, OR VIBRATES*

RECRUIT A HUNK (OR HUNKESS)

What you'll need:
- Strong member of either sex
- Pliers or wrench
- Level and/or cold drink of choice

What you'll do:
- Unplug your washing machine.
- Have hunk or hunkess help you pull out the washer so you can adjust the feet and check the level.
- Use a wrench or pliers to adjust each of the two to four feet located on the bottom.
- Place the level or drink du jour on top of the machine. Adjust until the level is level or the liquid in your glass doesn't tilt. Be sure to check both the back and front!
- Have hunk or hunkess push the washer back in place and plug it back in.
- Wash down the drinks.

DRYERS

PROBLEM: LIGHTS OUT

SWITCH

What you'll need:
- Screwdriver (you'll have to check individual model to see what kind you need)

What you'll do:
- Check the circuit breaker and look for a switch that is in the OFF position. If you find one, flip it all the way back to the ON position. For more info on circuit breakers, flip to "Homeschooling: Day Tripping—Circuit Breakers" on page 194.

---

*This fix-it also works for your dryer. So if you find it's making lots of noise or shaking, keep your hunk or hunkess around to help you level this out, too. Have drink refills available.

- If no switch has "tripped," change the bulb. Depending on your model you'll probably need a screwdriver of some sort to get to it.
- If that doesn't shed any light, it's time to make that call!

PROBLEM: NOT HEATING

HANG THEM OUT TO DRY

What you'll need:
- Two hands and eyes

What you'll do:
- Check to see if you "accidentally" put cycle on "fluff," short drying time, or other low heat mode.
- If you didn't, go to the circuit breaker to see if one of the switches is in the OFF position. If so, flip it all the way to the ON position
- If that isn't the problem, call your handy-dandy repairman and hang your clothes in the sunshine to dry. I'll keep my fingers crossed that it's spring or summer!

PROBLEM: CLOGS

BLOW IT OUT

If you find that at the end of a cycle your clothes are still damp, too hot, or your dryer's making more noise than usual, your exhaust hose and vent could be clogged. (This also assumes, which I should never do, that you have checked your circuit breaker to see if anything is in the OFF position, the correct drying mode is selected, and/or if dryer is off-balance. If the latter is so, go to "Recruit a Hunk (or Hunkess)" on page 205.

What you'll need:
- Dryer vent brush, vacuum with small upholstery attachment, or high-powered blow dryer or leaf blower

What you'll do:
- Unplug the dryer.
- Unclamp the metal bands that are around the exhaust hose so you can remove it. FYI: The hose looks like a bigger, firmer Slinky without any openings and it is connected to an exterior vent.

- Check to see if there are any crinkles, rips, or tears.
- If you find none, clean the vent and exhaust hose with your "blower" of choice. FYI: The vent is located outside but its exact location depends upon where your laundry room is, so you'll have to take a field trip around your home to locate it.
- Reclamp and attach the exhaust hose. Be sure you don't have too many crinkles or bends because they can create clogs or lint buildup and minimize airflow.
- Move the dryer back and plug it in.

If you're still experiencing all the same problems, reach for the phone!

PROBLEM: GAS SMELL

This is a potentially *big* problem that no accidental housewife should deal with, so call your local utility man the minute you smell gas (unless you and yours have just eaten beans and the fumes are the aftermath of this or a similar culinary delight!). Then evacuate your household pronto.

Kitchen Repairs

The kitchen is a place where repairs generally result from appliances breaking down. These repairs usually involve gas lines or electrical know-how and expertise that we accidental housewives should not get involved with due to the potential for personal and/or household harm. That said, there are a few simple things that you can do to prevent key appliances from breaking down sooner rather than later and to keep everyday things running smoothly without spending money on a repairman or obtaining a degree from MIT.

OFFENSIVE REPAIRS TO REMEMBER

FRIDGE
- ***SAVE YOUR ENERGY:*** I've said it before and I'll say it again, if your fridge is close to or past its maintenance contract, buy a new Energy Star model—it'll be worth the investment, since the average savings on your electric bill will be pretty amazing. A nineteen-year-old fridge can cost you about $288 per year while an Energy Star model will run you about $91 per year, which, according to my calculator, means you'll save about $200 annually. That's some cool savings.

- **KEEP YOUR SEAL SOFT LIKE A BABY'S BUTT:** If you keep the rubber seals that outline the inside of your fridge's door clean and well lubricated you shouldn't have to repair them. So every few weeks while making that daily call to your mother:
  - Take a microfiber cloth dampened with a little water and detergent and wipe.
  - Next, put a very thin coating of Vaseline on the seal to keep it from drying out. This will also help prevent any mold and mildew from growing.

FREEZER
- **DEFROST DEUX TIMES A YEAR:** If your freezer does not have an automatic defrost feature, defrost it one to two times a year to ensure that airflow and temperature remain consistent. I'm pretty sure you'll have to shut it off to do this—check your manual for exact instructions.
- **BREAK THE ICE WEEKLY:** To avoid clumping in your ice maker and potential breakdowns, stir up the ice or start serving more drinks during cocktail hour. Better yet, why not throw a party monthly and use all those suckers up so you can let your icemaker make new ones and thereby avoid clumping altogether.

A WORD OF CAUTION: When defrosting your freezer or icemaker, do not use any sharp objects to chip off ice or loosen it unless you're an accomplished ice sculptor. You don't want to puncture your freezer or yourself!

STOVE
- **SING THE BLUES!** If you don't have your sunglasses on and you notice that the flame on your stove is yellow instead of blue, this probably means that your stove is not operating properly. So before it explodes, check your warranty/service contract (if you can find it) or call a repairman pronto while you order dinner in or, better yet, play it safe and eat out.

SINK
- **PUT IT ON A FAT-FREE DIET!** Never throw grease or fat down your sink unless you'd like it to clog. Grease and fat act like glue and will cause the other food particles you send down to stick to your pipes (sort of like the fat and grease from a juicy cheeseburger sticking to your arteries!). Same thing goes for what you feed your garbage disposal, so put it on a grease and fat-free diet, too! Instead:

- Pour the grease or fat into a plastic bottle, jar, milk carton, wine bottle, or anything else that you can throw it away in.
- Use your sink strainer to block out all the foodstuff that comes off your dishes, pots, and pans.
- *Weekly:* Boil up a kettle of water, make yourself a cup of tea or coffee, and pour the remaining water down the drain to help melt away the grease.
- *Monthly:* Pour 1/4 cup baking soda or 1/2 cup salt down ye ol' drain. Add a cup of white vinegar, let it fizz and bubble, and then pour a kettle of boiling water down.

Garbage Disposal

- ***ONLY SEND DOWN SHRED-WORTHY STUFF!*** We sometimes forget that our garbage disposal isn't a trash can, but rather a place where food goes to be shredded into bits. That's why it's important not to send stuff down there that it can't handle. No-nos include grease, fat, coffee grounds, and potatoes (they'll form a starchy paste). For the stuff that is shred-worthy:
- *Daily:* Run lots of cold water after you send gook its way to help it go down the pipe and prevent stuff from getting stuck.
- *Weekly:* Send a pot of boiling water down to break up any grease or fat that's holding on. (Obviously, when you're doing this for the sink you're also doing this for your trusty disposal, so look at this as multitasking!)

Dishwasher

- ***TURN ON YOUR KITCHEN FAUCET!*** This is more of a tip to ensure that you don't waste energy and time. The kitchen sink and dishwasher usually share the same water flow so you can "heat up" the dishwasher water by running hot water in your sink for a minute before you turn it on. Doing this will also help minimize greasy film and soapy residue on your load.
- ***TOSS SOME VINEGAR DOWN YOUR DRAINO!*** Bi-monthly, pour a quart-size bottle of white vinegar in the tank and run it through one regular cycle *without* any dishes. It'll help get rid of any grease, detergent, or debris from the foodstuff you left on your pots and plates as well as that fishy smell.

Keep an Emergency Kitchen Kitty

Put all the following in a handy-dandy caddie under your sink:

- ***FASHIONABLE AND FUNCTIONAL RUBBER GLOVES*** to maintain your manicure

- *NONCAUSTIC DRAIN CLEANER*
- *CUP PLUNGER:* The red cup is the only one you need in the kitchen. Of course, you may be one of those who have chosen to own only the flange since you can push up the inside rim and use it as an all-purpose plunger—but I ask: *Why would you want to use the same plunger that you use for toilet duty (pardon the pun) for kitchen duty—particularly with "vagina" as its slang British name?*
- *SEVERAL HAND TOWELS:* These should be given out to all household members in case you overcook something, causing smoke to billow and set off your smoke alarm. Have them unfold the towels and do the wave simultaneously until you can see one another. Also, open windows to avoid smoke inhalation!
- *FIRE EXTINGUISHER:* You don't have to go for the garden variety red ones, there are those out there that look sleek and functional. Be sure to keep them within arm's reach and view near cooking areas including where your toaster oven sits! I like First Alert's Tundra Fire Extinguisher Spray since it's about the size of humongous can of hairspray and there's no pin to pull. All you do is just point and spray. Very manicure-friendly and small space-friendly. Go to www .firstalert.com to check it out or Google Tundra Fire Extinguisher to learn more.

How to Repair It Just Enough

KITCHEN SINK

PROBLEM: CLOGS

POUR
There are two options:

What you'll need:
1. Two or three cans of cola
2. Drain cleaner

What you'll do:
1. Empty the cola down the sink and let sit for two to three hours.
2. Pour drain cleaner down the drain per its instructions (I prefer the noncaustic

stuff like Bio-Clean, but Drano and Liquid-Plumr are fine, too. Just remember to read the directions and wear rubber gloves!) Unless otherwise instructed or warned against, flush with hot tap water for five to ten minutes.

BOIL

What you'll need:
- Tea kettle or large pot
- Hot water

What you'll do:
- Boil water in a tea kettle or large pot
- Slowly pour it into the drain and see if the clog dissolves.

BUBBLE

What you'll need:
- Baking soda
- White vinegar
- Measuring cup
- Boiling water

What you'll do:
- Pour 1/2 cup baking soda down the drain followed by 1/2 cup vinegar and let sit. It should get bubbly and foamy.
- When the bubbling stops, immediately pour down a fresh kettle of boiling water. Depending on how clogged your sink is you may need to repeat.

PLUNGE

What you'll need:
- Cup plunger
- Vaseline
- Rag or duct tape

What you'll do:
NOTE: *If you have a double sink, seal the unclogged drain with a rag or use duct tape.*

- Fill the sink with enough clean water to cover the plunger's head (approximately two to three inches). Apply a thick layer of Vaseline to the plunger's head to create more suction. The water level will help you know if the clog is unclogging since it will start to drain if it is.
- Next, start plunging! Push up and down until your arms begin to tire—be forewarned, it may take your building up a sweat to break up the gook and grease. Think of it as exercise!
- Flush through any remaining stuff with hot tap water.

If this doesn't work here's the final fix-it to try before calling your plumber:

SNAKE

What you'll need:
- Sink auger/hand snake (see "Homeschooling: A is for Auger" on page 227.)
- Bucket or some kind of yuk receptacle

What you'll do:
- Run the cable down the drain until you feel a block—the clog. Be patient and slow since it has to bend around the pipes and you don't want to cause another problem by breaking a pipe.
- Keep extending the cable until you've gotten through the clog. When you think you've got it, crank the handle counterclockwise to grab the yuk that should be on the end of the cable. Toss in bucket or wherever else you've designated as the yuk receptacle.
- Rinse the drain with hot water for three minutes.

NOTE: *If your cable's clean or your arm is worn out from repeating this fix-it a few times, fawgetabout it and call your plumber!*

Oh, I almost forgot, I do have one more manicure-friendly fix-it.

UNSCREW

I noticed that my kitchen sink does not have a U-shaped pipe since we put in a water-softening system. I have a straight-looking pipe that I don't want to mess with.

Clearly you're in luck if you have the same since I don't have any repairs for this, so you'll need to call your plumber. For those of you who have a U-bend pipe, this fix-it is for you.

What you'll need:
- Bucket
- Towels
- Pliers
- Wire hanger—unwound
- Toothbrush
- Optional: small pillow or stool to sit on

What you'll do:
- Sit on a stool or place a pillow under your knees and look for the U-shaped tube under your sink.
- Place the bucket under the U-shaped tube to catch anything that might come out when undone.
- Loosen the outer rings at each end of the U-shaped tube either by hand or with a pair of pliers. Slide them up or to the side so you can remove the U-shaped tube.
- Clean the pipes (both the one you removed and those it's attached to as best you can) with the hanger and/or your toothbrush. Dump the gunk into the bucket as you go.
- Rinse out the U-shaped tube in hot water and replace it by screwing the rings tightly enough to prevent it from leaking.
- If you have a problem with the tube—it is cracked or you want to replace it—it's best to bring it to your local home improvement store so they can tell you exactly what you need.

If this doesn't solve the problem, your work here is done. Time to call your plumber!

PROBLEM: FAUCET HEAD LEAKS

What you'll need:
- Duct tape

What you'll do:
- Wrap the source of the leak tightly and call your plumber.

'Til Trap Do Us Part

Like many of us I often take my jewelry off when I wash dishes. Well, one of those times I accidentally dropped my symbol of betrothal down ye ol' kitchen sink. As a result, I was forced to figure out how to retrieve my wedding band before my hubs noticed it was missing from my hand since I'd expressed to him numerous times that this piece of jewelry had become more of a symbol of a jail sentence and less a token of our undying love and devotion. So I called my plumber, who, though appreciative of the hundred bucks he earned, showed me how simple it is to unscrew the pipe where it had fallen and retrieve my band, which had found its way to the trap below my sink. This trap is the one shaped like the letter *U* and its real job is to stop the toxic gases our sewer system emits from getting into our homes. (My friendly Ace Hardware guru shared that.) In my case it trapped my wedding band among the gook and yuk that had taken up residence there. Trapped again 'til death or divorce do us part!

PROBLEM: FAUCET HEAD DEPOSITS

What you'll need:
- White vinegar
- Hand towel, rag, or plastic bag
- Hair clip or duct tape
- Toothbrush
- Disinfecting wipes—low streak formula

What you'll do:
- Drench a towel with vinegar.
- Wrap the towel around the faucet head and use a hair clip or duct tape to secure it. Leave overnight.
- Scrub remaining debris with toothbrush.
- Clean with disinfecting wipes.

GARBAGE DISPOSAL

Lots of times problems with your disposal can be solved by clearing up clogs in your sink, so if it's backing up you might want to try one of the clogged sink fix-its on pages 210–213 either before or after trying one of these.

PROBLEM: NOT CHOPPING

PRESS-TO!

- Reset the small red button on the bottom of your disposal simply by pressing it and pray it works.
- Check your circuit breaker to see if the switch for the disposal has flipped off.

SEE THE LIGHT!

If your sink has a removable stopper try this:

- Turn the disposal switch to the OFF position and flip the circuit breaker switch that controls the power to the OFF position to ensure you don't chop off your hand. FYI: I would still not put my hand down the disposal just in case.
- Use a flashlight to check if anything's causing the clog and use tongs or chopsticks to remove.
- When you think you've got it all, turn the circuit breaker switch back to the ON position and give it a chop.

"S" MARKS THE SPOT

- Turn the disposal switch to the OFF position.
- Flip the circuit breaker switch that controls the power to the OFF position.
- Find the little red button and look for a hole next to it. This hole is for the squared-off s-shaped hexagonal tool that came with your disposal—if you've "accidentally" misplaced it, you can most likely get another at your local hardware store.
- Put the "s" tool in and turn it a few times to manually move the blades and to hopefully break up any yuk that may be causing it to clog.
- Remove the "s" tool and switch the circuit breaker ON. If that doesn't work and you've tried some of the repairs I've shared for clogged sinks, start dialing! It's time to call your repairman.

DISHWASHER

If your sink or garbage disposal starts to back up when your dishwasher is running, it's probably because one of them is clogged (they share a common drain). So the first thing you want to do is turn your dishwasher off.

PROBLEM: NOT DRAINING

TEE OFF

What you'll need:
- Toothbrush or spike cleaning brush (golf)

What you'll do:
- Wait until the dishwasher cools and then flip off the dishwasher's circuit breaker switch so you don't electrocute yourself.
- Look on the bottom of your dishwasher where the spray arm is and unhinge or unscrew the hub cap (the arm will come with it).
- Release the strainer's clips. Use your toothbrush or spike brush to brush away the yuk that's in there.
- Replace and turn your power back on. If that doesn't work, check to see if your sink's U-shaped tube is clogged. (See "Unscrew" on page 212.) If all fails and you can still float your rubber duckie in there. . . . You guessed it! Time to call your repairman.

REFRIGERATOR

PROBLEM: TIPSY FRIDGE

If your fridge isn't level it can cause:

- Doors do not close properly, which means your food won't stay cold.
- Clogging in your ice-maker.
- Increased energy bills.

ON THE LEVEL

What you'll need:
- Level
- Pliers
- Hunk or Hunkess
- Optional: Accidental Housewife Dirty Martinis or libations of choice

The Dirt on Dirty Dishes

There are several reasons your dishes may not come out spanking clean when you put them in the dishwasher, so if you're noticing that they still have crud on them, one of the following may be causing it.

1. BLOCKAGE: I always feel there's room for one more dish in this most manicure-friendly appliance, but the truth is that the more you pile in, the less clean they'll be. That said, before you think your pal isn't working properly, make sure that none of your dishes are blocking one of the following.

- *Detergent dispenser*
- *Spray arm(s):* You may have two—one on the bottom and one under your glass rack, so check both to make sure they can rotate freely.
  - Every now and then you should clean the holes in your spray arms using the end of a heavy-duty paper clip or a stiff wire. Be careful—you don't want it to break and get stuck, which will cause you more problems.
- *Water flow*

2. HARD ON: The amount of minerals in your water can affect how much or how little detergent you need. I can't tell you what amount you have, but your local water utility man (or woman) can, so ask them to pay you a visit and find out how hard you are—so to speak! Then you'll know how much detergent to use and all will be well.

3. HEAT IT UP: In order to wash stuff well, your dishwasher's temp has to be hot enough to dislodge the debris you left since you were too lazy to rinse your dishes thoroughly before putting them in. *How hot is that?* According to the pros it's 140 degrees minimum. *So how are you going to know?* By doing a simple test using your sink and a meat thermometer (if you have one):

- Let the hot water run until it gets hot.
- Place the thermometer under the hot water and keep it there for two minutes.

If it's too cool, you'll need to either turn up the heat on your dishwasher or, if it doesn't have a heat control, find your hot water heater and turn it up. Most water heaters are in the basement. If you live in an apartment, talk with your super! FYI: Water pressure may also have an effect, but to fix that you'll have to call in the pros so we'll move on!

What you'll do:
- Unplug the fridge to avoid electrocution and then place the level on top of it near the front and then in the back.
- Level by adjusting the feet (bolts) on the bottom with your fingers, or if it's been a while use a pair of pliers. To be safe as you adjust it, have a big strappy guy hold the fridge in case it tips.
- Recheck with the level or make a couple of martinis and place them on top of the fridge in the front and back. If all's well and nothing's tipsy, give one martini to your assistant and one to yourself to celebrate the fruits of your labor.

Problem: Blown Gasket

SEAL THE DEAL!

What you'll need:
- Screwdriver
- New gaskets/seals (found at your local hardware or home repair retail center)

What you'll do:
- Depending on if you have strips or seals that are attached by adhesive or screws, carefully remove, unscrew, or unstick and then install the exact same kind you had in the same way.

Problem: Clogged Ice Maker

What you need:
- Hands

What you'll do:
- Check to see if the arm in the ice maker is in a lowered position and nothing—like too much ice—is blocking it. FYI: The arm rises each time ice is dumped into the bin so if too much is in there, the arm will stay up yonder where its little brain knows to automatically shut it off.
- If a major iceberg has formed take it out of the bin and empty it. You might have to let it melt first.

- When you replace the empty bin, make sure the arm is in the DOWN position and keep your fingers crossed that it will resume working in time for cocktail hour.

PROBLEM: LIGHTS OUT
One of three things might have happened:

1. *FLIPPED CIRCUIT BREAKER:* Check the switch and flip it back to the ON position.
2. *BUTTON STUCK:* There's a little white button on either the top or bottom of your fridge that gets pushed in and out every time you open and close the door. If you see that it's in, it's stuck—genius, eh! Tap it to see if you can release it, then clean it with a small brush to get rid of any yuk.
3. *BULB BLEW:* Sometimes the obvious is overlooked. If the bulb hasn't blown, it may be loose. Use a dishtowel to protect your hands as you check to see if it's in tightly since it may be hot and I don't want you to burn yourself. If it's screwed in tightly and there's still no light, unscrew it and replace with the appliance bulb that's right for your fridge. Bring it in to your local hardware store to buy the correct one.

COOKTOPS/RANGES—GAS

PROBLEM: CLOGGED GAS PORTS
These will cause the flame to die out when you cook or it won't work at all. Hmmm, on second thought, this may be a signal from above that you shouldn't be cooking but eating out!

DO THE HOKEY POKEY

What you'll need:
- Safety pin, paper clip, or pipe cleaners
- Dampened microfiber cloth

What you'll do:
- Check the manual to see how to turn off the gas.
- Do the hokey pokey—poke out goop in gas ports with a pin or paper clip.

A NOTE OF CAUTION: *Do not use matches or toothpicks to dislodge goop since they could break and get stuck in holes. Not to mention that these pieces could ignite next time you cook if you overlook or forget the fact that they broke.*

- Wipe any goop with a dampened microfiber cloth. Feel free to clean knobs, grills, and any other removable parts by soaking them in hot water and cleaning them with dishwashing liquid.

PROBLEM: GAS SMELL

You want to get to the source of a gas smell as quickly as possible, since it could cause physical harm to all. The culprit could be one of two things:

1. A blown pilot light: Check your manual to see how to relight it safely. (FYI: If a burner doesn't ignite it could be the same problem, so this fix-it will work for that as well.)
2. A gas leak: This means you should *evacuate the household and call your utility company pronto*!

FRIENDLY REMINDER: If you shut your gas off during a repair don't forget to turn it back on per the instruction manual unless you're using it as an excuse to order in or eat out.

MICROWAVE

I've always loved my microwave since it makes feeding my family so easy. And now I have even more reason to love it and so will you: According to the Consumer Product Safety Commission, it seems you should never ever try to fix the microwave. Apparently, even if it's unplugged you can still electrocute yourself, since our mealtime pal uses such high voltage to work that it still has the potential to harm. Their recommendation: Call a professional. If you want to see if there's any other good news from our consumer product pals, you can visit them on the Internet at www.cpsc.gov.

TOASTER

PROBLEM: BREAD WON'T POP UP

THERE SHE BLOWS

Starting my day without gobbling down my toasted bagel is not a good thing! So here's a simple fix-it for you and me.

What you'll need:
- Blow dryer

What you'll do:
- Unplug and gently shake out any crumbs or bugs (just kidding, I hope!).
- Use a blow dryer to blow out the stuff that the shaking didn't dislodge.
- Replug and put in your bagel.

If that fails, go to Goldberg's Bagels in Wyckoff, New Jersey, and tell them I sent you. Then go and buy a new toaster—it'll be cheaper than taking it to repairman.

FLOORS

Problem: Chips in Linoleum or Vinyl Floor

GIVE IT A COAT

What you'll need:
- Clear nail polish

What you'll do:
- Apply one coat at a time and let dry.
- Keep reapplying until the chip is filled.

Bathroom Repairs

A human being . . . An ingenious assembly of portable plumbing. —W. C. Fields

Plumbing issues are the key problem in this toxic zone—both literally and figuratively. And, you'll pardon the expression, their end result can be truly disgusting, which is one of the reasons I saved them for last. We'll start with some fairly mindless ways to prevent toilets, sinks, tubs, and showers from either overflowing or stuffing up, which will make your lives happier, drier, and cleaner.

Homeschooling: Crossing the DWV—the Main Drains

In the event that your home is quickly filling up with water it may be helpful to know where the main drains are located. Everything in your home that uses water is connected to a central water supply system that is in your basement. The main drain can be turned off by turning a large wheel-like valve clockwise. This wheel is usually next to the water meter in your basement. Here, courtesy of my wonderfully poetic editor, is a simple, catchy reminder to help you know which direction turns your water off and on: Righty tighty, lefty loosey! Since I'm dyslexic, this doesn't help me much but I love saying it!

By the way, you also have local shut-off valves throughout your home that are usually found under or next to your faucets, sinks, toilets, and other key water dispensing places.

We continue: The main drain is connected to a septic tank or public sewer system—sounds like the game Operation! You'll be happy to know that the main drain in your home is separate from your drinking/water supply system. In the plumbing world this is known as the DWV—which stands for drain waste vent—system. So there you have it—riveting information, I know, but it may save you from rowing in your living room someday!

OFFENSIVE REPAIRS TO REMEMBER

REGULARLY
- *IF YOU CAN, REMOVE THE STOPPER IN YOUR SINK AND TUB* to remove any gunk that has accumulated. Weekly will be okay, but daily is better.
- *REMEMBER TO FLICK YOUR DISPOSABLE CONTACTS INTO THE GARBAGE OR TOILET AND NOT YOUR SINK.* They may seem like flimsy nothings but those babies can clog up your sink's drain quickly and what you'll be seeing is a nice puddle of water forming. So toss or flush them down the toilet—as far as I've been able to learn they don't clog up your septic tank but to be safe ask your local waste management folks.
- *CLEAN THE HAIR FROM YOUR DRAINS DAILY.* Okay, that may require too much thought, but try to do it weekly—either that or consider shaving your head!

- *DON'T FLUSH ANYTHING THICKER THAN TOILET PAPER DOWN THE OLD THRONE.* Things like paper towels, Tampax, Q-tips, turtles, and baby alligators are major cloggers and could back up your entire sewer system. Clearly this would be a nightmare to fix—not to mention the time and expense required.

EVERY NOW AND THEN

For those of you who are a bit more anal and have some brain cells left to remember these things, here are a few simple longer-term offensive repairs.

- *MONTHLY:* Pour boiling water or a mixture of $1/2$ cup white vinegar and $1/2$ cup baking soda down each of your drains to help clean them out.
- *EVERY SIX MONTHS OR SO:* Pour a noncaustic drain cleaner down your drains. Use one of the ones suggested for your bathroom's defensive emergency kit.
- *ONCE A YEAR:* Have your plumbing system inspected, cleaned, and checked by the pros. In my neck of the woods, there are plumbers that offer annual service agreements for automatic checkups. I suspect your area may have the same. Check the yellow pages and let your fingers do the walking so you won't have to remember this offensive tip every year.
- *EVERY TWO TO THREE YEARS* (that should give you enough of a buffer to remember!): If you have a septic tank, call in the professionals to inspect it. Trust me, this can save you tens of thousands of dollars. I know from experience and from the fact that I was forced to give up my dream of new diamond earrings on my tenth anniversary for a septic system renovation nightmare. Instead, I now own a lovely pair of zirconiums.
- And remember to keep an emergency defensive bathroom kitty. Fill it with the key things that you'll need and know how to use. The critical words here are *know how to use*, which is why I've tried to keep this list fairly short:
  - BUCKET: For bailing
  - RUBBER GLOVES: So you don't have to touch that yuk
  - DRAIN CLEANER: This is your first and simplest defense when any of your drains stuff up. I prefer using the noncaustic kind, which is different from the store-bought varieties, which work well, but they require me to think. Thinking fast is often a problem when I'm in a state of panic. I don't read directions, which means I'll probably forget to put on my rubber gloves and goggles to avoid possible burns and eye and nose irritations as the warnings mention

before pouring. But if you're cool, calm, and collected during these times—go for it. One more thing to remember—before using these store-bought varieties check that it's okay to use them if you have a septic system.

Now back to the noncaustic: Here are a few I've tried:
- Bio D—Available online
- Bio-Clean—Available online
- Two cans of cola (rum optional!)
- HANGER: Unwound wire hanger to snake down ye ol' drain
- PLUNGER: Like most things these days, even plungers have their specialty. To those in the know they're sometimes called plumber's helpers. Fortunately, you don't need a degree in engineering to figure out which you need for what since there are only two:
  - *Cup plunger*—these are the red ones we always see. They're used to unclog kitchen and bathroom sinks, showers, and tub drains.
  - *Flange plunger*—these are black (wonder why?) and specifically shaped for toilet clogs.

  NOTE: If you decide you can deal with only one, go with the flange. You can flip the flange—which is the inside cup—up into the interior and it will act like a cup plunger. Because of its flexibility it can be used for all common household clogs. I don't recommend this, however, since the plunger that has come into contact with all the crap in my toilet is not the same one I want to use where I brush my teeth or wash my family's dishes.
- FLASHLIGHT: It's good to have so you can see what you're doing and if you're curious as to what's causing the clog.
- FLOATIE GEAR: Have personalized floaties, wet suits, and snorkel gear at the ready, stored in sealed plastic bags.

How to Repair Just Enough

And now my friends, it's time for the poop on dealing with your home's grossest medley of repairs. We begin with the number-one cause of bathroom ruin and rage: ye family throne. Put on those gloves, grab your septic septer (your plunger), and tally-ho—let's get to the bottom of it!

Homeschooling: A Flange Is a Flange Is a Vagina!

My fascination with the word *flange* led me to learn that the primary definition of the word is a protruding rim or edge that holds something in place or helps it attach to another object. Digging a bit deeper, I also found that it means the underside of a golf club. And, as I dug a bit deeper, I learned, much to my chagrin, that it's British slang (vulgar, I'm told) for vagina. Truth be known, ever since I learned of the Brits' defintion I've not been able to look at the flange or the hole in my t-bowl quite the same way, if you catch my drift!

TOILETS

PROBLEM: CLOGS
IMPORTANT REMINDER: *Do not flush again until it's fixed.*

JE NE SAIS FLANGE

What you'll need:
- Towels (old, raggedy ones recommended)
- Flange plunger (that's the black one with the inner cup)—see "Homeschooling: A Flange Is a Flange," above.

What you'll do:
- Wait a few minutes to see if the water level goes down a bit. While you're waiting, put some towels down.
- Place the flange (I love the name of this plunger—it *almost* makes using it sound like a heroic act until you learn its British translation!) over the hole in the toilet, making sure it's under water and sealed.
- Plunge up and down for a minute or two, gaining gusto with each push.
- Lift slightly to see if the water level is going down. If it isn't: *Do not flush again* and read on!

SNARE 'EM

What you'll need:
- Water closet auger or toilet snake
- Towels (ragged ones suggested)
- Bucket
- Rubber boots

What you'll do:
- Put towels around the floor surrounding the toilet.
- Put the auger over and into the drain and feed the cable down into it. *WARN-ING: This will take a bit of arm muscle so if you're feeling tired or not in the mood, call your plumber pronto!*
- If you're still threading and think you've reached China, stop. If you've hit the clog, hook it, and continue twisting the auger as you pull it up. Put the yuk immediately into the bucket.
- Flush the toilet to test—have your rubber boots on just in case.

PROBLEM: RUNNING TOILETS

JIGGLE AND WIGGLE

What you'll need:
- Your right or left hand

What you'll do:
- Jiggle the handle. Sometimes the chain or guide wire attached to the handle gets stuck. These two things are located inside the tank and are in easy sight should you wish to see what I'm talking about. Take a peek by lifting the lid—be sure to take off the box of tissues, magazines, or air freshener before you do.
- If a jiggle doesn't work, take the lid off to see if the black, rubber, floating ball is touching the side of the tank. If it is, wiggle it and gently bend the arm so it's free to go up and down.

Homeschooling: A IS FOR AUGER AS IN AUGER-WHELMED!

An auger is like a snake since it has a flexible cable with a steel bit on the end that helps break up and clear clogs in a sink, tub, or toilet. Like the plunger, there are two types of augers:

1. Sink auger—sometimes called a drum or canister auger, it can be used for kitchen and bathroom sinks, showers, and tubs

2. Water closet auger—used only for your personal throne (toilet)

You can use a snake or auger interchangeably in most places, but it's best to use the one that's a water closet auger for your toilet. The non–water closet variety can scratch your precious porcelain poopster. And besides, why would you want to use your sink auger or a snake in your toilet and risk having poopy remnants grace your sink or tub next time that clogs?

In any case, and if I haven't bored you enough, the reason it's called a water closet auger is because way back in the early days bathrooms were generally tiny rooms or closets with a toilet and perhaps a sink—fascinating isn't it?

On a lighter note: Since I discovered the auger it has become both my son's and my favorite bathroom tool since it reminds us of fishing—I know what you're thinking—what a great family activity!

PROBLEM: PUDDLES FORMING AROUND YOUR TOILET

CHILD'S PLAY: THE LEAKY TOILET TEST

What they'll need:
- Food coloring of choice
- Art paper

How they'll test it:
- Add a few drops of food coloring to the tank.
- Let it sit for a few minutes. If your bowl's sporting a red, green, or yellow cast, then you guessed it—you have a leaky toilet, so call your plumber.

- Flush pronto, since the food coloring can stain your tank and that'll mean you'll have to clean it!
- Use the rest of the food coloring to paint with your kiddies!

LEAKY BALL BUSTER

Another thing that may be causing the problem is that your ball's leaking in your tank. Checking this is easy:

1. Shut off the water by turning the shut-off valve clockwise—this valve is located below the tank and near the wall. Clockwise is turning it to the right and counterclockwise is toward the left.
2. Take the tank top off, unscrew the ball, and shake that baby. If you hear any water swishing around inside it's time to get a new ball! Don't forget to screw the ball back on in the meantime.
3. Turn your water back on by twisting it counterclockwise—or as Beyonce sang in her 2007 hit song of the same name: *to the left, to the left.*

By the way, any yuk on the ball or other parts is neither poop nor anything else that will disgust you. It's lime or some kind of mineral deposit that you can easily clean with white vinegar and an old toothbrush.

SEAL THE DEAL

What you'll need:
- Vaseline

What you'll do:
- The last stop in the tank and before you call it a day (and your plumber!) is to check if your flapper is sealing. Your flapper is that black rubber plug on the bottom of the tank that lets water in and out of your toilet—sort of like a sink stopper.
1. Before you reach down, turn your shut-off valve clockwise to off and then flush so your tank is empty. Reminder: The shut-off valve is located directly below the tank and close to the wall.
2. Dry the flapper and surrounding area and coat it with Vaseline to give the rubber a better seal.
3. Turn the valve counterclockwise to turn the water back and pray this works. If not, dial *P* for plumber!

Homeschooling: Crap and Crapper

There's lots of debate about the origin of the word *crap* that you may or may not care about, but for those who do give a crap, here's a bit of history, or at least hearsay:

- It's from a low German word: *krape*, meaning a vile and inedible fish

- It came from a British businessman named Thomas Crapper who didn't necessarily invent the toilet, but owned a plumbing company and several patents that had his name on them. One of those was for the toilet.

Tommy's toilets were used by World War I doughboys—slang for infantryman—who were passing through England and they had the manufacturers' name printed on the tank: T. Crapper—Chelsea. So as they say, the rest is history: The doughboys began referring to the toilet as the crapper and it became slang for our beloved throne. The End!

PROBLEM: FLAPPER'S FLAPPING, NOT FLUSHING

If when you push the handle down, it doesn't do anything it usually means you've got a disconnect, which you can fix with minimal effort.

FIXING THE FLAPPER

What you'll need:
- Both hands

What you'll do:
- Remove the tank cover and check to see if the lever that has the wire and chain has come unhinged from the flapper. (Friendly reminder: The flapper is the black rubber plug on the bottom of the tank.)
- If it has, just put your little ol' hands in there and reconnect it. If you don't see anything disconnected, put the lid back on.

Any other parts that may be causing this problem are below my "c" level—as in my comfort zone—therefore I will leave the solution to the pros. Feel free to share with

---

General Advisory

I f more than one sink, tub, or toilet is clogged, pour yourself a drink and immediately call the plumber.

---

me any simple ideas that won't ruin my manicure or mindset on my website www
.theaccidentalhousewife.com!

SINKS, SHOWERS, AND TUBS

These bathroom fixtures have their share of clogs, leaks, and drips, but they're far less disgusting to deal with than those you face with your toilet. Here are a variety of ways to fix any of these problems fast.

PROBLEM: CLOGS

Here are several simple solutions to deal with them beginning with the easiest to those that may require you to put in a little bit more TLC before losing your mind or ruining your manicure.

TWIST 'N' TURN

What you'll need:
- Tweezers or small scissors
- Screwdriver (for showers only)

What you'll do:
- *For sinks and tubs:* If you can, remove the stopper and clean off the gunk. Sometimes you have to turn the stopper counterclockwise (that's to the left) to remove it. If you can't, try to prop it as far as you can to reach the gunk. Use tweezers or small scissors to keep it propped up.
- *For showers:* Check the strainer cover to see if there's any hair clogging it up. You may have to unscrew the cover to get to it.

POP GOES THE STOPPER (FOR POP-UP STOPPERS ONLY)

What you'll need:
- Small pillow or stool
- Screwdriver
- Old toothbrush

What you'll do:
- Get on your knees or sit on a pillow or stool and look under the sink to find the screw that holds the stopper's rod in place. Clue: It's connected to the drainpipe.
- When you find it, unscrew, stand up, and pull out the stopper from above! Put the screw somewhere away from the sink so you don't accidentally wash it down.
- Clean off any gook with a toothbrush and check to see if anything looks worn or damaged.
- Put the stopper back and rescrew the stopper's rod below.

BAIT AND HOOK

What you'll need (for all):
- Wire hanger (unwound) or sink auger
- Flashlight
- Bucket

What you'll do:
- Use an unwound wire hanger or sink auger and snake it through the pipe to push any yuk through or to hoist the gunk up. You may want to use a flashlight to see what you're doing and what's down there.
- Put gunk in bucket.

Please note: You may need to run the hanger or snake through a few times.

DOWN THE DRAIN
There are two options:

What you'll need:
1. Two or three cans of cola
2. Drain cleaner (Noncaustic if available)

What you'll do:
1. Pour the cola down the sink, tub, or shower drain and let sit for two to three hours, or
2. Dispense drain cleaner down the drain per its instructions (again, I prefer the noncaustic stuff like Bio-Clean, but Drano and Liquid-Plumr are fine, too. Remember to read the directions and wear rubber gloves!).

Regardless of which you follow, you should run lots of hot water down to rinse any remains through.

TIME FOR TEA

What you'll need:
- Tea kettle or large pot
- Water

What you'll do:
- Boil water in a tea kettle or large pot.
- Slowly pour it into the drain and see if the clog dissolves.

If this doesn't work, get a tea bag and make yourself a cup of tea and save the rest of the boiling water for the following tip:

CHILD'S PLAY: MOUNT SINK HELEN'S

What you'll need:
- Child (twelve or older)
- Baking soda
- White vinegar
- Measuring cup
- Boiling water (adult required to boil and pour)

What they'll do:
- Pour ¹/₂ cup baking soda down the drain followed by ¹/₂ cup vinegar and let sit. It should get bubbly and foamy just like those erupting volcano experiments you did back in grade school! This is one of those fix-its that you can engage your kiddies to do since they love seeing what happens and it's safe.
- When the bubbling stops, it's time for adult intervention. Pour in a kettle of boiling water or the leftover boiling water from the preceding "Time for Tea" tip. **DO NOT LET ANY CHILD NEAR BOILING WATER.** Feel free to boil up another pot and send it down there as well . . . as my grandmother always says, "It can't hoit!"

NOTE: For shower and tub clogs double the dose: Pour a cup of baking soda and a cup of vinegar down . . . all else stays the same.

TAKE THE PLUNGE

What you'll need:
- Duct tape or waterproof large-sized bandages (sink only)
- Bucket or wet-dry vac (shower and tub only)
- Cup plunger
- Vaseline

What you'll do:
For the sink:

- Use duct tape to seal the hole located at the top of the sink and under the faucet. (This hole is known as the sink overflow outlet.)
- Remove the stopper if you can.

For the tub:

- Remove the stopper if you can or prop it up as much as possible with tweezers or small scissors.

For the shower:

- Unscrew the strainer cover.

For the tub and shower only:

- Suck up any standing water (that's the yucky water that won't go down due to the clog) with a wet-dry vac or empty as much as you can with a bucket. TIP: If you have a wet-dry vac, it may even suck out the problem so that you won't have to continue with what follows! DO NOT TRY THIS WITH ANY OTHER SUCKING DEVICE, SUCH AS YOUR HOUSEHOLD VACUUM CLEANER OR HAND VACUUM.

Then for all the above (sink, shower, or tub):

- *Fill 'er up!* Run enough fresh, clean water to cover the plunger's head (approximately two to three inches should do). The water level acts as a mindless way of letting you know when your clog begins to unclog, since it will start to go down ye ol' drain!
- *Start plunging!* That means push your plunger up and down several times with feeling, since it may take a bit of elbow grease to break up that yuk.

TIP: To help seal the plunger's head and give you more suction, put a thick layer of Vaseline around the rim.

If the plunger doesn't work here's my final fix-it to try before calling your plumber.

GO FISH!

What you'll need:
- Sink auger or hand snake
- Bucket or some kind of yuk receptacle

What you'll do:
For sinks and tubs:

- Remove the sink stopper if you can or at least prop it up.

For showers:

- Unscrew the strainer cover.

If using an auger:

- Run the auger cable down the drain until you feel a block—the clog. Pull out another foot of cable and tighten the set screw, which is located near the bottom.
- Keep extending the cable until you feel you've gotten through the clog.

If using a hand snake:

- Feed the end into the drain and when you feel the clog, crank the handle counterclockwise to "hook" that baby.
- Crank and pull as you "reel" in your catch.
- If you've gotten through, run hot water to see if the drain's good to go—that is, not backing up.
- Repeat running the auger cable or hand snake down. If you've run out of cable it probably means your clog is beyond your available "fishing" line so it's time to reel it in and call your plumber!

Okay, I lied again. . . . Here's one more clog-buster U can try but please note that this repair works only for your sink.

TAP INTO U TUBE

What you'll need:
- Small pillow
- Bucket
- Towels
- Wire hanger (unwound)
- Toothbrush

What you'll do:
- Put a pillow under your knees and look under your sink for a tube (pipe) that looks like the letter *U*. This is part of what Dan, my Ace Hardware Man in River Edge, refers to as a "trap" and its job is to stop toxic sewer system gases from entering our homes. In this case, it may be the cause of your clog.
- Place the bucket below the U tube to catch any water or gook that may be in there.
- Loosen the outer rings at each end of the U tube either by hand or with a pair of pliers (mine were plastic and actually had two raised areas to hold on to, so

---

Eh, What's Up, Doc?

Our favorite wabbit, Bugs Bunny, was always coming up with harebrained schemes to get even with his many foes. In one of his classic escapades, Bugs keeps distracting the famous opera singer Giovanni Jones from practicing. Well, being a cartoon character, Giovanni tries to stop Bugs from his antics by clobbering him with a variety of instruments. At first, Bugs, in his usual mild-mannered way, doesn't let it get to him, but by the third blow he declares, "*Of course you know this means war!*" And the battle begins: Bugs launches his attack by hammering the roof of the "acoustically perfect" concert hall and then sprays Giovanni's throat with alum, which shrinks his head. For those not familiar with alum, it's a salt-based product that you can find in the spice aisle at your supermarket and it's found in baking powder. It's also used for pickling, if you're interested in turning those cucumbers into garlicky delights. I use it to get rid of the scum and mineral residue on my shower head. (See "Eh, What's Up, Doc?" fix-it on page 239.)

Now, back to our tale: Well, clearly Giovanni's shrunken head didn't make him very happy but Bugs wasn't through with Giovanni—Bugs followed up his attack by having Giovanni hold a note until he burst, then the ceiling came crashing down on him, and then Bugs administered his final and most fatal blow—he played his banjo, which is how the whole ruckus started!

---

see if yours do as well). Slide them up or to the side so you can remove the U tube (pipe).

- Clean the pipes (both the U trap pipe and those it's attached to) with the hanger and/or your toothbrush, dumping the gunk into the bucket as you go.
- Rinse out the U trap pipe in hot water and replace by screwing the rings tightly enough to ensure it doesn't leak.
- If the problem prevails you may need a new tube, which is easy to replace. Bring the tube with you so your Dan can be sure to give you the right replacement tube.

If your sink's still clogged I give up—Call Roto Rooter!

PROBLEM: CLOGGED SHOWER HEADS

And so our shower clogs don't feel left out, here's one to help clear your head—so to speak—of soap scum and mineral deposits. Hope there's gold in them thar hills!

HomeSchooling: Compression, Ball, Cartridge, Disk, Sensor, Oh My!

Here's just enough info to ID your faucet should your plumber ask or should you want to make an impression by telling him what you have and what you want. By the way, if you opt for a new faucet ensemble, do your part as an accidental environmentalist and install a low-flow, metered, or sensor faucet.

Oldies and somewhat newies:

- **COMPRESSION FAUCET:** These are the granddaddies of faucets that we all are familiar with (at least those of us born in the last century!). They have separate hot and cold knobs that control the flow of water. They have washers and are the most leaky. Therefore, they require the most maintenance. My advice: As soon as you can, replace them with one of the newer guys on the block.

- **BALL FAUCET:** These are usually found in kitchens and were the first washerless faucets. This means they have more parts than newer models and therefore more places to leak. These faucets have one handle that has a rounded ball-shaped cap located above the spout. You use this ball-shaped cap to regulate the flow and temperature (left is hot, right is cool), thus the name ball faucet. Brilliant!

- **CARTRIDGE FAUCET:** These are washerless but they can be confused with a compression or ball faucet, since they come in two forms to help confuse you further:
  - **STEM:** These look like compression faucets since they have individual knobs for hot and cold. They say you can tell the difference by how smoothly the handle turns off, since it requires less pressure. I guess that also requires that you have a compression faucet in your home to help you tell the difference. I do and in a blind "turn" test, I failed and couldn't tell them apart!
  - **SINGLE HANDLE:** The easiest way to tell that it's not a ball faucet is by its handle, which has no ball—I love when they make it easy!

The latest and greatest least-likely-to-leak models (at least at the time I'm writing this):

- **DISK FAUCET:** This is often considered the Rolls-Royce of faucets and the one you want to install, since it doesn't break down very often. Why, you may ask? Because it uses only two disks to control the flow and temp and no washers, which are *soooo* yesterday. You can tell a disk faucet by its wide body and the single handle that sits above it, which has no ball. Starting to sound kind of sexy!

- **SENSOR FAUCET:** These are *très* cool! More important, they limit germs from spreading and are environmentally friendly, since they wait for your hand or toothbrush to glide under them and then they dispense a tempered water flow. No washers or disks, just good old-fashioned high tech! Batteries included! If you just want to update your existing faucet, you may be able to attach a sensor adapter—ask at your local home improvement store (Lowe's, Ace, or Home Depot) or go online and Google *sensor faucets and adaptors* to learn more.

  For those of you who are still having a hard time figuring out what kind of faucet you have or are using an old-fashioned water pump, I suggest you either call your plumber or, if you're in the mood, take pix and visit your local hardware store to have them ID it.

HEADS UP!

What you'll need:
- White vinegar
- Hand towel, rag, or plastic bag
- Duct tape, large rubber band, scrunchie, or hair clip
- Old toothbrush

What you'll do:
- Drench a towel or fill a plastic bag with vinegar.
- Wrap the towel around the shower head or top of the bag and secure with tape, a rubber band, a scrunchie, or a hair clip and let soak overnight.
- Use a toothbrush to scrub away the scum or minerals.

EH, WHAT'S UP, DOC?

What you'll need:
- Small bowl
- Alum (it's a salt-based spice used for pickling)
- $1/4$ cup lemon juice
- Dish towel or rag

What you'll do:
- Mix 1 teaspoon of alum with the lemon juice.
- Drench the rag in the mixture and scrub the shower head until the "mouth shrinks", i.e., deposits disappear. (Check what happened to Bugs Bunny to learn about shrinkage on page 236!)

PROBLEM: DRIPPY LEAKY FAUCETS

If you have older-style faucets you have to turn them gently because they have washers that wear out. That's why I suggest you consider replacing your older faucets with washerless faucets. Newer ones use cartridges instead of washers, which means they don't rub against one another. That means fewer leaks, parts, and repairs.

WRAP THE TAP

What you'll need:
- Duct tape

What you'll do:
- Wrap the source of the leak tightly.
- Call your plumber.

PART 5

EASY
ENVIRO-KEEPING

Chapter 12

A Convenient Truth

*Uh, Lisa, the whole reason we have elected officials is so we don't have to think all the time. Just like that rain forest scare a few years back: Our officials saw there was a problem and they fixed it, didn't they?—*Homer Simpson

The environment is big news these days, and with good reason. We've taken too much for granted for too long and we can't afford to ignore it, no matter how much we might want to. So it's time to wake up and smell some organically grown, fair-trade coffee that we can brew in our solar-powered coffeemaker. I know thinking green can be intimidating and everyone has their advice, which is why I'm not suggesting that we take Sheryl Crow's lead and count out toilet paper squares for our loved ones. But the truth is that with relatively little effort or inconvenience in our everyday lives we can help save our planet, one drip, watt, or gallon at a time. And, if the truth be further known, you'll also save money on your energy bills that you can use toward a facial, massage, or even that long overdue vacation, which, to quote Ms. Crow is "all I wanna do." And that, my accidental housewifely environmentalist, is a convenient truth!

The Bathroom

There are lots of simple things you can do in this toxic though largely degradable dumping zone that can help save the planet without stopping anyone in your home from showering, brushing, grooming, or pooping.

- *GET NEW HEADS:* Clearly, there are days I wish I could replace my head with a younger, less cluttered one, but I'm not referring to our noggins but our shower heads and our toilets, which naval types refer to as the head!*
- By replacing your standard shower head with a low-flow water-saving shower head you can save on your water heating costs. The down and dirty kind can cost you under ten bucks (installation not included). By the way, just because they're low-flow doesn't mean you have to feel like you're standing in a light drizzle, so ask for one that offers a strong enough stream.
- Changing your toilet to a low-flow model is a bit more expensive than changing a shower head, but it can reduce water consumption by about 40 percent. But if you'd rather walk before you run, simply replace a water-saving device like your toilet's flapper ball and flush valves. A simple fix-it, by the way, to help with leaks (which are a major water waster) is called "Leaky Ball Baster" on page 228.
- *CUT SHOWER TIME:* Before I realized how much money my son's marathon showers were costing me, I was glad that I could actually get him to take one. That was then, this is now: By taking a five-minute shower vs. a twenty-five-minute deluge, we're saving more than $200 a year. If you're a newlywed or living with a significant other, think of the romance of showering together. Not to mention how you're helping to save our planet! If estimating time is difficult for you, buy one of those waterproof shower radios and lather and rinse to no more than *two songs.*
- *BAN BATHS:* I suspect you don't have the opportunity to take one very often so you're "mindlessly" doing your part! But once the kiddies get beyond their need for rubber duckies and bubbles, switch to five-minute showers, since baths use about three times as much water.
- *STOP THE DRIPS:* If you're a light sleeper like I am, that drip from the bathroom faucet will keep you awake for hours. To preserve both your beauty sleep and water, stop the drip! Believe it or not, one drippy drop per second can add up to more than two thousand gallons of water in a year. Wow! To fix the drips, check out my simple manicure-friendly fix-its, on page 239 and read about some fab faucet options on page 237.

---

*The nautical term *head* goes back to 1485, when it was first used to describe the front part of a ship. That was where the ship's toilet was located, since it could be naturally cleaned by the splashing salt water. . . . I guess you could say they were enviro-mates! Arrrrrh!

- *A MATTER OF DEGREE:* Check to see if your water heater's temp is 120 degrees—keeping it there saves energy and anyone from burning themselves accidentally, particularly your little ones who enjoy turning those tub knobs! On the flip side, don't go lower than 120 degrees, since it won't help stop bacteria from growing.

- *WRAP IT UP!* According to the experts, if your water tank is more than fifteen years old you should "wrap it up" in a fiberglass blanket that you can get for less than $30 at your local hardware store, Lowe's, or Home Depot. And, yes, even an accidental housewife can handle this wrap since they generally come in a kit complete with easy-to-install instructions. Then again, since the instructions are so simple a child can do it, you might want to have your preteen son handle this one while you watch!

- *TURN THE OTHER CHEEK:* *No*, I haven't changed my mind. I'm not suggesting you do the Sheryl Crow toilet paper portion-control jingle. What I am suggesting is that you buy recycled toilet paper, which may not look as pretty but it's a much more enviro-friendly flush!

- *BEAUTY UNPLUGGED:* Whenever you're not using your curling iron, blow dryer, or flatiron—and once your shaver or toothbrush is charged according to your manual's instructions—unplug those suckers! If they're plugged in they're draining energy even when you're not using them. And, according to actor and environmentalist Ed Begley Jr., every time you use your curling iron it's like leaving on a lightbulb for a week. What can I say, it's not easy being green—or was that Kermit?

The Kitchen

Unless you eat out frequently or have roped it off, the kitchen is probably one of the largest energy-eating zones in your home, since it's filled with a plethora (I couldn't wait to find a place to use that word!) of appliances and gadgets, large, medium, and small. But by following, or at least being aware of, the following guidelines, you can be an eco-friendly housewife in the kitchen without breaking a nail, sweat, or your bank account.

- *REACH FOR THE STAR!* As in Energy Star—look for the Energy Star label when you buy an appliance and you'll be saving money and energy (see "Homeschooling: Starstruck Energy Star" on next page.)

- *SAVE A TREE!* Use recycled paper towels and you'll be saving our forests.

Homeschooling: Starstruck Energy Star

Look, it's a dishwasher, no it's a fridge, no it's Energy Star! You've probably seen the logo and may or may not have known exactly what it means, so here I go.

Energy Star was introduced in 1992 by the EPA (Enviromental Protection Agency). It is a joint program between the EPA and the Department of Energy to help us save moola and, most importantly, our planet. When you see the Energy Star logo it means that the item you're eyeing is energy efficient and it will help reduce greenhouse emmissions. For those who love trivia, computers and their monitors were the first products to wear the "energy star." If you'd like to learn more, follow your curiosity star to www.energystar.gov.

Fridge and Freezer

- *NOT TOO LITTLE, NOT TOO MUCH:* It may seem confusing, but it costs more to run a fridge when it's empty. So if you don't cook or eat at home a lot, put a bunch of water bottles in your fridge or use it as a wine cooler. On the other hand, if you put too much stuff in, the cold air can't circulate, and foods won't stay chilled. That means you need to keep it *not too full and not too empty*—I know what you're thinking: *Is nothing ever easy?*

  The same holds true for your freezer. Use bags of ice—*but not too many*—to keep it working efficiently.

  Oh, yes, one more thing that sort of relates to this. If you're going to buy a new fridge (or any appliance for that matter) don't buy one bigger than you need, because size counts (not in a sexual way). Bigger isn't better if it's just taking up space, since it'll use more energy and also cost you more money to run.

- *SHUT IT:* Every time your loved ones leave the refrigerator, freezer, oven door open, 30 percent of the cooled or hot air can escape. Be sure they close those doors pronto or you'll be hearing your energy bill go *ka-ching, ka-ching!*

- *CHILD'S PLAY: HAVE THEM STICK IT:* Bet your kiddies a dollar to see if your fridge's door seals are airtight. If the buck fits and you can't remove it, you lose or win depending on how you look at it. Bottom line: A buck that's stuck means all is well. If you win and the dollar comes out this means your doors are losing suction. Time to go directly to "Problem: Blown Gasket" on page 218.

Ovens, Ranges, and Stoves

- *DOWNSIZE:* Instead of using that oven, particularly if it's electric, do yourself a favor and tape it shut! Use your microwave, toaster oven, or your Crock-Pot, which can use up to 75 percent less energy to work. That or go out for dinner.

Dishwasher

- *ALL ABOARD!* Run your dishwasher only when you have a full load. If you want to multitask and save energy you can also throw in a dirty baseball cap or your child's sneaks.
- *AIR DRY:* Put it on the air-dry cycle and check to see if your dishwasher has any other energy-saving options. If you've added a baseball cap or sneaks, dry them in the sunlight. Then put a crumpled piece of newspaper in each shoe to absorb any lingering dampness (as well as any M & M buds—that's mold and mildew in case you've forgotten—that are thinking about moving in!).

Living Spaces

Televisions, DVDs, remotes, stereos, lights, computers—your living spaces are an electronic overload at your fingertips. And since none of us are going to sacrifice our next episode of *Grey's Anatomy* or *Oprah*, or connecting with our YouTube pals, you can connect with saving our planet by doing a few simple things:

- *CAN YOU HEAR ME NOW?* You're draining energy by leaving your cell phone, iPod, BlackBerry, laptop, and all your other favorite electronic gadgets plugged in all the time, so unplug both the device and the charger once they're fully charged.
- *TAKE A COMMERCIAL BREAK:* If you should be so lucky as to go on a vacation, unplug your DVD, TV, stereo, computer (and monitor), and any other device in your entertainment center to save energy and money, which will help you afford another vacation. By the way, by using a laptop instead of a regular computer with a monitor, your energy savings can be as much as 90 percent, so next time you're in the market for a computer consider this route for your home office, personal use, or for your kids. Also keep your computer in hibernation mode when you and yours aren't using it.

- *REACH FOR THE STAR:* Again! If your heating or air-conditioning system is ten to fifteen years old you may want to consider investing in a new Energy Star–certified one. In the meantime, have the pros check to see if it has any leaks or drafts. The same thing applies if you're in the market for a new in-window air-conditioning unit or dehumidifier. Be sure to buy one with that good ol' Energy Star label. If you'd like more info on the enviro-worthiness of these and other appliances and electronics, visit our Energy Star buds at www .energystar.gov.

LIGHTING

- *CHECK WATT'S UP!* If you're using incandescent bulbs you want to switch pronto to compact fluorescent lightbulbs—otherwise known as CFLs. They're four to six times more energy efficient, which means you don't need as much wattage. In fact, by replacing five bulbs in your home you'll save around $60 a year, which you can use to reenergize yourself. I see a hot stone massage or seaweed facial in your eco-beauty future!

    I've done some math to save you the trouble of using your little ol' brain or a calculator to help figure out what CFL you need. (FYI: The "equivalent" rate is also printed on the package for these bulbs, so you can look there as well.)
    - 60 watts incandescent = 15 watts compact fluorescent
    - 75 watts incandescent = 20 watts compact fluorescent
    - 100 watts incandescent = 26–29 watts compact fluorescent
    - 150 watts incandescent = 38–42 watts compact fluorescent
    - 250–300 watts incandescent = 55 watts compact fluorescent

    If you require wattage higher than these you're on your own; my brain can't compute that much!
- *LIGHTS OUT:* Always turn lights off in any and all rooms that aren't being used. Lighting can account for as much as 20 percent of your energy bill.
- *FLICK 'N' FLIP!* Next time you're planning on watching TV or a movie, microwave some popcorn and flip the light switch off to create a theater-like setting!

HEATING

- *CUT A RUG:* Put area rugs down on hardwood, stone, or tile floors to keep your feet warm and limit your need to raise the heat. I'd also suggest you put those cute little bunny slippers on as well.

Homeschooling: Fluorescent and Incandescent

like the way these two words roll off my tongue—but that doesn't really help those of you who are interested in "watt" the difference is between them. Here it is:

The good old-fashioned incandescent bulb that you grew up with (or at least I did, thanks to Thomas Edison) creates light when the electricity heats up the wiry-looking filament inside the bulb. Fluorescent bulbs—including compact fluorescent ones—don't use heat, which is where all the energy is wasted, to create light. They have a gas that produces invisible ultraviolet (UV) light when you turn on the electricity. The UV light then heats the white coating inside the bulb and changes it into light. Hallelujah—I see the light!

For those who enjoy a bit of trivia—according to a favorite Web site, TreeHugger .com, if every home in the United States replaced just *one* incandescent bulb with a fluorescent one it would eliminate the equivalent of the emissions created by *one million* cars! Considering that the average household has fifteen to thirty bulbs, this little piece of trivia should help us all see the light!

- *LET THE SUN SHINE IN:* Leave your blinds up and curtains wide open during the day so the sun can warm up your rooms. At night, let them down and close them to keep the heat in and the cold out.
- *NIX SPACE HEATERS:* Space heaters are energy eaters so don't use them unless your central heating is on the fritz.
- *TAKE CONTROL*
  - *Get with the Program:* Put in a programmable thermostat so you can control your home's temp—they aren't terribly expensive and by turning it down just 10 degrees the pros say we can lower our heating bills by 10 percent.
  - *Turn It . . .*
    - UP: In warm months, raise the thermostat to 78 to 80 degrees when you go to bed, out, or on vacation.
    - DOWN: In cooler months, if you're going on vacation set your thermostat to around 55 degrees—this will save money on your energy bill, and also help keep your water pipes from freezing.
  - *Shut Doors:* If you've got zone heating (that means that you can control the heat and A/C in different areas of your home individually), be sure to adjust

the thermostat in rooms you're not using and shut their doors so the cooler or warmer temp doesn't affect the rest of your home. You might also want to put a towel or some kind of stripping at the base of the closed doors to block any hot or cold air from traveling.

COOLING

- *CHILD'S PLAY:* If you've got a central air-conditioning system, let your kiddies take a break from hosing you down in the summer and let them hose down your outside compressor. That'll help keep it clean and the air flowing unencumbered—as my dad would say, "That's a big word like *delicatessan!*"
- *PLANT A TREE:* Okay, this may not be a manicure-friendly enviro-saver for everyone, but that's why we have landscapers! Believe it or not, according to the PowerTV.com gurus, you can reduce your cooling cost by 25 percent if you plant a tree near a very sunny room. They also suggest placing leafy trees to the south and west, and evergreens to the north—I don't know about you but that's too much for me to remember.
- *FAN FARE:* Install ceiling fans to help circulate air—it's also a hands-free way to dust since it will "spread the glove." Another option is to get a whole-house attic fan, which will lower your home's temp about five degrees in less than ten minutes, and they can cost less than twenty-five cents a day to operate.

SEASONALLY

- *SUCK IT UP:* During one of those rare times when you're vacuuming your couch, keep on going and hit your heater's vents and air-conditioner's screens and filters. By sucking up the debris that's settled there the air will flow better and your unit will work more effectively.
- *CALL IN THE INSPECTOR!* Have your heating and cooling systems inspected by the pros before you start cranking up the heat or A/C. Nowadays, given the ups and downs of world fuel prices, this a particularly good idea.

The Bedroom

- *SAY NIGHT-NIGHT TO LIGHTS:* Whenever you or any member of the household leaves the bedroom be sure to turn off all the lights. If you feel more comfortable with some kind of light on 24/7, think about buying a night light. It's okay, I won't tell anyone that you're scared of the monsters under your bed or in your closet! Also check out a motion light sensor, which will

The Dirt on Houseplants

Want to cut your electric bill, reduce noise, beautify your home, and keep your indoor air clean without even trying? Then go out, buy yourself some houseplants, and scatter them about your living spaces pronto! According to a two-year study that NASA and the Associated Landscape Contractors of America did, it seems that given the right environment certain houseplants can clean up to 87 percent of indoor pollutants. Apparently, plants absorb chemicals in the air, balance humidity, and turn carbon monoxide into oxygen. I'm breathing better already!

Truth be known, I have a black thumb, not a green one, and before I knew about plants' eco-friendly health benefits, I bought some plants based on their ability to stay alive with very little water or attention. (No, I don't sing or play music for them, nor did I buy a cactus!) But I was pleasantly surprised to learn that I had "accidentally" bought what many in the know consider to be environmentally friendly plants. I also have come to learn that almost any plant will do us some good and that every expert has his or her faves. But for those of you who want to know if certain plants are better than others, here are recommendations by those in the know:

- Dracaenas
- Palms (that's what I have!)
- Ferns
- English ivy
- Peace lilies
- Mums and daisies
- Spider plants

Please note: If you have allergies, check with your local plant shops for their opinions. One word of advice: No matter what they say, stay away from Venus flytraps unless you're in the mood to trade in your sneezes for some blood, as did our flower shop bud Seymour in the 1960s cult classic movie *Little Shop of Horrors*.

automatically turn lights on and off when you enter or leave. And don't forget to switch out your incandescent bulbs to compact fluorescents. See "Check Watt's Up" on page 248.

- KNOW WHEN TO DRAW 'EM: In some ways this runs contrary to the above since I'm suggesting you let light in, but then again I never said I was practical or consistent other than in trying to help you save your sanity and your manicure!

- In cool months, keep your blinds up and curtains open to let the sunshine in and naturally warm your room.
- During warmer months, keep blinds down and curtains drawn to keep your bedroom cool.
- *A/C BUSTERS:* Here are some ways to reduce your A/C bills.
  - FAN FARE
    - Think about putting a ceiling fan in your bedroom to help circulate air and cut down on the A/C.
    - Install an attic fan, which can lower the temp in your bedroom and throughout your entire house 5 degrees in less than ten minutes.
    - EASY BREEZY: Open windows that are at opposite sides for cross ventilation and to create a natural indoor breezeway.
- *UNTROUBLED WATER BEDS:* If you have a water bed you can save more than 30 percent by keeping the bed covered with a comforter, since most water beds are heated by electric coils. An insulated mattress cover is another good enviro-saver. If you have temp control keep that turned down as well or do it the old-fashioned way and help save the environment by keeping a warm, well-built body nearby to keep you comfy.
- *BUY IRON FREE:* As in sheets and pillowcases. It'll save you the boring task of ironing them and save you money on your electric bill.
- *CHILL OUT:* To help cool down your room at bedtime without raising the A/C, check out Chillows at www.chillowstore.com. They're water-cooled pillows that you slip between your regular pillow and pillowcase. You can also put your pillowcases in the fridge for a bit.

Laundry Room

The laundry room, like the kitchen, has several energy guzzlers, so unless you opt for your birthday suit 24/7, here are several ways to help keep your laundry room green enough like the rest of your home.

WASHING

- *REACH FOR THE STAR ONE MO' TIME:* You know the drill by now—if you have a washing machine that's more than ten years old you can save *beaucoup* on your utility bills by buying one with an Energy Star label. In fact, according to our buds at energystar.com, it could save you as much as $110 a year.

- *LOAD 'EM:* Don't do partial loads, but be careful not to overload either.
  - Top-load models—fill to the agitator. (FYI: This agitator is not your child who may be annoying you!)
  - Front-load models—check your manual, but the good news with these models is that they generally have a larger capacity.
  - If you enjoy doing laundry, insist on doing small loads, or have an immediate need for that fave pair of jeans, adjust your load setting so you use less water.
- *COLD WASH:* Unless you're washing your mite-infused bed stuff or following a stain removal tip in Chapter 10, always use cold water.
- *SPIN THEM:* The more moisture you can get out of your clothes the less drying time they'll need. Check to see if your washer has a spin option and if it does let it rip!

DRYING

Energy Star doesn't label dryers since they all use pretty much the same amount of juice. But here are a few ways you can be your own "star" without using too much personal energy.

- *CLEAN SCREEN:* Before or after every dry cycle, clean out the removable lint filter. Believe it or not, by doing this you use up to 30 percent less energy—plus the lint in there can be a fire hazard!
- *STAY HOT:* If you can, dry loads one right after the other to maintain the heat and minimize the time your dryer needs to heat up.
- *DAMP DRY:* Try to remove your stuff while it's damp, which will save energy and reduce shrinkage, ironing, and static cling.
- *RACK THEM:* For items like sneakers, baseball caps, stuffed toys, and pillows, use the stationary dryer rack that comes with most new models. If yours didn't, buy one! It'll speed up drying time, which in turn will reduce your energy bill.
- *ENJOY SUNSHINE:* In warmer months (not during allergy season, however), and if you don't live in an apartment building, let your clothes and linens hang out in the good ol' sunshine. Then grab your favorite sunscreen and hang out with those rays, too!

IRONING:
I trust these are self-explanatory!

- *BUY WRINKLE-FREE*
- *SHAKE AND DAMP DRY*

PART **6**

LAST RESORTS

Chapter 13

Stuff That Bugs Us

JUST ENOUGH PEST CONTROL

Men should be like Kleenex . . . soft, strong, disposable.—Cher

No, by pests I'm not talking about your significant other, your children, or your mother-in-law, but things like mice, roaches, and ants, which can infiltrate our homes and turn grown women into screaming idiots upon seeing them scampering about. So if you've ever found yourself jumping on a counter to avoid the path of those not-so-cute, real-life mice or have been totally grossed out by roaches greeting you with your morning coffee, here are a few ways to stop those vermin without calling in the X-Terminator.

Mice

If you invent a better mousetrap the world will beat a path to your door.—Ralph Waldo Emerson

I don't know that anyone has invented a "better mousetrap," but there are some simple options to catch them if you don't mind seeing mice squirm and squeal in a trap—personally, I can't handle it, so I let my son do the dirty work.

Before I continue here's something that I found pretty interesting and thought you might as well: Apparently only cartoon mice really like cheese—I learned this from a study done by Manchester Metropolitan University and underwritten by the Stilton Cheese Makers Association. It seems a mouse's food of choice is stuff with lots of sugar, like chocolate, fruit, peanut butter, and muesli. I don't know about you but seeing Jerry (of *Tom and Jerry* fame) or Mickey chewing on a peach or a bowl of muesli versus a Cheddar wedge doesn't seem as endearing!

- *GIVE 'EM LUNCH:* Mice can see only a few inches in front of them, which makes trapping them fairly easy and probably explains why they're drawn to small places like paper lunch bags. My bud Amy suggests "giving them lunch." Place some sweet stuff on a trap inside a good old-fashioned brown paper bag. Then when they come in for lunch you fold the top down and chuck the bag. At least this way you won't see them suffer!
  - CAUTION: If it's morning and you haven't had your first cup of coffee yet, be sure not to "accidentally" leave the bag with the mouse on the counter. You may mistake it for your kiddie's lunch and give it to him or her to take to school!
- *STICK IT TO THEM:* For those who are sadistic and enjoy torturing small, innocent animals that are only trying to survive, you can use sticky paper. That'll trap them and if you forget to check it for a few days, they'll slowly starve to death. Personally, I can't handle this method even if someone else is doing it.
- *SET 'EM FREE:* For those like me who don't have the heart to kill these little varmints there are traps that will catch them but not kill them. However, you, your significant other, or your child will have to take them outside and set them free. Check out www.havahart.com (love the name) to learn more about this humane trap.
- *HERE KITTY KITTY!* If no one's allergic, get yourself a kitty to chase them away. Cats are actually a purr-fect accidental housewifely pet, since they can stay by themselves, do their doo without your having to walk them, and prefer to be alone. Just try not to go for the ones that shed a lot, which may be cuter but also are higher maintenance!

Moths

I think of moths as powdery mini-bats, since they hate the light and love dark, humid places, just like M & M and dust mites. They also like to:

- HANG in corners and folds where it's dark
- COCOON, which enables them to blend into fabrics, making them hard to spot

- EAT wool, fur, down, and dander (like our mighty mites)
- PROCREATE—they're love machines and "make love" as often as they can

BIRTH CONTROL

This last fact about their penchant for making love is a key reason you need to stop these sexual studs—particularly when you read the following piece of info, which will gross you out: *One female moth laying eggs can set the stage for future generations to lay 20 million eggs in just one year's time.*

You will now run, not walk, to learn how to stop their madness:

- *GO LAVENDER:* Lavender naturally repels moths, though it doesn't kill their eggs or larvae. Hang it from rods or place it in drawers as a birth control measure.
- *HANG A BUNDLE OF CHALK:* Chalk will help draw out the moisture in your closet, which will make it less attractive to these pests. Just keep it away from everything so it doesn't get your stuff covered with its dust.
- *STUFF SHOES:* Put crumpled up newspaper into sneaks (and any shoes that your footsies perspire in) to absorb the moisture, which will again make it a less appealing spot for moths to reside.
- *DEHUMIDIFY:* If possible, keep a dehumidifier in or near your closet.
- *LIGHTS ON:* Keep a light on—this sort of contradicts our eco-friendly efforts, but since moths don't like light it will help keep them away. Please remember to use only eco-friendly compact fluorescent bulbs!
- *FREEZE THEM:* If you have a decent-sized freezer or work in a meatpacking plant, put clothes in Ziploc bags and freeze them for a few hours. It'll freeze the larvae and enable you to shake them out. It's also a great way for you to cool off during hot summer months!
- *GET BOARD:* If you're in the mood, bring out the ironing board and burn those suckers by ironing your clothes. I'm not a big fan of this idea.
- *SEAL STUFF:* Keep clothing you're not using in sealed plastic storage coverings and containers to prevent your little studs from finding a place to nest.
- *SUCK THEM UP:* Vacuum regularly to get rid of dander and other stuff they like to eat.
- *FORGET VINTAGE:* Don't buy vintage clothing from resale shops or garage sales, since the likelihood is they haven't seen the light of day for years and are home to our sex magnets.

You can also try:

- **CEDAR BLOCKS:** Seems they've got some kind of oil that kill the larvae, which is what destroys your clothes. It will not kill the moths or their eggs, however. (I don't know about you but I think I need a refresher course in bug science.)
- **PHEROMONE TRAPS:** Okay, you know now that they're love machines so the pheromones, which are a naturally occurring chemical that triggers sexual response, speak to your studs' nymphomaniac tendencies and cause them to come to Mama, or rather to the pheromone trap!

Ants

The most common kind of house ants are pharaoh ants, which can also be called

- sugar ants because they like sweet stuff like syrups, jellies, and honey, or
- grease ants because they like grease.

They also like toothpaste, but I've never heard them referred to as toothpaste ants. At any rate, here are some simple ways from those in the know to enjoy "sweet" revenge.

- Mix one teaspoon of boric acid* with five ounces of any or all of the following and keep your fingers crossed that they bring it back to their queen for din-din—wait a minute, I thought these were called pharaoh ants; guess the female rules the roost here too.
  - Apple jelly
  - Peanut butter
  - Karo syrup
  - Honey

CHILD'S PLAY: WALK THE LINE

A friend of mine told me that if you draw a line with chalk, the ants won't cross it—by the way, if you do this outdoors you'll have to redraw it after a downpour.

---

*Be sure not to leave it where your kiddies or pets can get at it.

Roaches

Fortunately, I haven't seen roaches speeding across my floors or cabinets since I left my Manhattan apartment. I do, however, have vivid memories of being totally disgusted by their seeming omnipresence. If only I had known then what I know now!

I begin by sharing some disturbing little tidbits to get you truly in the mood to squash each and every one of these prehistoric critters.

- Roaches have been around for more than 250 million years.
- If you have one, you probably have more than twenty thousand.
- They can live off the leftover toothpaste on your toothbrush.
- They can live up to twenty days without food, fourteen days without water, and several days without a head!

Gross, huh? Now here are three manicure-friendly ways to squash them:

1. Put some Vaseline on the inside lip of a jar baited with apple, banana, or potato slices. Keep the food fresh since, with or without a head, they find fresh stuff more alluring.
2. Keep cucumber peels on your countertops—it repels them.
3. Mix brown sugar with borax and flour, then dust it around your sink, fridge, stove, and any corners these prehistoric midgets travel. They'll carry the toxic mix back to their nest and extinction from your home should follow.

Chapter 14

If You Do Nothing Else . . .

My idea of housework is to sweep the room with a glance.—**Anonymous**

Even though this guide has shared a variety of tips to maintain a clean-enough home, that doesn't ensure that you'll be able to put them into action since life gets interrupted. On the other hand, things like bacteria, mold and mildew, drains backing up, our planet melting away, and that red wine stain don't care about your everyday real-life interruptions. That's why the following will help keep health inspectors at bay, the earth intact, and your favorite silk blouse from disaster long enough until time or desire permit.

The Bathroom

- *DROP* two effervescent tablets into your toilet bowl and let sit for twenty minutes, then flush.
- *PLOP* an automatic toilet bowl cleaner into the tank (read the directions regarding how long they last so you have a vague memory of when to put a new one in!).
- *KEEP* disinfecting cleaning wipes on your vanity and swipe your sink, faucets, toilet bowl exterior and seat, light switches, and anything else within range.
- *PREVENT* mold and mildew by using M & M resistant products, keeping your shades up and your windows open (in warm months), and hanging towels to dry.

- *REMOVE* hair from sink, tub, and shower drains.
- *VACUUM* or sweep floors.
- *EMPTY* trash.
- *UNPLUG* any beauty tool not being used (such as the curling iron, blow dryer, flat iron, and electric toothbrush once it's fully charged).
- *SPRAY* with aromatic disinfecting spray.
- *POUR* boiling water or a mixture of vinegar and baking soda down your sink, shower, and tub drains to prevent clogs every two weeks or thereabouts.
- *PRESERVE* your manicure—hire a monthly cleaning service!

The Kitchen

- *WIPE:* While yakking on the phone or yelling at your kids to do their home-work, take out a disinfecting cleaning wipe and wipe anything in swiping sight: faucets, fridge handles, counters, sinks, microwave, cabinet doors, jars and bottles in the fridge.
- *ZAP:* Put your sponges in the microwave daily for three minutes. Let cool before touching. Do the same with cutting boards if you use them daily and they're microwaveable.
- *POUR:* Avoid clogs by pouring white vinegar and baking soda down the drain. Follow with a pot of boiling water.
- *TOSS:* Check expiration dates on foods in the fridge every two weeks. Toss any that are past due, lumpy, green when they should be white, or require you to wear nose clips.
- *REMOVE:* Take out garbage daily (CHILD'S PLAY).
- *LAYER:* Line your trash can with five garbage bags.
- *CARPET:* Buy decorative, machine-washable kitchen floor mats and cover all the key dirt-gathering spots, such as in front of your sink, oven, stove, prep area, homework corners, and trash can.
- *PASS THE ROLLING PIN:* Hire a chef and domestic assistant.
- *UNPLUG:* Any small appliance not being used (coffeemaker, coffee grinder, toaster oven, etc.)
- *EAT OUT:* Often with and/or at friends, relatives, or restaurants
- *SERVE:* Dirty martinis anytime anyone comes over to shift and blur focus—somewhere in the world it's cocktail hour!

Living Spaces

- *WIPE:* Dust furniture and windowsills.
- *SWIPE:* TV screens, phones, remotes, doorknobs, and switch plates with disinfecting wipes. You can also use fabric softener sheets or baby wipes.
- *SUCK:* Vacuum the floors and carpets.
- *UNPLUG:* Any small electronic device, and unplug chargers once your gizmos are fully charged.

The Bedroom

- *SMITE THE MITE:* Every two weeks wash sheets and pillowcases to prevent mites from sleeping with you forever.
- *PLAY DUSTY FOR ME:* Go over night tables and dressers with a microfiber cloth.
- *PICK ME UP:* Weekly, pick up stuff on floors and hang or toss in laundry or bins immediately.
- *GIVE IT A SPRITZ:* Spray with aromatic disinfecting spray.
- *EMPTY TRASH*
- *TURN OFF LIGHTS*

And if you really can't or don't want to do anything else:

- *WIPE WHEREVER:* Countertops, faucets, sinks, toilet seats, appliances, handles, switch plates, and anything else in your path with a disinfecting cleaning wipe
- *ENGAGE A CHILD:* Have your kiddie vacuum
- *TRASH TRASH:* Empty only trash cans filled with food
- *SPRAY AWAY:* Spritz your home with an aromatic disinfecting spray
- *GO DARK:* Turn off any lights in rooms you're not in

HIRE HELP: Once a month use those pennies, dimes, and quarters you've collected from your laundry pockets and bring in the pros.

Enough Is Enough!

And on that note, this guide will come to a close. I hope that it has given you a chance to take a breath and look at homekeeping with a smile and some calm. If so, spread the glove and encourage your family and friends to embrace the fact that *we* are the face of today's housewife, the accidental housewife and proud of it!

Appendix

THE ULTIMATELY SHORT AND SWEET RESOURCE GUIDE

THE BATHROOM

Mrs. Meyer's: www.mrsmeyers.com
Greening the Cleaning: www.imusranchfoods.com
Method: www.methodhome.com
Seventh Generation: www.seventhgeneration.com
Life Tree: www.lifetreeproducts.com
Velcro: www.joann.com.
Damp Rid: www.damprid.com
Moldzyme: www.ecodiscoveries.com.
Storage bags: designer quart-sized storage bags (vintageweave.com)

THE KITCHEN

Color-coded flexible cutting boards: www.surlatable.com
Multi-colored coded cutting boards: www.target.com
Rachael Ray Gusto Grip 7-Piece Clean-Cut Cutting Board Set by Füri: www.amazon.com
Touchless trash can: www.simplehuman.com
ScatMat: www.safepetproducts.com
Fridge Liners: www.Mom4life.com
Fridge It: Available at Linens 'n Things or online at www.innofresh.com
Timestrips: www.timestrip.com

Method's granite and marble cleaner: www.methodhome.com
First Alert's Tundra Fire Extinguishing Spray: www.firstalert.com
Scooba Robotic Floor Washer: www.irobot.com
Coffee grinder cleaner: www.espressoparts.com

If you'd like to learn more about preventing bad bacteria from taking over your kitchens go to www.fightbac.gov. They've got lots of great info for your kids, too, and food cooking safety charts that you can print out so you don't have to remember anything.

LIVING SPACES
Charitable Floor Mats: www.carpetone.com

THE BEDROOM
Organizing Resources: www.napo.net

JUST ENOUGH LAUNDRY BASICS
BraBall: www.braballs.com
Nellie's Dryer Balls: www.nellieslaundry.com. Also available at Target.

UNITED STAINS OF AMERICA
Fabric Freshener from Whirlpool: www.whirlpool.com

A CONVENIENT TRUTH
energystar.com
www.chillow.com

STUFF THAT BUGS US
Humane mouse traps: www.havahart.com
Energy saving tips: www.energystar.gov
Chillows: www.chillow.com

Index

JULIE EDELMAN is the *New York Times* bestselling author of *The Accidental Housewife*. She appears regularly on national television shows, including *Rachael Ray*, *The View*, *Today*, and *Real Simple TV*, and in magazines such as *Family Circle*, *Glamour*, and *New York*. Edelman lives in New Jersey with her family.